Concerned Women for America has been a strong voice for biblical values for many years now. In this engaging new book, Penny Young Nance gives a rallying cry for women everywhere to make their voices heard and impact the world around them on the issues that matter most.

—JIM DALY, President, Focus on the Family

This excellent book is for all women who want to stand up and be counted. Penny Nance has handled most of the controversial issues with dignity and honesty. As you read this thought-provoking book, you will find many ways to express your convictions as a Christian conservative woman. I heartily recommend this book for women who want to make a difference.

—DR. BEVERLY LaHAYE, Chairman, Concerned
Women for America

Penny Nance is a fearless culture warrior who takes opponents apart and shreds their shallow left-wing nonsense for the drivel it is. And she does it with a smile that belies her toughness. Penny proves that a conservative woman can be intellectually and spiritually prepared for anyone or anything—anytime. You'll love her book, *Feisty and Feminine*, and will realize why liberals don't want to be on the stage with her. They don't like losing!

—MIKE HUCKABEE, Governor of Arkansas,
1996–2007

Penny's book is conversational and fun, yet deep and insightful. She is a masterful (and very feisty and feminine!) ally in our work to build a culture of life. *Feisty and Feminine* communicates a timely and necessary message for women today who are seeking real truth and fulfillment.

—JEANNE MANCINI, President, March for Life

Feisty and Feminine is an inspiring look at how a woman can be a conservative Christian while still being a powerful advocate for the rights of women and all other people. It is easy to read and very informative.

—BENJAMIN S. CARSON SR., MD, Emeritus
Professor of Neurosurgery, Oncology, Plastic
Surgery, and Pediatrics, Johns Hopkins
Medicine; President and CEO, American
Business Collaborative, LLC

Penny Nance is one of today's boldest and most outspoken conservative women of faith. In this book, Penny exposes who is really waging the "war on women," and it's not who you've been led to think it is. More feisty and informed women are exactly what our country needs.

—WILLIAM J. BENNETT, former secretary of education; host of the nationally syndicated talk show *Morning in America*

I've known Penny Nance for twenty years, and I absolutely love her passion for Christ, her passion to advance freedom and opportunity for all Americans, and her passion to educate and empower a new generation of conservative women to help get America back on the right track. She's a rare voice in Washington—courageous and classy. May her tribe increase!

—JOEL C. ROSENBERG, *New York Times* bestselling author, *Implosion: Can America Recover from Its Economic and Spiritual Challenges in Time?*

My friend Penny offers answers to any conservative, pro-life woman who has ever had an uncomfortable encounter over religion and politics with a friend or neighbor at a PTA meeting or child's soccer game. Penny's prayerful, practical advice disarms liberal opponents, fosters thoughtful conversation, and inspires women to lead in their families and communities. *Feisty and Feminine* is a hopeful and pragmatic response to the most difficult, hot-button issues facing our culture.

—MARJORIE DANNENFELSER, President, Susan B. Anthony List

Women are right to be concerned about the state of America and their families. Feminism has failed them. The good news is that women have a fearless champion in Penny Nance, who is proving every day that feisty and feminine is a winning combination!

—GARY L. BAUER, President, American Values; Former Chief Domestic Policy Advisor to President Reagan

Often the pages of a book will reflect the personality of its author. This one fits the bill—positive, straightforward, and dynamic. A real joy to read!

—DR. RICHARD G. LEE, There's Hope America; Editor, *American Patriot's Bible*

FEISTY &
Feminine

FEISTY &
Feminine

A Rallying Cry for Conservative Women

PENNY YOUNG NANCE

ZONDERVAN

Feisty and Feminine
Copyright © 2016 by Penny Young Nance

Requests for information should be addressed to:
Zondervan, 3900 Sparks Dr. SE, Grand Rapids, Michigan 49546

ISBN 978-0-310-34613-5 (audio download)
ISBN 978-0-310-34489-6 (ebook)

Library of Congress Cataloging-in-Publication Data
    Names: Young Nance, Penny.
    Title: Feisty and feminine : a rallying cry for conservative women / Penny Young Nance.
    Description: Grand Rapids, Michigan : Zondervan, 2016. | Includes bibliographical references.
    Identifiers: LCCN 2015049865 | ISBN 9780310345138 (hardcover)
    Subjects: LCSH: Christian women—Religious life—United States. | Christian women—Political
        activity—United States. | Conservatism—Religious aspects—Christianity. | Esther, Queen of
        Persia. | Concerned Women for America.
    Classification: LCC BV4527 .Y68 2016 | DDC 261.70973—dc23 LC record available at http://lccn
        .loc.gov/2015049865

The author is represented by Alive Literary Agency, 7680 Goddard Street, Suite 200, Colorado
Springs, Colorado 80920, www.aliveliterary.com.

Cover design: Curt Diepenhorst
Cover photo: Dan Davis Photography
Photo stylist: Rita Vogg
Interior design: Denise Froehlich

First printing February 2016 / Printed in the United States of America

Contents

1. Feminine Conservatives Face an Esther Moment 9
2. The Devaluation of Women 17
3. Sexual Assault and Politics 35
4. Marriage and True Tolerance 55
5. Abortion and the Sanctity of Life 79
6. The Real War against Women 105
7. The Rise of Islamic Extremism and the Need to Fight Back 125
8. Beyond Our Borders: Why Israel Matters to Christians 143
9. Seasons: Work, Family, Life, and the Art of Balance 165
10. A Vision for the Future 187

    Acknowledgments 193
    Notes 195

CHAPTER 1

Feminine Conservatives Face
an Esther Moment

I had forgotten what it feels like. For the past several years, I have been fortunate to be surrounded by likeminded people in my job, church, and social life. By likeminded I mean thinking, compassionate, conservative people of faith. Because of my support for Israel and religious freedom, I have some less conservative friends and some friends of different faiths, but true political liberals have been out of my orbit except as opponents on TV debate segments. And the secret of those debate segments is that we are professionals and know better than to take things personally. It hasn't always been the case, but over the last five years, my life has been protected and insular.

Boy, did I get a wakeup call when I attended my husband Will's annual work-related "holiday" party this past year. It's a long drive from our house, but we faithfully dress up and attend every year in order to spend time with some nice people and their spouses, same-sex partners, or significant others. The hosts work hard and always create a beautiful party. This crowd of about one hundred is typically made up of smart, successful people with a variety of religious and political perspectives. Like every other spouse at an office function, I try not to be insensitive. In fact, I try not to stand out at all. But let's face it: conservative women bother some liberals just by breathing, so I don't always succeed.

All said, though, it's usually a nice evening. But not this year. This year, I found myself in a room full of people who felt free to denigrate my beliefs right to my face. No sensitivity or tolerance. No political correctness. Apparently, "I'm okay; you're okay" is over for them.

Like most women, I switch hats a lot. I'm a mom, a friend, a daughter, a sister, and a wife. All of those roles require a different persona. But in one of my most public of roles, I have the privilege of representing the more than half a million conservative women who are members of Concerned Women for America (CWA), the nation's largest public policy women's organization. I'm often called on to share CWA's perspective before Congress, on TV and in print media, and in other public venues.

While I'm comfortable wearing this hat, I don't usually talk about my work while fulfilling a family obligation. Like anyone else, I don't feel the need to talk politics on planes (especially on planes), at my kids' soccer and lacrosse games, and in my role as supportive wife. In those venues, I don't talk about my work at all unless I am asked. Even on those rare occasions when someone says I look familiar, I usually deflect by making a joke about Fran Drescher or Janice Dickinson.

So to be fair, the people at the party had no idea how I earn a living. But this makes what followed all the more outrageous. The conversation started out innocuously enough. As we were waiting for dinner to be served, we found the common ground that most parents do: our kids. Everyone in the group had children in college or applying for college. So we swapped stories of SAT stress, college application angst, and where they got in or didn't. One mother was especially proud that her daughter had just been accepted into the College of Charleston. My husband and I smiled and offered our encouragement to the other parents on our shared journeys. It was all very collegial until someone asked what our seventeen-year-old daughter would like to do as a career.

I replied something vague about broadcast journalism, and then after a couple of follow-up questions, my husband had the *nerve* to say that Claire would very much like to work as on-air talent for Fox News or CNN. Now, I had to give Will credit for trying to appear normal by mentioning CNN, because Claire had absolutely no interest at the time in CNN. At that moment, she simply wanted to be one of the elite group of smart, successful broadcast journalists who report the news to millions of viewers every day, specifically Elisabeth Hasselbeck, Harris Faulkner, Greta Van Susteren, Megyn Kelly, and her absolute favorite, Supreme Court expert Shannon Bream. These journalists appear in more homes than do journalists for all the other cable news providers combined, and I thank God that my daughter and other young women have such fabulous role models.

But at the mention of Fox News, you would have thought Will had said Claire hoped to club baby seals to death for a living. I swear, if we had said she planned to be a stripper, these parents would have been less shocked.

"Fox? Fox?!" they crowed, looking like they were about to choke on their bacon-wrapped scallops. The College of Charleston mom's eyes almost bugged out of her carefully coiffed head as she shrilly reminded us that "we are in Maryland." I wasn't sure what that had to do with anything, but I politely explained to her that we had driven up from Virginia. One of the men leaned toward my husband and asked in a concerned voice whether we supported what was clearly, to him, a wholly unacceptable career goal. Always charming, Will laughed and assured them that Fox is the news channel that we watch most in our house.

Ohhh . . . *now* they got it. Somehow Will had gotten past Human Resources. The company must be doing a special outreach program to idiots. Most of the crowd quickly closed ranks, leaving only one of the original members to continue the conversation. He was new to the company and was desperately trying to put the pin back into the grenade. He lamely offered that he had once met someone in North Carolina who worked for Fox and that she was nice. Maybe he could even dig up her number and introduce us. I smiled and thanked him for his generosity and open-mindedness, and then found an excuse to get up. But before I left, I mentioned just loudly enough for everyone to hear that Claire was also planning to register as a Republican and would be voting in the 2016 election. I'm sure that gave everyone nightmares that night.

Facing Derision for Your Beliefs

While I admit this was an isolated interaction, as I reflected on what had happened on the ride home, I became more and more upset. My good-natured husband shrugged it off; we wouldn't have to deal with that group again for at least another year. But I just couldn't let it go. Why did their disapproval bother me so much? Finally, I hit on it: while their derision was hurtful to both me and my family, I realized that if I was having to deal with this nonsense, then on any given day so were the millions of other conservative women around this country.

At the same party, a mom had confided to me that she felt funny for mentioning the word prayer. What?! I heard God's name taken in vain more than once that night, yet the sweet woman who prays was made to feel odd for publicly mentioning her Christian beliefs. This didn't make sense.

When did simply referencing one's faith become taboo? Somehow polite society has decided that while most any other belief system is fine, traditional views are unacceptable. Because this group's distaste for Fox News was code for a deeper distaste for conservatives. What's more, we have let liberals get away with it for so long that they are oblivious to what they are doing. My husband's work associates did not set out to be unkind and disrespectful. They were just so used to being unchallenged in their thinking that they had no idea they were being rude. I couldn't help but wonder why liberals feel so free to espouse their views in non-political settings, but we conservatives have to keep our mouths shut so as not to offend.

There are times in which we all should refrain from political commentary and deep theological discussions, but I don't think the other team got that memo. Furthermore, they aren't ever going to get it if something doesn't change.

What's even more concerning is that the left seems to have a particularly nasty spite reserved for conservative women. This means that women who love their country, love God, believe in the Constitution, trust the free market, want small government, respect life, think there are necessary reasons to exalt and encourage traditional marriage, and work to put their families before their own desires are shamed and condescended to by the cool kids. Just think of the attacks launched at prominent conservative women by mainstream media, whether at Ann Romney for not being a working mother, Michele Bachmann for her appearance and clothes, or radio host Laura Ingraham and columnist Michelle Malkin for daring to express opinions with which the left disagrees.

The vitriolic attacks on conservatives—especially conservative women—from the left have got to stop, and that will happen only if we take a stand.

We need not cower in the face of darkness. We know the truth via the author of truth, and, therefore, we have power. Even more important, we are facing a tipping point in our culture. Objectification and hypersexualization of women has never been higher. Marriage rates are falling. The sanctity of life is under attack at every turn. Islamic extremism threatens women abroad and at home. And Christianity is routinely vilified, belittled, and ridiculed. But you know what? As Christian women living in America today, we are in a unique position to change history.

The Power of Feisty, Feminine Conservatives

Women make up 51 percent of the population. We earn more college and advanced degrees than men and have carried every presidential election

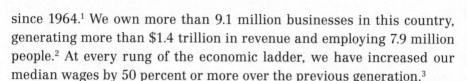

since 1964.[1] We own more than 9.1 million businesses in this country, generating more than $1.4 trillion in revenue and employing 7.9 million people.[2] At every rung of the economic ladder, we have increased our median wages by 50 percent or more over the previous generation.[3]

Christian women in particular are positioned to make a difference in our country. It may well be that all our experiences have been leading up to this very moment in our nation's history. The author of the book of Esther reminds us that perhaps we were born "for such a time as this" (4:14), a time to stand tall and explain to a broken culture who we are and what we believe. A time to advocate for all that is true and pure and good.

If you find yourself coming home from biology class, PTA events, neighborhood gatherings, work, or the playground with hurt feelings and thinking up clever, stinging retorts, this book is for you. And here's the thing: you are not alone. On any college campus, in any neighborhood, and in every region, FemCos—feminine conservatives—abound. We don't fit neatly into stereotypes. We may not feel free to express our opinions. But we desperately want to be heard. We are weary of choking down words of truth and often words of grace because we're afraid others won't approve. We are tired of walking on eggshells about our faith and our beliefs. So maybe it's time we stop and learn what it takes to say respectfully what we think. It's time to challenge the status quo and in the process become more honest and transparent and, ultimately, more relevant to the discussion.

It's time to become Esther Women.

Time to Find Your Voice

You remember Esther from the Old Testament. She was a sixth-century BC orphan, a nobody whom God plucked from obscurity and made the queen of the vast Persian Empire. Born a humble Jew, she was picked by King Xerxes to become his queen, raising her to a position of incredible prominence and power. She made history because she, through prayer, gathered the courage to speak truth to power at great risk to herself: when Haman, an adviser to the king, crafted a plot to kill all the Jews in Persia, Esther risked her own safety by revealing her Jewish heritage to Xerxes and begging him to spare her people. Xerxes granted her request, delivering the Jews from certain destruction. Though it could have cost Esther her position, her power, even her very life, she trusted that God had raised her up for a reason, and by finding her voice and speaking up, she saved herself and her people.

We too were born "for such a time as this." Christian women must take our stand and *lead!* We live in a broken world that needs more of God, not less of him. We are capable and called to point others to Jesus' sweet message of redemption and restoration embodied in the gospel.

So why are we so afraid?

My prayer is that this book will be both a wake-up call and a tool to empower the Esther Women across this country to find their voices and speak up. There are so many issues facing our nation and our world today that we have the power to change if we just take a stand, and I will touch on many of them in the following chapters. Each chapter is a self-contained primer on one of the hottest issues of our day. I can't hit everything, but the topics that follow are ones that are near to my heart and to the mission of CWA. I'll look at questions of culture and the sexual objectification of women, the rise of sexual assault on campuses and in the country more broadly, the assault on traditional marriage, the need to protect the sanctity of life, and the challenges of balancing work and life. I'll also consider questions of international importance, including the rise of Islamic extremism, human rights violations against women around the world, and the need for Christians to stand with Israel. These chapters will serve as the educational foundation you need to speak authoritatively on these issues in any forum, Christian or secular. You will learn to support your beliefs not only scripturally but also using irrefutable data.

You'll also meet some of the faces of the conservative movement today, women who are leading the charge and standing up to fight for causes that matter. They are diverse, talented individuals across a variety of fields who represent some of the best role models for Esther Women. I've highlighted some of them in profiles placed between each of the chapters. We aren't without leadership in the feminine conserv-ative movement, and I hope their work inspires you to pursue causes of your own.

I have also done something risky. I have included stories from my personal life that support the issues we are discussing. I pray that my honesty and transparency will give you a clearer understanding of both the issues and of me as the author. You may not agree with every point I make, and that's okay. If I've made you think differently about an issue or about conservative women in general, then I have succeeded.

Most important, I hope I have made you think about your faith. In order for conservative Christian women to powerfully impact an increasingly secular world, we must understand what happens beyond our pews. And we need to know how to raise cultural issues with nonbelievers in ways that encourage understanding and dialogue while also pointing them toward the sweet forgiveness of Christ. Our message must always be redemptive, because that's the ultimate truth.

Each chapter ends with a section titled "What Can Esther Women Do?" offering action points and encouragement that I hope inspire you to take a stand, speak up, and effect real change. I want to give you the resources and the courage to share your beliefs in a way that at the least makes others stop and think, and perhaps leads to fruitful conversation and action. We are complicated and imperfect people, but we are sincere. Let's together learn to winsomely share our thoughts and surprise people who think they already know it all. Because the truth is they don't know you, and even more important, your voice needs to be heard!

Beverly LaHaye

FOUNDER AND CHAIRMAN OF THE BOARD OF DIRECTORS, CONCERNED WOMEN FOR AMERICA

Beverly LaHaye is one of the most important pioneers of the feminine conservative movement. She founded Concerned Women for America (CWA) in 1978 because she believed that women needed voices in the public sphere that represented their beliefs and values. Concerned about the direction our country was headed, Mrs. LaHaye organized a meeting of nearly twelve hundred like-minded women to forge a new way forward, and CWA was born.

The mission of CWA was then, as it remains today, to protect and promote biblical values among all citizens—first through prayer, then education, and finally by influencing our society—thereby reversing the decline in moral values in our nation.

Mrs. LaHaye worked tirelessly to build CWA into the most powerful women's public policy organization in the country. With the formation of prayer-action chapters around the nation, CWA engaged women at a grassroots level. Nearly forty years later, this is the very same model of activism CWA uses today.

Mrs. LaHaye had never intended to be a national public figure. She was a reserved woman with little desire to step into the limelight. But she felt the pull of God upon her heart, and she agreed to step out in faith and answer his call.

Under her leadership, CWA grew to an organization of more than five hundred thousand members and thirty-six state directors, four hundred chapters, and twenty Young Women for America college chapters. Over the course of her career, Mrs. LaHaye met with presidents, testified before the Congress, led a delegation to the Fourth United Nations World Conference on Women in Beijing, and helped influence public policy at many levels.

Mrs. LaHaye faced significant opposition in her work and fought against the same simplistic stereotypes that many conservative women face today. Yet she refused to let the other side define her. And even in the face of setbacks, she continued to fight for the issues God had placed on her heart. "God didn't call us to win the battles; he called us to fight the battles," she said. Through this perseverance, she created one of the most formidable women's groups on Capitol Hill, one that continues its remarkable work today in service of women around our great country.

CHAPTER 2

The Devaluation of Women

I have always been very sensitive to the objectification of women in our culture. In the seventh grade when a classmate grabbed my backside while I was walking by him returning from the concession stand at a ballgame, I reacted instinctively by pouring my full glass of Coke over his head. He was so drenched, he had to go home, but he learned some manners—and I learned that I could stand up for myself. It's a lesson I've held onto.

I had to rethink my instincts a couple of years ago, though, in the Phoenix airport. I had just gotten off a long flight and was traveling alone, pulling my rolling bag behind me. Walking distractedly on my way to the hotel shuttle, I passed a man wearing a rock 'n' roll T-shirt and smoking a cigarette. As I passed him, I heard him say something I can only describe as filthy. *Excuse me?* I was shocked out of my travel haze. I stopped. Then I looked him squarely in the eye and proceeded to upbraid him for his boorish and vulgar behavior.

His reaction to my tongue-lashing made me even madder. He had the *nerve* to look confused and then tried to defend himself! Oh, no. I was having none of that. I cut him right off and suggested he should grow up.

I walked off feeling smug. I had once again taken up not only for myself but also for women everywhere. After all, who did he think he was, saying something so dirty to an innocent woman? Just because I am a woman traveling alone doesn't give him the right to be disrespect-ful, I thought. I loaded my bag into the airport shuttle and continued to mull over the entire episode. And then, as the van pulled out of the parking lot, it hit me. He had said, "Nice boots."

Oh no. What had I done? I had been so quick to jump on this man, assuming he was making vulgar remarks and objectifying me as a woman, and I had been completely wrong. Let me take this opportunity

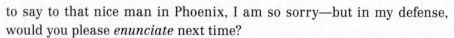

to say to that nice man in Phoenix, I am so sorry—but in my defense, would you please *enunciate* next time?

I had a good laugh about the whole episode. I thought back to the man's shocked face when I ripped into him. I can't even imagine what he told his wife when he got home that night!

In this instance, I was wrong to assume that I was being objectified and belittled because of my appearance or gender. However, in many instances in my life that hasn't been the case. Every woman has a few stories. My quickness to assume this man's intentions were less than honorable made me realize that I needed to rethink my conditioned responses, but it also suggests that there are some serious cultural issues in play.

It's bad enough to be treated with disrespect by another person. The real problem, however, is not that the objectification of women is commonplace, as my response to this man assumed; it's that for the most part, we've stopped caring. Women today are becoming complicit in our own devaluation.

A Downward Spiral

A clear indicator that our culture is at a dangerous tipping point is the new trend in movies and books marketed specifically to women glorifying BDSM (bondage, dominance, sadism, and masochism). At the risk of outing myself as uncool, let me state that this trend is downright alarming. Something has flipped in our brains, and we don't even realize it. The success of this genre signifies a new low point for women in the way we view ourselves, our worth, and our dignity. Hang with me a minute, and I'll show you what I mean. Many women are no longer opposed to women being objectified, manipulated, and even physically beaten to fulfill a man's sexual fantasy. Many have given into and even embraced abuse. Think about this.

How many women do you know who have read the book *Fifty Shades of Grey* or who have gone to see the movie? I know entire book clubs of bored women who read the book and then went together to watch the movie in theaters. My favorite hair stylist, Alex, a pretty twenty-something with two children, was one of the millions of women who joined the trend. She didn't read the book, but went with her husband to watch the film. Alex said she expected sexy, but what she got was Hollywood's prettied-up version of vile abuse.

"I wanted to wash my brain out after I watched it," she told me. "I can't get the images out of my head. It manipulates the viewer into rooting for a man who is a misogynist." She said her husband found it alarming and wanted to leave. She later posted on Facebook a piece by Michelle Lewsen from the mommy blog *Scary Mommy*, which called out the movie for its negative message and stated that the future of our children is at stake when adults confuse abuse with love.[1] The reaction from Alex's friends to the post was mixed.

For those of you who have been in a media blackout, here's the background. On Valentine's Day 2015, the media was abuzz with accolades for the movie *Fifty Shades of Grey*, based on the *New York Times* bestseller about an innocent young woman (in fact, a virgin), fresh out of college, who falls for a wealthy businessman whose erotic predilections happen to include BDSM. The film was marketed as "an incredible fairytale love story." The movie instead glorified stalking, emotional dominance, and sexual abuse. Yet, it broke the box office record for Valentine's releases, grossing more than $85 million in its opening weekend.[2]

Compare that to the bestselling movies of past Valentine's Days: the Oscar-winning *Driving Miss Daisy* in 1990, the family-friendly comedy *Groundhog Day* in 1993, the romantic comedy *Hitch* in 2005. These movies offered more positive views of love, relationships, and women than the garbage we see in the theaters today. Have we lost our minds? American taxpayers spend an estimated $4 billion a year on programs to end domestic violence, yet we turn around and spend money on books, music, and movies glamorizing abuse.[3]

I would love to blame Hollywood, but women, even Christian women, are buying this trash. While I wish women like Alex weren't subjected to glorified depictions of sexual subjugation unwittingly, it's not them I worry about. It's the millions of lonely women with little or no self-respect or self-esteem who are now being told they can or even should allow themselves any manner of defilement to please men. And I worry for the young men who are being told that degrading and beating a woman is a legitimate choice.

Sadly, we live in a culture that glamorizes sexual abuse and permits its existence everywhere. In the last several decades, society switched its expectations of women from June Cleaver to Beyonce. Both the 1950s perfectionist who does housework in her pearls and the hypersexualized, airbrushed performer are false depictions of women, but the latest version seems desperate. Don't get me wrong, Beyonce has amazing talent, which is why I find her tendency toward packaging it as raunchiness surprising. She doesn't need to sell her body to sell records. She is indicative of a culture in which the value of women is based on their ability to elicit a sexual charge.

As I consider the state of our culture today, I have to wonder: what's the fallout going to be?

How Men Treat Women, and How We Treat Ourselves

How have we fallen to this new low? This goes far beyond a cultural problem; it's a spiritual one. Somehow we have forgotten that women are God's crowning achievement in creation. God made Eve and broke the gender mold. He was done! She was perfectly made. And the relationship between man and woman was perfect too. As we read in Genesis, "The man said, 'This is now bone of my bones and flesh of my flesh; she shall be called Woman, because she was taken out of Man. Therefore a man shall leave his father and mother and be joined to his wife, and they shall become one flesh" (2:23–24 NKJV). Men and women together were the ultimate combination, and their sexuality and chemistry with each other was all part of God's marvelous plan.

But then sin entered the world. Eve's (and Adam's) epic stumble in the garden of Eden fractured not only humankind's relationship with God but also the relationship between men and women. The brokenness that resulted is visible everywhere. I hear it when I appear in segments on Fox News for debates. I read it in quotes from thought leaders. I even notice it in conversations with my girlfriends. Relationships between men and women have become combative and unhealthy, based on power dynamics, sexual objectification, and distrust on both sides. Certainly we can criticize both genders, but the polarization we face today, in which a man subjugates a woman or in which a woman responds with loathing to a perceived slight, has gone too far.

Some of this battle of the sexes is benign, but there is a much more poisonous version emerging in American culture. Over the last few years, as the divide between the sexes has grown steadily more toxic, it has spilled over and now infects not only how men treat us but how we treat ourselves. Somewhere along the way we took a dark turn. In an effort to relate, counter, or perhaps compete with men, we started to copy their character flaws and to embrace their objectification of us. Suddenly we aren't battling the other sex; we're battling, berating, and beating ourselves. And it's downright dangerous.

We have developed a new kind of Stockholm syndrome in which we have come to identify with those who abuse and misuse us. Instead of speaking up against this troubling state of affairs, we are jumping on the bandwagon.

Self-Empowerment or Self-Loathing?

This mindset is visible everywhere. Consider, for example, the pop star Rihanna. Long before the *Fifty Shades of Grey* craze, Rihanna released the single "S&M," in which she sings about chains and whips as part of her sexual repertoire. This is the same Rihanna who made headlines in 2009 when she was choked and beaten by her then-boyfriend, singer Chris Brown, and then began dating him again a few years later. When asked how she could take him back, Rihanna insisted that she was the one in control and was doing what was best for her. "Even if it's a mistake, it's my mistake . . . I'd rather just live my truth," she told *Rolling Stone*.[4] Here's the truth, sweet girl: that's messed up. You deserve so much better.

Hollywood has always been the least common denominator, but the intellectual elite and feminists are still working to protect women. Right? After the many years of lecturing from feminists about sisterhood, surely they recognize the harm this culture is inflicting upon women.

Think again.

Along with the embrace of promiscuous and often violent sexuality, the self-degradation in female culture is also emerging under the guise of feminism itself. In a March 2015 *National Review* article, Mary Eberstadt wrote of a new trend among women that she termed "jailhouse feminism"—a tough, even "thuggish" filtering of reality deliberately stripped of niceties, where promiscuity is promoted, offense is easily taken, and anger abounds.[5] And Eberstadt is right. Somehow it has become trendy for women to bandy about derogatory language, venomous attacks, and promiscuous mantras.

Consider the way we speak and present ourselves. Mean girls are in vogue. Just note the rise in the use of profane and derogatory terms that populate the language of educated women today. From slut walks to slut pride, book titles like *Moody Bitches* and *Bitchfest*, and songs with talk so raunchy they make me squirm, the language of women today has become, as Eberstadt puts it, "a cacophony of rage punctuated by curses—especially when progressive-minded women are talking among and about themselves."[6]

Feminists seem to think the prolific use of words like *slut* by women is a good thing, an example of taking back language that was once used to disparage us, thereby rejecting society's right to criticize women for their sexual choices. Rather than endure so-called slut-shaming, they seem to argue that we should instead embrace the mantra of slut ourselves.

While it's admirable and important to reject abuse that women have endured in the past, this jailhouse feminist mindset has led to a wave of women who are foulmouthed, angry, and offensive, and who insist that they cannot be made to feel bad about any kind of sexual conduct.

The aggressive, indignant, and sexually empowered stance that seems so common among women today has also filtered down to young women on college campuses. Gail Dines, in her 2010 book *Pornland*, recounts a lecture she was giving on pornography at an East Coast Ivy League school, where female students became increasingly angry during her presentation. They weren't angry about the way porn demeans women or sets up false expectations that hamper our relationships and marriages; no, "they accused me of denying them the free choice to embrace our hypersexualized porn culture," she writes.[7]

The most educated and advantaged young women in our country today are convinced that embracing pornographic representations of women gives them agency and power. Dines writes that in rejecting the image of the Stepford Wife as the ideal form of womanhood, women today have instead embraced "the Stepford Slut: a hypersexualized, young, thin, toned, hairless, and in many cases, surgically enhanced woman with a come-hither look on her face."[8]

The Porn Problem

Why does this matter? Because it has led to what radio host Laura Ingraham has called the "pornification of America."[9] A 2007 Nielsen and NetRatings joint study found that approximately 13 million American women visit pornographic sites each month.[10] The huge success of the *Fifty Shades of Grey* series, which has sold more than 100 million copies worldwide, is also changing the way women encounter porn. Suddenly it's acceptable to read violent pornography on the subway, airplane, or at Starbucks while drinking your Venti latte.[11]

Unfortunately, when it comes to our response to this problem, the attitude of "you do you" (in other words, "it's none of my business") doesn't work, because a coarsening culture will eventually impact you and your home. Let's be clear: the days of *Playboy* are over. Porn today is not the 1950s version. It's much darker and intimately connected to the kind of aggressive, violent sexuality that used to be reserved for a small sadistic following.

According to a recent study, the majority of top-watched porn scenes contain aggressive acts—including slapping, gagging, and verbal abuse.[12] Unsurprisingly, studies have shown that men are more likely to have increasingly aggressive behavior after viewing porn, and pornography consumption has been linked to both violence against women and sex trafficking.[13] Is this the kind of culture we want to promote in the name of female empowerment, or worse yet, that we want our young men to view as normal? Certainly, a steady diet of porn changes how men view sex and women. Research shows that regular porn use hijacks the brain's pleasure centers, leading to addiction and often to tolerance, so that men require increasingly higher levels of stimulation for satisfaction.[14] We also know that porn addictions devastate marriages.[15]

Consider Proverbs 23:7: "As he thinks in his heart, so is he" (NKJV). The secular version of this verse is "garbage in, garbage out." Advertisers spend billions of dollars per year on visual images for one reason: they affect behavior. By accepting the pornification of America, we normalize it for ourselves, our spouses, and even our children—with devastating results.

And lest you think this doesn't affect you because you don't read porn, think again.

Pressure to Be Perfect

The acceptance of pornographic representations of women and the trivialization of sexuality in our culture has led us down a precarious path. Women are valued for their appearance and ability to please men, and we've embraced this idea ourselves.

We are bombarded with messages about our worth, sexuality, and appearance on a daily basis, from all corners of the culture and popular media. Society insists that we must be gorgeous, sexy, and alluring to be worthy of attention and love. From photoshopped magazine covers to celebrities who rarely venture above a size 2, the media's single-minded message to women is that no matter how smart and successful we become, we still have to look perfect for our accomplishments to matter.

I would love to say that due to my relationship with Christ and my understanding of who I am in him, I am immune to such pressure, but that would be a lie. I certainly feel it, and I have since I was a teen. Being married to a supportive and accepting husband hasn't fixed it either. Criticism of my appearance regularly comes up on social media after I have done a TV debate, with Twitter trolls usually ignoring the debate topic. One never gets used to mean tweets, but honestly, it isn't even about what others think. It's about my own insecurity.

TV plays a role, but the pressure to be perfect is particularly acute when it comes to images online and in print media. Do you read fashion magazines? I do, and I love them, because I love fashion. When I was growing up, my godmother owned a small clothing store called The Peggy Lou Shoppe in my wonderful hometown of Paintsville, Kentucky. I loved spending time there with her; it's where I learned to love fashion. Unfortunately, after reading fashion magazines today, I usually feel vaguely dissatisfied. I swear, I want to go run about ten miles when I finish browsing *InStyle*. And apparently I'm not alone. Studies at Stanford University and the University of Massachusetts revealed that about 70 percent of college women say they feel worse about their own looks after reading women's magazines.[16] Most of us know those ads have been photoshopped, but still, the illusion works.

It's Not Just About Us

Even more worrisome is the fact that this emphasis on appearance and the pornification of America affects our kids too. According to the American Psychological Association, girls in the United States see around 40,000 commercials a year, the majority of which emphasize that female self-worth is based on appearance and sex appeal, and which encourage girls to aspire to have a body size most of us can never achieve.[17] The effects are incredibly detrimental: studies have found that nearly half of girls in fifth to twelfth grades report wanting to lose weight because of magazine pictures, and almost the same percentage of first- to third-grade girls—as young as six!—want to be thinner.[18]

Of course, it's not just the pressure to be thin or pretty that our kids face; it's much, much more. As a mom of two teenage kids, I know the dangers out there, and I have been shaken to my core by the things my kids have come into contact with. Trust me, I'm right there with you. Some days I want to move my family to a cave in the desert and hide my kids from all the evils the world will throw at them. But the truth is, we have to keep our heads above the sand.

When my daughter Claire was around eighth or ninth grade, she came home one day in a bad mood. Granted, at that point in her life being moody was not that odd, so I didn't question her, but when she came to me to talk, I realized something was wrong. Claire told me that a girl one year younger than she, whom I'll call Jane, had come to her for help.

Apparently a boy had asked Jane to send him a naked picture of herself. Jane is a smart, cute young woman, but insecure. Her parents are divorced, her dad was never around, and her family life has always been unstable. Sadly, on impulse Jane sent this boy the picture he requested. What happened next is typical. The young man, finding this salacious picture too interesting to keep private, shared it with his friends on his sports team. Some of his teammates were horrified, but none of them told an adult. They did, however, let Jane know what they had seen, and others too. Jane was humiliated and reached out to Claire for help.

Inside, I was frantic, but outwardly I kept calm. Not only was Jane's reputation and emotional state in tatters, but the young man had potentially committed a felony by possessing and distributing child porn. Thank God I took a deep breath and kept my face sympathetic. I asked my daughter a few questions, ending with "May I share this with the proper adults?" She was torn between not wanting to breach a confidence and knowing she was in over her head. Together we prayed for Jane and decided that I should let the school know so they could intervene. I explained to Claire that if adults didn't get involved, that picture might continue to circulate and haunt Jane forever. I also told her that Jane needs help. She and the young man involved were headed down a dark road that could eventually destroy them.

And so I reached out to the school. All parents involved were contacted, the memory cards of phones were confiscated, the state law regarding child porn was examined, which fortunately allowed the school to decide how to respond, and both children were counseled. The saddest part to me was that Jane eventually switched schools. Despite love, support, and a message of redemption, she just couldn't get past the event, and she wanted to start over. This grieved me, but even so, I knew that the outcome could have been so much worse. The experience made me more vigilant as a parent and opened my eyes to the fact that this doesn't just happen to other people's kids. It's happening in Christian homes and schools.

There is no way to bubble-wrap our kids and protect them from everything. Believe me; I would have done it if I could. But it is crucial that we stay informed and sensitized to what our children are up against, so that we can respond well when situations like this arise. We have to be aware of the fact that the violent, hypersexualized world we live in trickles down to affect them as well.

As my children began to ask for iPhones and social media, I really had to do some soul searching. I knew from my work that the internet is the Wild, Wild West in many ways. It can be like allowing your kids into the best library in the world or the very worst criminal-inhabited alley. This dilemma sometimes makes good parents overcompensate and view modern technology and communication as the enemy. It's not. But the internet is undoubtedly a dangerous place, and there are a lot of roads our kids can take on it that will lead them to dark corners. For instance, according to one national survey of kids aged ten to seventeen, one out of four said he or she had encountered unwanted pornography in the past year, and one out of five had been exposed to unwanted sexual solicitations or approaches.[19] When kids are looking for this stuff, it's too easy to find. And this is where it starts to get complicated.

How can we expect our kids to develop good discernment when today's women think it's perfectly acceptable to lust over the *Fifty Shades of Grey* series? We *have* to help our kids navigate this territory, and we can only do that by knowing what they are seeing and reading and listening to.

So here is the deal in our house. We don't have all the answers, obviously, but we've created some ground rules that have helped us navigate this tricky territory. Our kids can use cell phones, iPads, and laptops and watch cable, but these devices are not theirs until they buy them. As long as my husband and I pay for them, they belong to all of us. Therefore, we are all accountable to each other. This means that Will and I get to put safeguards in place to protect our kids from inappropriate content or predators, and there are plenty trolling out there. It also means that we all share passwords with each other. My kids have my passwords, and I have theirs. At any point if they want to look at my phone, they have my permission, and I expect to have theirs. Newsflash, Mom and Dad: that might mean you watch what you say in your own texts. My kids aren't perfect, and neither am I. It's okay to help each other.

Let me say this now, though: I am in full support of snooping on your kids if you have any reason to believe that they are getting into trouble. It is your job to protect your children while they live under your roof.

The consequences for denying early intervention can have lifelong implications. The stakes are too high to wimp out or worry about temporarily upsetting your kids. They are not your friends yet. This will come later, when they are grown. For now they need a mom and dad.

We've got to be realistic about the world we live in. Incidents like the one at my daughter's school aren't isolated; a national study by the journal *Pediatrics* in 2014 found that 20 percent of middle-school students have engaged in sexting.[20] It's not just that our kids are surrounded by messages of violence and promiscuous sexuality; they are falling prey to them.

A recent undercover video by Lila Rose's Live Action gives us a glimpse of the depth of depravity to which our society has fallen. The video highlights the kind of sexual counseling that our government is paying Planned Parenthood to give our kids: At Planned Parenthood of the Rocky Mountains, a counselor tells a client she believes to be fifteen-years-old that it's okay if her boyfriend chokes, whips, or gags her as long as she has a safety word. She encourages the young woman to do some internet research on what BDSM involves, suggests she and her boyfriend go to a sex shop to look at different outfits and toys and "get educated together"—it is illegal for a minor to enter a sex shop, by the way—and even goes so far as to tell the fifteen-year-old that she and her boyfriend should watch porn together and then "act it out."[21]

If this is the kind of sexual advice our kids are receiving, how can we expect them to escape unscathed? Will our daughters learn to value themselves when society doesn't?

Our children are learning about sexuality and pornography at a very early age, and if something doesn't change, the long-term effects will be disastrous. As Diane E. Levin and Jean Kilbourne write in their book *So Sexy So Soon*, "boys raised in a sexualized culture often become men who are unsatisfying and sometimes even dangerous partners for women."[22] Girls exposed to sexual images from a young age, meanwhile, are more prone to three of the most common mental health problems for girls and women: depression, eating disorders, and low self-esteem.[23] More generally, as Levin and Kilbourne write, the lessons our kids learn at a young age from our oversexualized society "shape their gender identity, sexual attitudes, and values, and their capacity for relationships, for love and connection that they take into adulthood."[24] We are setting our children on a dangerous path, one that will affect them for years to come, if not the rest of their lives.

What Can Esther Women Do?

This is really scary stuff. Trust me, I feel it too. As a woman, I am burdened by the pornification of America and the way women are portrayed and treated by the media and society. As a mother, I am terrified of the way this culture can potentially threaten or damage my kids. The reason I bring all of this up is to consider how we can and should respond. For you Esthers out there hoping to impact the culture and speak truth into our messed-up world, the importance of recognizing where things stand today is critical. Even more important is what we choose to do with that information.

Hear me when I say this: your perspective as a conservative Christian woman is desperately needed. As believers, we understand our value as women, because we have experienced it powerfully and transformatively through the sacrifice and redemption of Jesus. As women who know the Author of love, we are equipped to speak authoritatively about true love and self-respect. So buck up. You can do this! Your sisters need to hear words of truth and, most important, words of grace. God loves us and wants to provide us a life's banquet of filet mignon, so we need to stop settling for pig slop.

Christians have a message that we should be blaring from the rooftops when it comes to what is happening in our culture in regard to sexuality and what is portrayed as normal and appropriate behavior.

SPEAK UP ABOUT OUR TRUE VALUE

First we have to start with the ultimate truth about our value: we are God's masterpieces. He created us, is pleased with us, and has raised us up for his glory. As he told the prophet Isaiah: "Bring my sons from afar and my daughters from the ends of the earth—everyone who is called by my name, whom I created for my glory, whom I formed and made" (43:6–7). Did you catch that? He formed and made us. He is the perfect Creator, and we are his precious creations.

This is a beautiful message for those of us who know God. It might not have the same oomph, though, when we're speaking with nonbelieving friends. Unfortunately, in an increasingly secular nation, we have less ability to use biblical teaching as a reference point. We can't just pull Scripture out of our back pockets and expect the world to be persuaded. But the Word of God is transcendent, eternal truth, and often people still recognize truth when they hear it. Our call is to point them toward that truth.

Though we might choose different words, the message is the same: you are God's magnificent creation, and you were meant for more than phony love.

Every woman is "fearfully and wonderfully made" (Ps. 139:14) by a God who loves her. The world recognizes this fact. Look at art through the ages, from the Venus de Milo to Degas's ballet dancers to Ruben's exquisite, full-figured women. The female form has always been recognized as something beautiful and unique. Music too has sung of love and female beauty across the ages; consider the love songs of Rumi and King Solomon, the troubadours of Europe, even the tunes of more contemporary eras like Eric Clapton's "Wonderful Tonight" or Frank Sinatra's "Fly Me to the Moon." Women are incredible creations and have always been seen as such, whether the world perceives God's hand in it or not.

By gently speaking the truth about our worth as women—God's crowning creation—we can encourage others to reject the unfulfilling lies of the media, Hollywood, and even damaging strains of feminism. We are uniquely and beautifully female, and God has given us certain qualities that we should embrace. We aren't just men with different plumbing; we are an entirely different and magnificent creation! Science supports what we feel intuitively: men and women differ hormonally, chemically, anatomically, and physiologically. Women typically have larger orbital frontal cortices than men, for instance, which may allow us to identify our feelings faster and better express emotion.[25] (Well, that explains a lot!)

The truth of our distinct differences frees us from feminism's claim that we have to be tough, protective, aggressive—basically, masculine. By appropriating the worst male behaviors and attitudes in our desire to protect ourselves, get to the top in the corporate world, or gain sexual empowerment, we detract from the unique identities God gave us as women.

HOLD OURSELVES TO A HIGHER STANDARD

We are God's masterpieces. That's the most important truth to get across to women in our culture today. But we must also realize that as God's masterpieces, we are meant for more. He created us for his glory, not for our own pleasure. The reason to abstain from pornography, promiscuous sexuality, or anything else that demeans the masterpiece God made is because we are not our own. Paul told the Corinthians, "Do you not know that your bodies are temples of the Holy Spirit, who is in you, whom you have received from God? You are not your own; you were bought at a price. Therefore honor God with your bodies" (1 Cor. 6:19–20). Wow. As a believer, I need to remind myself that it's not just about me. I belong to God, and therefore how I treat my body, what I choose to say, and the media I consume matters. Any trash I put into my mind that demeans me is an affront to my Maker.

Okay, so most of us church ladies don't dabble in visual or written porn, but what about those cable shows? You know the ones I'm talking about, those series that we compulsively binge-watch despite the fact that they've got enough sexual innuendo and risqué bedroom scenes to make us cringe. Paul told the Philippians, "Whatever is true, whatever is noble, whatever is right, whatever is pure, whatever is lovely, whatever is admirable—if anything is excellent or praiseworthy—think about such things" (4:8). Uh-oh. Now I'm starting to squirm. What *about* those magnificently entertaining cable series? One of my good friends recently confessed to me that she felt so convicted she had to stop watching a really good one—one that I watched as well. I felt sick. I knew that I had heard the same still voice, and I ignored it. I fall short every day; we all do. This doesn't mean we give up the quest to please God in every area of our lives and to free ourselves of negative messages that harm.

We must be ever vigilant to protect our hearts and minds, and in today's world, that's not easy. Our culture has pitted men against women, women against men, and even women against one another, and boiled down our relationships to their most base and selfish versions.

We must be the ones to raise the bar. We must be the ones to declare truth and exhort beauty because we know what real Truth and true beauty look like. We can't settle for a world of men versus women or accept that women will always be demeaned as objects for sexual use and subsequently discarded. No, together we must demand something different. Together we are a living testament to God's love for the church and Christ's sacrifice for her. Together we are more, not less, and we must insist on that principle and embrace it ourselves.

Consider Jesus' prayer for all believers: "I have given them the glory that you gave me, that they may be one as we are one—I in them and you in me—so that they may be brought to complete unity" (John 17:22–23). We are called to unity, and when we embrace this call, God can and will work through us for his glory.

POINT OUT WHAT DOESN'T WORK, AND OFFER ALTERNATIVES WORTH EMULATING

As we work together to proclaim the truth of God's love for us, we can also gently point out that the truths by which many people order their lives today simply don't satisfy. For instance, in our hypersexualized society, women are promised more—more sexual empowerment, more freedom, more love or attention from men, more satisfaction. But in reality, we feel like we have a lot less. We aren't happier or more fulfilled; we're the opposite. Rates of depression and anxiety are on the rise; one in four women today take antidepressant medications.[26] And a 2009 study by Wharton professors Betsey Stevenson and Justin Wolfers found that over the past thirty-five years, women's happiness has steadily declined—both in comparison to where we were thirty-five years ago and in comparison to men.[27] Clearly, something isn't working.

Part of our role in discussing these issues is to help women recognize that the world's lies are just that—lies. But more important is that we offer them an alternative, a redemptive message that speaks of their own unique value. What does work is a life where God's view of women takes center stage. When we embrace the truth about who God says we are, we find a lot more contentment than when we're trying to live up to all of the wild expectations of the media or society.

We were meant for more. We need to encourage each other to stop looking at the Kardashians as role models and look to our grandparents, our mentors, real-life women who embody the kind of love that *does* satisfy. All around us, especially in our churches, we have beautiful examples of true women and true love—lasting and agape (God-sized) love. There are beautiful couples who have loved and sacrificed for each other for more than fifty years, not fifty shades.

I witnessed this kind of love up close in the lives of my great-uncle Robert and his wife, Carolyn Young. Robert was a part-time pastor, and they owned a small country store in the mountains of North Carolina. They persevered as life partners through infertility, war, illness, and even the Great Depression. Carolyn's health was fragile for decades, but Robert lovingly cared for her even when he was elderly. Finally one day she became so ill that she lapsed into a coma. He took her to the hospital and stayed until the staff made him take a break and go home. While at home, he sat down and simply died. I believe it was because he couldn't face life without her. A few hours later she too was gone. The homecoming in heaven must have been glorious and unexpected. What a gift. They are strolling the golden streets arm in arm as they did on earth.

We need to celebrate relationships like theirs, ones that value women as treasures and view true love as a reality, not an unrealistic or outdated trope.

One last point. It is crucial that we speak about these issues from a place of humility. Whether speaking with our Christian sisters or non-Christian friends, the only way we're going to get anywhere is if we remember that we are *all* sinners, and that the reason Christ died was to redeem us all from our fallen state. The apostle Paul's letter to the Romans should always be at the front of our minds: "But God demonstrates his own love for us in this: While we were still sinners, Christ died for us" (5:8). We aren't arguing to score a point or prove ourselves right; we are speaking truth because God has called us to, and because through us, others can encounter the incredible message of redemptive love.

At the end of the day, we are surrounded by a world that embraces promiscuity, violence, self-degradation, vulgarity, and shallow, materialistic definitions of beauty. Too many women have fallen prey to this culture, attempting to embrace it as a way of self-empowerment or self-protection—but as we've seen, it doesn't work.

We need to realign our perspective with reality and focus our efforts on becoming the kind of women God has called us to be. Let's work together to become brave women whose primary aim is to glorify God, who recognize that our femaleness is a unique gift, who speak wisdom and truth, who enjoy sex in a way that honors the Lord, and who know that we are perfectly made in the image of God. When we align ourselves with this image of womanhood, we will be truly empowered—able to stand up as role models for the young women around us, able to speak truth to the lies that come from every level of society and government, able to give women a voice that demands respect and has the power to bring about change. As Erick Erickson has written, "a Christian on the sidelines is a Christian not going forth."[28]

It is time for us to get off the sidelines. It is our time to stand up to a world gone crazy. Will you join me?

Lila Rose

FOUNDER AND PRESIDENT, LIVE ACTION

Lila Rose founded Live Action in 2003, when she was just fifteen years old, in order to end the culture of abortion in our nation. Live Action uses investigative journalism to expose and educate the public about the abuses perpetrated by abortion providers and to encourage a culture of dignity for all people. "As I entered my teen years, I felt convicted and inspired to do my part to educate about this human rights abuse and help other young people see the truth," she says.

Live Action has exposed, among other things, the widespread racism, medical misinformation, and sexual-abuse cover-ups committed by Planned Parenthood and other abortion providers. Their work has helped defund the abortion industry in many states and has made millions more people aware of the horrific acts of those within the abortion industry.

With her deep faith, strong moral convictions, and willingness to speak out, Lila has been a light for conservative women. This doesn't mean she hasn't experienced significant pushback, however. "It can be challenging as a young woman to lead today. Some people, particularly certain left-leaning media groups who oppose our organization ideologically, have tried to marginalize or downplay the substance of our work, focusing instead on my youth, my sex, or my appearance as the founder," she says. Yet Lila refuses to be silenced by these voices of opposition. "I'm proud to say our team takes it all in stride, focusing instead on our work and mission."

Lila's work has helped make the pro-life movement stronger and more effective than ever before. Hearts and minds are being changed, and she witnesses it every day. "Every time we get an email or comment from someone who tells us our undercover or educational videos have changed their minds on abortion, or helped them choose life for their baby, it makes all of the work more than worth it!" she says.[29]

CHAPTER 3

Sexual Assault and Politics

I remember it was warm that day. I had been sick for a few weeks with my first pregnancy, and I had found that exercise helped quell my nausea. I was tired, but thinking that a run might help, I laced up my running shoes and put on headphones. Since my late twenties, I have always loved to run in the mornings. My whole day seems better if I can get a run in first. That day, however, running would not bring me relief. This morning jog would end up changing the way I view the world.

I started out slowly on my usual running path in suburban Virginia outside Washington, DC. After a few minutes I began picking up speed and feeling better. My route included a pedestrian bridge over a busy highway, and as I crossed bridge, I saw him. He passed me and looked at me strangely. He was pulling up his shirt, oddly, exposing a flabby stomach and chest, kind of flashing me as he ran by. It all seemed strange, but my instinct was just to look away and avoid eye contact. I continued my run.

A section of my route skirted a quiet and isolated cemetery, and normally I would have followed the path around it, but that morning I had a bad feeling about going in there. I decided to skip that part of the route and instead thread my way down to the running path along a busy street. It was there on the path that I heard or sensed footsteps behind me. I looked over my shoulder. It was the same man.

I wasn't afraid; it was nine in the morning, broad daylight, and cars were intermittently passing us, but still I could feel that something was off. When I got to a section of the running path that dipped down a hill and through some trees, obscured from the road by hillside and highway guardrail, I paused. I heard an almost audible voice say, *Let him go first.* Now, I am not the kind of person who starts sentences with "God told me." I know and respect those kinds of people, but I am usually not sure exactly what God is saying, other than what he says in the Bible, and I often wish he would speak to me more directly. However, there are a few times in my life when I know that I heard from him, and this was one of them. Although I didn't know it at the time, I believe this was the Holy Spirit warning me and telling me what to do.

Without turning around to look at the man, I paused at the top of the path and moved to the side so he could go by me. But instead of running by, he grabbed both of my arms from behind. Despite the weird vibe I had felt earlier, I was shocked, so shocked that my first reaction was to shrug him off and yell, "What are you doing?" He lost his grip slightly as I jerked away, but then grabbed me again, more firmly this time, and started dragging me down the path behind the rail.

Now, I am a fighter and have prided myself for not taking harassment from men. I had always thought that if something like this were to happen, I would kick and scream, but that moment, there on the running path as the man dragged me by my arms, I couldn't physically fight. I had a million thoughts running through my head, but I was almost paralyzed with fear. I felt weak, like a rag doll. Physically, I was completely out of control. Still, I remember crying, begging him to leave me alone, and telling him I was pregnant.

He outweighed me easily by a hundred pounds and had no trouble forcing me to the ground on my stomach, face to the pavement, shielded from the road by the hillside. The next thing I knew he was on top of me. I found my voice again and this time I was screaming. I wasn't aware of what was going on around us; all I could think was, *I don't know how this is going to end.* I would like to say that I prayed, but I didn't. I just screamed.

Again, I heard a quiet voice in my head. *Keep screaming.* So I did, as hard as I could, so hard that it wasn't even very loud, but the register was high. It seemed like hours, but it had to have only been a few seconds, and then it was over. I heard him curse, and he jumped up and ran off. I jumped up too and clawed my way up the dirt embankment to the sidewalk.

On the side of the road was a beautiful African American woman sitting in her car with her young son. She told me that her name was Mary. She had seen something that looked wrong, stopped her car, and honked her horn, and that was enough to make my attacker run away. She was the miracle I was hoping for but didn't have the presence of mind to pray for. She was my guardian angel. I wasn't raped. I was physically battered and left bleeding, but I wasn't sexually assaulted.

That same man attacked two other women before the police caught him, at which point I identified him. The police told me that they found evidence in his apartment linking him to campus assaults that had happened while he was in school at a major university in the South. They also told me that they found lots of porn. Eventually he was sentenced to eighteen years (less with time off for good behavior) in prison in Virginia. He's out now. I know where he lives. He is a registered sex offender.

I hesitate to share this story because it feels somehow inappropriate to dwell on my experience compared to the deep trauma that other women suffer. Because of my report to law enforcement after the attack, our county's social services offered me free group counseling. In retrospect, it would have been helpful. Yet I declined, for one reason: I couldn't imagine sitting in a room with women who had suffered so much more than me and complaining about my trauma. Maybe they would have understood that I was scared and shocked, but I didn't think I had a right to feel what I was feeling, and it made me ashamed somehow.

I recognize now that this may have been a form of survivor guilt, and that I still feel that confusing guilt albeit to a lesser degree. I know that what I experienced can in no way compare to what other women have survived. I am incredibly thankful for God's provision for me, but I don't know why I was spared and others aren't. I know God loves them as much as he loves me. I simply don't have the answers; but one thing I do have is a platform from which to advocate for others. In sharing my story, I hope to bring awareness to the stories of those who have suffered far worse, and I also hope to encourage others who may have felt, like me, that their trauma wasn't real or traumatic enough. Your experience matters, and together we can help others.

Two important things resulted from my attack and have driven me to write about it now. First, that day changed me. I knew then that I wasn't immune to evil and that the world really is a dangerous place. Fear crept in and was only exacerbated with the birth of my two children. As a mom, I have lived in fear of sexual predators. In the early years of motherhood I would get anxious if a stranger wanted to look at my baby. Everyone was a potential pedophile in my mind. Now as a mom of a freshman in college, I worry about campus assault.

After the attack I couldn't sleep for months, especially if my husband was gone. Even now, all these years later, I still don't sleep well when I am on the road for work. I watch the door before I fall asleep, worrying that someone will break into my room and hurt me. This deep-seated anxiety has stayed with me at home too, where everyone in my family knows to warn me if they're in the house when I'm not expecting them. I have flipped out on more than one occasion when someone surprised me. And I experience all of this as a woman who escaped rape. What would have happened to me if he had succeeded?

The second significant result of my attack is that I have a deep empathy for women who have been sexually violated in any way. I am so sorry for those who have suffered, and feel such compassion for their pain. I believe them. I feel a responsibility to help them. One would think that everyone would feel this way toward survivors of sexual assault, but that's not always the case. Some have used this horrific issue for their own gain, and for that I have no tolerance.

Campus Rape and Victim Exploitation

The Washington political class has used rape victims as props for their own purposes, politics, and even profit. Campus rape is the perfect example. As the groundswell of attention around this topic in the past two years has illuminated, tragically, instances of campus assault are still prevalent today.[1] It's a reality that hits home. Recently, another mom shared with me that her older daughter, while away at college, was sexually assaulted at a campus party. The child has had to drop out of school for a semester to recover. She is planning to attend a different school in a year.

We hear these sorts of stories all the time, and they tear at a mother's heart. And yet such incidents are either brushed aside or used to promote agendas, instead of forcing us to deal with assault as an intolerable crime.

Even if we disagree on the frequency, it is irrefutable that rape occurs too often on college campuses. Unfortunately, colleges have been reluctant, ill-equipped, and sometimes downright unwilling to do much, if anything, about it. Concerned about their reputations, fundraising, and rankings, colleges and universities have had little incentive to report sexual violence on their campuses. A 2014 Senate report found an overall failure of schools to encourage reporting of sexual assault, and it remains one of the most underreported crimes in the country; more than 80 percent of campus assaults are never reported to campus or law enforcement.[2] And even when assaults are reported, they are often not handled properly.

Just think of the infamous case of Jameis Winston, the Florida State University (FSU) star quarterback. Winston was accused of raping a freshman girl in 2012. Though she reported the alleged attack, there was hardly any investigation; the police waited two weeks to interview Winston, never collected a DNA sample, and quickly dropped the case. Winston was allowed to continue to play for the football team, which won the national championship in 2014. Only after the accusation became public and FSU was placed under national pressure did they reopen the investigation. This kind of incompetent and incomplete work in response to rape allegations is rampant across the country today, and is one of the reasons victims are reluctant to report rape in the first place. The victim and the accused deserve swift and meticulous investigation. In this case the young man was not charged, but the shoddy process left doubt he may not deserve.

Awareness has been growing about the culture of silence and mishandling of rape on campuses, and the attention focused on the issue has led to some change in policies and practices, although certainly not enough. The Obama White House has made sexual assault one of the administration's priorities and set up a task force in early 2014 to investigate the issue and come up with solutions. While this is admirable, and some of the suggestions to come out of the task force's report have started to move us in the right direction—suggestions that include proper training for school officials and increasing transparency around enforcement efforts, for instance—the government's response has mainly been to increase bureaucracy.

The attention the left has focused on this issue has so far done little to address the roots of the problem: preventing rape before it can happen and getting rapists off the streets. The attention has often served advocacy and political groups far more than the victims. Instead of emphasizing that rape is a horrendous and despicable crime, campuses and advocacy groups have spent time focusing on partial measures, politically correct messaging, and bad policies.

Take the recent wave of mutual affirmative consent policies, for instance. Championed by liberal advocacy groups and adopted by many campuses in response to the White House's report, these policies suggest that the solution to campus assault lies in intricate contracts between young men and women based on continual consent for any sexual activity. Moving away from the old mantra "no means no," these new policies instead insist that without an enthusiastic and continual yes from both partners, there is no consent. Although the strategy was widely adopted, college safety experts noted that it "is too new, and too little studied" for us to have any measure of its effectiveness.[3] That didn't stop Governor Jerry Brown in September 2014, however, from making California the first state to legally require that every college adopt such a consent policy or lose state funding.

Absurdly, this policy requires that separate consent be given for each type of contact, meaning, as the *New York Times* put it, that "an encounter that progresses from kissing to intercourse would require not one go-ahead but several."[4] Even if we believed that college kids would stop at each step of a sexual encounter to receive "affirmative, conscious and voluntary agreement" from their partners, as the law states, do we really think that such a government-mandated intrusion would stop campus assault?

Feminists groups have championed the law, claiming that it removes victim blame and puts more pressure on the accused to prove that his partner did want to engage in activity, rather than the victim having to prove that she did *not*.[5] This sounds good, but in reality, it expands the definition of sexual consent and detracts from the crucial issues at stake. Such laws turn any sexual encounter into a potential rape. As legal scholar Jed Rubenfeld wrote in the *New York Times*, "Under this definition, a person who voluntarily gets undressed, gets into bed and has sex with someone, without clearly communicating either yes or no, can later say—correctly—that he or she was raped."[6] Such policies do not prevent campus assault; instead, they encourage people to think of themselves as potential victims after the fact.

These types of policies ignore the fact that the campus hookup culture has led a generation of young men and women into a murky and dangerous sexual landscape in which too often sexual encounters leave them unsatisfied, confused, angry, or hurt. As Mona Charen wrote in *The Federalist* last year, rather than condemning "rape culture," we ought to point to "the sexual revolution itself. The agonies college campuses are now routinely experiencing are the result of a hyper-sexualized culture that has robbed the young of romance, courtesy, privacy, and yes, love."[7] Yet colleges, feminist activists, and government administrators overlook the cultural breakdown that led us to this place and instead use claims of a widespread rape epidemic to promote their own agendas and policies.

Take the way colleges now handle rape accusations, for instance. We ought to view assault as a criminal offense that occurs outside of the scope of a bad date or miscommunication about consent, and we should be willing to bring in law enforcement to handle investigations and determine which accusations merit criminal prosecution. And yet in 2011 the Obama administration's Department of Education released federal regulations requiring colleges to step into this role and handle sexual assault claims themselves. Asserting that sexual assault is a form of "sexual discrimination" prohibited by Title IX, the government now requires colleges to address assault claims or risk losing federal funding. Schools may coordinate with law enforcement if there is an ongoing criminal investigation into an incident, but they must conduct their own Title IX investigation regardless. Further, if a criminal investigation ends without an arrest or conviction, schools must continue to carry out their separate proceedings nonetheless.[8]

Unsurprisingly, the results of such proceedings have been consistently dreadful. Administrators are effectively conducting criminal trials and investigations, which they are not equipped to do, and in many cases, the rights of the accused, the accuser, or both are ignored. When a guilty verdict is reached, the punishment is often laughably light—a slap on the wrist, perhaps expulsion in extreme cases. Colleges mishandle cases and focus on adjudication when efforts should instead be aimed at preventing rape from happening in the first place.

Stumbling over Political Correctness

Such efforts are only hampered by the wave of political correctness and the cries of victim blaming that have overtaken the conversation. When Emily Yoffe wrote a piece in *Slate* suggesting that binge drinking might contribute to a woman's likelihood of being assaulted, she was eviscerated for her "rape denialism manifesto" and for "betray[ing] all survivors."[9] This kind of one-sided, reactionary rhetoric prevents us from accurately assessing sexual assault claims and properly punishing perpetrators, and from avoiding false accusations and convictions of innocent men, whether in the court of law or in public opinion.

Alcohol or drug use does increase the chance of assault; this fact is indisputable. A recent poll by the Washington Post-Kaiser Family Foundation found two-thirds of sexual assault victims say they had been drinking alcohol just before the incident.[10] Yet telling women to consider drinking less as a protective measure is considered offensive and antifeminist.

It has gotten to the point that almost nothing can be said encouraging women to watch out for the dangers around them. As Fox News reported, students at Colgate University were outraged in 2014 when an email sent by university officials warned students of an attack earlier that day and urged them to be "aware of [their] surroundings," and "look out for one another at social events." Students criticized the email as victim blaming. "It's unfair to make potential victims responsible," one student said.[11] Well, unfortunately, life's not fair, and there are people who mean young women and men harm. Reminding kids to look out for each other and to use good judgment is in no way victim blaming; it's prevention.

Similarly, liberals pilloried Miss Nevada in the 2014 Miss USA pageant for suggesting that women learn self-defense to protect themselves. Feminists took to Twitter, claiming it was uneducated, disrespectful, and inappropriate to suggest women are responsible for physically fending off sexual predators.[12] Seriously?

Now, hear me clearly: no woman deserves to be assaulted, raped, or touched in any way she doesn't want. Nor should survivors be blamed or accused of having caused their rapes. However, there has to be an end to playing the victim-blaming card in order to promote political ideologies and feminist thinking that misdirects the public's attention and does little to stop assault. I wasn't surprised last year when the American Enterprise Institute's Christina Hoff Sommers was the subject of protests and threats at Oberlin College. Outside the venue where Sommers delivered a lecture on the pros and cons of feminism, protestors held up signs calling for trigger warnings because they felt the talk might upset listeners and invalidate the experiences of rape victims.[13] That's right—they bullied her with trigger warnings. Well, I think we need to have all sorts of discussions on the issue, not just the comfortable ones.

I taught my daughter to look both ways before crossing the street. I taught her not to talk to strangers when she was little. I also talked to her about being aware of her surroundings and not walking alone at night. Perhaps most important, I have warned her that anything she might be tempted to do that diminishes her judgment or awareness makes her more vulnerable to danger. People who think that it is wrong to give our daughters this kind of advice are, as my Israeli friends say, "so open-minded their brains fall out." Ignorance makes us vulnerable.

A Deep-Seated Evil

What hasn't occurred to the left is that sexual assault is indicative of a deeper problem of the heart. This isn't going to be solved by politically correct rhetoric, campus kangaroo courts, or making students secure consent ten times for each sexual encounter. Nor will it be fully solved by reducing levels of binge drinking or drug use on campuses. Chuck Colson of Prison Fellowship was fond of saying that at its core, criminal behavior is a moral issue, and he is right.[14] He should know. Prison Fellowship is the world's largest prison ministry, working to bring restoration and share the love of God with inmates in thousands of prisons in 127 countries around the world. Colson understood what drives the human heart to evil, and he recognized that the only thing that can stop this kind of evil is a complete transformation of the heart through the power of Christ.

Transformation, by the way, should happen to sexual predators in prison in order to keep citizens safe. These are the people we fear. This is why we build prisons. I support alternative sentencing for nonviolent criminals, but I strongly support long, and in some cases life-long, sentences for sexual predators.

Here's the thing: sexual assault is not caused by miscommunication; it is a horrible crime often committed by serial assaulters. This goes far beyond campus assault, and unfortunately much of the rhetoric around the campus rape epidemic has distracted us from focusing on the dangerous men who serially rape. According to a January 2014 federal report on sexual assault, more than half of men who admitted to committing rape or attempted rape said they committed multiple offenses, averaging six rapes each.[15] Sexual assault is a deep-seated, addicting, and ensnaring sin. We must take sex offenders off the streets after the first attack.

Measures enforcing political correctness, mutual consent, and minor punishment miss the point. This issue is about the darkness in our hearts and needs to be treated as such. The horrifying case in Steubenville, Ohio, in 2012 illustrates the vileness at the heart of sexual assault. In August of that year, a sixteen-year-old girl was sexually assaulted by two football players from her high school while she was drunk and incapacitated. The boys used their cell phones to take pictures of the unconscious girl and then shared those images with others, along with descriptions of the assault and comments about the young woman. A video of the incident, taken by a student bystander who is shouting encouragement and laughing, is shocking in the depths of its depravity. Eventually the photos and video found their way onto Instagram, Facebook, and YouTube.

Concerned Women for America (CWA) waded into the Steubenville case and urged Ohio Attorney General Mike DeWine to get to the bottom of the assault. Prior to our involvement, only the National Organization for Women (NOW) was politicizing the event, and the school officials were covering up the crime. Attorney General DeWine had worked with CWA previously as a member of the US Senate, and he trusted our judgment enough to go in swinging. He charged not only the boys responsible but also others involved in the cover-up. In March 2013, the two boys were found guilty of rape and given mandated minimum sentences, and that November DeWine brought additional charges against four school officials for obstructing justice and tampering with evidence.[16]

Now clearly, there was no consent asked for when these boys assaulted an unconscious sixteen-year-old girl, and obviously none was given. Nor would a law requiring such consent have prevented the evil that emerged in Ohio when those boys were left to their basest sinful desires. Rape is a sickness of the soul. We can't politicize it away. In our focus on political agendas, we are missing the larger picture.

The Misdirected Federal Response

I can't say it enough: Rape is a serious crime. And crime does need to be addressed by the government—sometimes at both the state and federal levels. Unfortunately the federal government can't seem to get it right. Its answer to sexual violence is just to dole out grants, sometimes to legitimately helpful organizations, but also to many left-leaning ones who talk a good game.

In 2014, under the auspices of the Violence Against Women Act (VAWA), the government awarded almost seven hundred grants to organizations connected with sexual violence, some more than $1 million each.[17] Yet the oversight of these grants is limited, and the effectiveness of recipients has not been carefully tracked. A 2010 report found multiple instances of fraud, embezzlement, or mismanagement of funds by grant recipients, with federal officials doing little to stop it.[18] Although CWA was smeared for questioning the VAWA's efficacy and instead suggesting block grants to the states and law enforcement, even the bill's supporters have admitted that it is too broad to be effective.[19]

The lack of oversight adds to the difficulty in holding colleges and universities accountable for their use of grants funded by VAWA. Such grants, sometimes more than $500,000 a year, are intended to equip colleges to better handle sexual assault claims and prevent incidents on campus. Yet that money is not carefully tracked, and results are hard to quantify. In 2014, twenty-four of the colleges and universities receiving such grants were simultaneously under investigation by the federal government for potential sexual-violence-related violations.[20] That's right; they were receiving money even while being investigated for violations that would strip them of that funding.

Furthermore, the powerful lobbying and huge amounts of money behind this cause have the potential to breed fraudulent claims and impure motives. There is money in victimization, and unfortunately, too often that colors the way sexual assault is addressed and discussed. This reality has sadly come to light through the proliferation of false narratives in order to promote rape advocacy. Consider Lena Dunham, who wrote in her 2014 memoir *Not That Kind of Girl* that she had been sexually assaulted in college but misidentified her alleged assailant; the false accusation of rape by members of the Duke lacrosse team in 2006 and the rush to condemn them; or the November 2014 *Rolling Stone* article that perpetuated a completely false story of gang rape on the campus of the University of Virginia.[21]

There are financial, political, cultural, and just plain sick motives for presenting a false narrative, hurting the least of these: the victims. This situation has only been exacerbated by the pressure the federal government has put on schools to change their policies; in their rush to deal with assault charges in order to keep their funding, schools have often been too quick to condemn innocent men. Such reactions only perpetuate the idea that most rape claims are false and further deter future victims from coming forward.

Feminists insist they want to take back the night, and Washington swears to help them. But the truth is that the government is spending hundreds of millions of dollars annually but not keeping women safe. They are throwing money to advocacy groups but are failing to double down on preventing future crime.

Federal money would be far better spent first on law enforcement and criminal prosecution. Prevention efforts seem useless when we can't prosecute perpetrators. Unfortunately law enforcement may not have the resources it needs to pursue justice for victims and prevent future attacks. It may not have the ability to work with colleges and universities to address the issue as a federal crime rather than a school disciplinary matter. And rapists are being left to walk free. As the White House task force report laid out clearly: "Across all demographics, rapists and sex offenders are too often not made to pay for their crimes, and remain free to assault again. Arrest rates are low and meritorious cases are still being dropped—many times because law enforcement officers and prosecutors are not fully trained."[22]

The bottom line is that government has a responsibility to enforce the law and deliver justice to victims, and it's time to get this right. Debbie Smith is the perfect example of what happens when justice is delayed.

The Rape Kit Backlog

In 1989, Debbie Smith suffered a brutal attack by a man who dragged her into the woods outside her home in Virginia and raped her repeatedly. He told her that he knew where she lived and threatened to come back and kill her if she told anyone. Bravely, Debbie reported the assault and went to the emergency room for a sexual assault forensic exam. But because of a backlog of DNA kits, it was more than six years before the kit was analyzed. For those six years she waited for the rapist to be identified, living in utter fear that he would hunt her down. "I was terrified for myself and my family, and was suicidal for a time," she later recalled.[23]

In 1995, a technician finally identified Debbie's attacker while analyzing DNA records. The attacker, who was then serving time for abducting and robbing two women, was now sentenced to 161 years in prison. Knowing that her rapist was behind bars "gave me back my life," Debbie said.[24] Yet the six years in which she lived in terror could have been avoided if her DNA kit had been tested in a timely manner.

Rape kits can be vital to successful prosecutions in cases of rape and sexual assault. Realizing that there was an immense backlog of these kits and insufficient funds to cover the cost of testing them, Debbie became an advocate for the issue. Eventually she became the face of a bipartisan bill, the Debbie Smith Act, introduced in 2001 to provide federal grants to help states reduce the DNA backlog and provide legal assistance to victims.

Along with Concerned Women for America, I worked with then Senate Majority Leader Bill Frist to get the Debbie Smith Act through the Senate. We were successful in our efforts, and a key moment came when over a small dinner on the issue I urged Senator Frist to champion the bill. He agreed that there simply was no excuse for our government to allow evidence to languish and for other women to suffer from predators

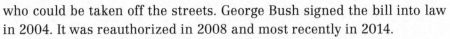

who could be taken off the streets. George Bush signed the bill into law in 2004. It was reauthorized in 2008 and most recently in 2014.

Unfortunately, despite everyone's good intentions this has become yet another example of misappropriation of government funding. It became clear in 2012 that the money from the Debbie Smith Act was not solving the backlog of kits; in fact, more than 400,000 kits were still sitting around waiting to be tested.[25] The Senate Appropriations Committee noted that funding specifically set aside to test rape kits and get rapists off the streets had been used instead for expenditures that had nothing to do with DNA backlog reduction.[26]

Are you mad yet? Well, the mismanagement gets worse.

In 2013 Congress passed the Sexual Assault Forensic Evidence Reporting Act (SAFER Act). The new law specifically dictated that the Department of Justice award 75 percent of Debbie Smith Act funds to cleaning up the backlog. It also required audits so Americans would know if victims were being served or not. After more than a year of working with representatives, trying to bring this bill to the floor with a number of setbacks, we at CWA were gratified to see it pass both houses in early 2013. Rape victims would finally get justice. We thought we had won.

We were wrong. After all of the hard work of CWA members and other advocates, including then *Washington Post* columnist Melinda Henneberger, Senator John Cornyn (TX), and Representatives Ted Poe (TX) and Bob Goodlatte (VA), as of this writing, the Department of Justice has inexcusably not implemented the law.

Since August 2014, we have been sending Freedom of Information Act requests to all fifty states to find out how many kits are left to be tested in each state, but the majority of states have said they do not know. Really? CWA's legal counsel, Mario Diaz, who filed the requests, told me, "The most frustrating part about our efforts is that everyone in theory wants to help; Republicans and Democrats both want to do something. But nothing is done. We need more than money to solve this problem, we need leadership."

Sadly, and infuriatingly for those of us who have worked so hard, the politics continue. The government pays, the advocates make bank, and the victims wait.

We are nevertheless slowly making progress. Several states, including Texas, Illinois, Colorado, and Ohio, have passed legislation requiring an accounting of rape kits and demanding that actions be taken to clear the problem. But we know that accountability must follow. When we can get the states' attorney generals to take ownership of this issue, tangible results will follow.

Former senator and now attorney general of Ohio, Mike DeWine, with whom we worked to bring justice in Steubenville, is a good example. When he took office in 2011, his Sexual Assault Kit Commission encouraged law enforcement agencies in the state to send their unprocessed kits to the state's Bureau of Criminal Investigation to be processed at no charge to them. In six months more than eight thousand kits had been submitted, half of them had been processed, more than a thousand DNA samples gave matches in the law enforcement database, and 135 had been indicted.[27] That is the sort of leadership needed in every state.

What Can Esther Women Do?

Aside from murder, sexual violence is the ultimate crime and human rights abuse. It is one person inflicting pain and dehumanization on another. The physical and psychological damage is scarring at best and incapacitating at worst. Sexual violence is the depth of evil, and it is a reality in our world today that we cannot escape.

So as Esther Women, what is our response? How can we approach the issue in a way that is effective, compassionate, and redemptive?

START WITH COMPASSION

Our message should be focused on a few key points, beginning with this: God sees the violence committed against women every day, and it breaks his heart.

In 2 Samuel 13, the Bible offers a devastating picture of sexual assault in the story of the rape of Tamar. Tamar, a daughter of King David, was raped by her own brother, Amnon, and left in disgrace and shame. At that time, like today in many Muslim countries, women had few rights and were often blamed by society for sexual violence committed against them. Through Tamar's story, we see how seriously God takes sexual assault and vividly feel Tamar's violation and disgrace as she wept, tore her robes, and put ashes on her head.

God's anger toward Amnon, mirrored by King David and culminating in Amnon's death at the hand of his brother's servants, underscores the fact that, as a good and compassionate God, he cannot allow such evil to stand. And while Tamar's cry in this passage, "Where could I get rid of my disgrace?" (2 Sam. 13:13) was left unanswered, many biblical scholars have noted that an answer is found in the sacrifice of Christ, whose abuse and shame at the hands of others bears striking similarities to Tamar's story. As Justin and Lindsey Holcomb have written, "Jesus Christ was killed, not for revenge but to bear [Tamar's] shame on the cross and to offer her a new robe of righteousness to replace her torn robes of disgrace."[28] God saw her pain, and his heart burned to heal her brokenness.

God's redemptive work is so beautiful, and it continues today in the midst of our broken world.

We need to have the same compassion for victims of sexual assault and abuse that God does, and we need to share our compassion with them. We must let them know that we see and acknowledge what they have suffered, or perhaps acknowledge what we ourselves have suffered, and that we want to see them brought to a place of healing and restoration.

If you were sexually assaulted and have struggled with fear, anger, shame, or even, like me, guilt for not having suffered enough, see the love our heavenly Father has poured out over you, and know that you can be made whole. Psalm 34 reads, "The LORD is close to the brokenhearted and saves those who are crushed in spirit," and it also tells us that he "will rescue his servants; no one who takes refuge in him will be condemned" (vv. 18, 22). God can redeem even the darkest and most horrible of experiences, and he will be by your side in your brokenheartedness and sorrow. I don't know why things like this happen to women and children or why justice isn't always served, but we can trust that God will ultimately judge all things and make all things right.

We must also do what we can to help anyone who has suffered sexual violence. That might mean helping victims find the support they need, whether pastoral or clinical counseling. It might mean helping them notify law enforcement. It might mean that we simply listen, hold their hands, "weep with those who weep" (Rom. 12:15 NKJV). When you encounter women who have had these experiences, let their pain touch you. Mourn with them. Pray with them. And support them as they seek recovery. When you don't know how to respond, simply say, "I'm sorry." While non-Christian victims might not find the same comfort in words about the way God redeems brokenness, we can still show deep love and compassion that reflects the heart of Christ and points them toward hope. Simply listening to women and guiding them toward resources can be a huge blessing.

TAKE A VOCAL STANCE

Beyond supporting victims in our own lives, we also need to publicly address the issue of violence against women and sexual assault. In this endeavor, we have a firm biblical basis to stand on. God calls on us to pursue justice, particularly for women and children. Isaiah 1:17 tells us, "Learn to do right; seek justice. Defend the oppressed. Take up the cause of the fatherless; plead the case of the widow." And again in Micah 6:8 we read, "what does the LORD require of you? To act justly and to love mercy." Justice is the cornerstone of God's kingdom, and those who follow him must work to see it served.

The issue of sexual violence and abuse is not meant to be a political football; it is the cry of God's heart and we are all called on to respond. As Christian women, let's stand up together to demand this issue be addressed in ways that work. Let's reject Washington's posturing and empty rhetoric. Rather than worrying about political correctness and political agendas, let's demand justice for victims, strict punishment for perpetrators, and an end to obfuscation and silence around this issue. If we speak up, God will be faithful to give us the words to say. As he told Paul, "Do not be afraid; keep on speaking, do not be silent. For I am with you" (Acts 18:9–10). God calls on us to fight for the oppressed; in this area especially, we must speak up for women.

While we have strong biblical backing, in the public square we should also rely on solid data to point to the root causes of sexual abuse that are not being addressed. For instance, statistics show that we need more resources for law enforcement. According to the National Crime Victimization Survey, only 12 percent of the 283,200 annual rape or sexual assault victimizations between 2005 and 2010 resulted in an arrest. Two-thirds of survivors had their legal cases dismissed, often against their wishes.[29] Officers and the judiciary don't have the resources, awareness, or training to properly pursue and prosecute these crimes, and it is our duty to see that this changes.

We should also emphasize the need to keep pushing for rape kit testing and demanding greater transparency from governmental grantees. Congress has agreed that rape kits should not sit untested on shelves while rapists walk free, and yet we have seen little come of the hard work invested in the Debbie Smith Act. Contact your state's attorney general and demand accountability. There are still hundreds of thousands of untested kits and unanalyzed DNA. We must continue to press this point.

BE REALISTIC, NOT POLITICALLY CORRECT

As my experience twenty years ago taught me, the world is a dangerous place. Ultimately, no amount of government interference or legal protection is going to keep women wholly safe from predators and abusers. And because of this, we need to be vigilant. For women in particular, it's so important to keep our wits about us, have an ability to defend ourselves, and try to avoid stepping into situations that could heighten our vulnerability. We also need to impress these things upon our daughters. Female empowerment means seeking to protect ourselves.

As parents, we need to educate our kids about the dangers of binge drinking and drugs, and the need to be aware of their surroundings. As I've mentioned, when people are under the influence of alcohol or drugs, they increase their chances of being victimized. It's a terrible thing, but it's true. Couple this with the fact that an estimated 44 percent of students at four-year colleges drink alcohol at the binge level or greater—meaning more than five drinks in two hours for men and four drinks for women—and it's not difficult to see how sexual violence and assault are an all-too-frequent outcome.[30] We need to emphasize commonsense prevention efforts.

Abuse of alcohol and other drugs can also increase the chance of becoming the victimizer. Such substances can impair judgment, increase violent behavior, and result in situations that end up ruining lives.[31]

We need to teach our sons to respect women and value the sanctity of sex. Chivalry might not be in vogue, but curbing your sexual urges and treating women with respect and love is a biblical commandment: "Do not use your freedom to indulge the flesh; rather, serve one another humbly in love" (Gal. 5:13). In teaching our sons to respect women in every situation, we may also help quell some of the left's frantic claims of a campus assault epidemic. Assault is a serious crime, and by emphasizing an elevated view of sex and the negative ramifications of casual hookups, we can move away from unhelpful measures like consent laws in order to focus on the criminal nature of rape.

The one true hope that we have in the face of this fallen world is the love of our Father and the promise that one day he will make all things right. Until that time comes, we need to protect ourselves against the darkness that surrounds us. This isn't victim blaming; it's common sense.

At the end of the day, the advocate community has missed the point. We must encourage people to step back and see the larger picture:

Sexual assault is a violent crime that threatens the life and safety of every woman, and of men too. It is not a political football, a problem of miscommunication or phrasing, or an issue to be used to gain funding or attention for specific groups, schools, or ideologies. This should not be an issue of the right versus the left or men versus women; it is a human problem that affects us all and threatens to tear the fabric of our society apart.

This is one of the greatest threats women face today, and we ignore it at our peril. Let's join together to speak up for the safety of the least of these. We must make campuses safer; we must make the streets safer; we must be aware of the dangers that lurk in every neighborhood, school, church, and home. Violence against women breaks God's heart, and it should break ours too. We were raised up to fight issues like this at such a time as this, and it's our duty to speak out and demand change.

Emily Dukes

YWA CHAPTER PRESIDENT, O'MORE COLLEGE OF DESIGN

Young conservative women around the country are engaged and passionate, standing up for the values and issues they believe in. One young leader is Emily Dukes, a student at O'More College of Design in Franklin, Tennessee, and the president of her campus's Young Women for America (YWA) chapter.

As the daughter of small business owners, Emily was raised to value the entrepreneurial opportunities our nation offers to those willing to work hard. Building on this foundation, Emily has already begun to establish a path toward success as a business-woman. She has launched her own clothing label, "Emily Dukes," specializing in custom garments and accessories, and she has also designed costumes for the Nashville Ballet.

Pursuing this dream, however, Emily found that there was often a conflict between her values and the industry she loved. "Conservative values and ethics in business are often not fostered in the fashion industry," she says. But YWA has given her a leadership role in her school and community that enables her to bring her faith into the public sphere and has given her the confidence to speak up on issues that matter, including traditional marriage and education. Now she encourages other young women to do the same. "Be confident in the biblical beliefs you have!" she says. "They are not outdated, and you do not have to compromise them to be successful in life."

If we are persistent in our work and stay informed, Emily believes, we can bring about change. "Educate. Read up. Follow the news on social media. Be aware of what's going on in our nation," she encourages young women. "You *can* have an impact on the direction our country is headed. Your voice *can* be heard."[32]

CHAPTER 4

Marriage and True Tolerance

Over the years as a conservative woman in the public square, I have been on the receiving end of a lot of vitriol. I have on many occasions received tweets, Facebook posts, comments, and even phone calls saying terrible things and calling me horrible names. Usually, the words used are those intended to specifically hurt women. The N-word is appropriately condemned to the dung heap of the English language, and people who use it, other than rappers, are considered vile. Yet I've been called the C-word, which many consider to be the most offensive term in the English language, more times than I can count, and few people seem to view it with the same shock or horror. It's a word used to shame and convey specific hatred, in this case based on gender. Why is it allowed in public conversation?

Bill Maher called Sarah Palin that word on stage during one of his performances and got away with it.[1] What if she were black and he had called her the N-word? Would people have laughed then?

As a Christian, I'm not sure how to process this kind of hatred. Jesus calls us to love those who hate us, but I struggle to understand how to love people who, instead of expressing displeasure with my ideas or beliefs, spew verbal vomit on me. It makes me angry, and I want to fight back and say mean, cutting things instead of turning the other cheek. And believe me, these kinds of people tend to be easy targets.

I know it is wrong for me to stew in anger over these kinds of attacks. If I do, it becomes my sin. And I know that God wants me to have a heart for these people and their own hurts. They are often sad and lonely people in need of redemption—just like me. I want to see them as God does and to love them as he does. But it's hard. These are the arbiters of tolerance?

> Stupid Fascist C***. Between you & Sarah Palin, you've probably got an IQ of 40.

The latest round of venom came in response to a piece that I wrote for the news outlet Breitbart at their request on the National Day of Silence held in public schools across America every April.[2] Sponsored by the radical Gay, Lesbian and Straight Education Network (GLSEN), the day is intended to "call attention to the silencing effect of anti-LGBT bullying and harassment in schools." I support an end to any kind of bullying, but I couldn't help but notice how ironic this day seemed in light of how mercilessly conservative Christians are bullied for holding any beliefs that differ from the liberal media's views. After my piece, which suggested we focus efforts on ending *all kinds* of bullying, was published, I was called a "Christian terrorist," an "insular bigot," and "bats**t crazy," among many other and far worse insults. There weren't even any leftist First Amendment advocates supporting my ability to voice an opinion.

The article on Breitbart struck a nerve, I think, in part because it discussed traditional marriage and families. Nothing elicits the kind of nasty, ad hominem attack from the left like a discussion on marriage—not even abortion.

The Marriage Debate

When it comes to the topic of marriage, the very people who champion tolerance can be the most intolerant. Take for example the national outrage over Phil Robertson from *Duck Dynasty* and his 2013 interview in which he, albeit inartfully, quoted 1 Corinthians 6:9–10 on homosexuality. "Neither the adulterers, the idolaters, the male prostitutes, the homosexual offenders, the greedy, the drunkards, the slanderers, the swindlers—they won't inherit the kingdom of God. . . . Don't deceive yourself. It's not right," Robertson said. It was his next comment that really set off a firestorm though: "Start with homosexual behavior and just morph out from there—bestiality, sleeping around with this woman and that woman and that woman and those men."[3]

Okay, that probably could have been said better.

During the controversy I was called by CNN to appear on the show *Crossfire* to discuss Robertson's words and the fallout. People had chosen sides, and I was supposed to go on national TV and represent people who believe what the Bible says—or, in the minds of the show's producers, to represent the bigots. I didn't want to go. The format of *Crossfire* is a talk show with four people, two liberals and two conservatives, and for that episode the other conservative was to be Newt Gingrich, former Speaker of the House. Gingrich is a brilliant man, but not the best advocate for marriage. He's on marriage number three and has two angry ex-wives with enough dirt on him to fill the Grand Canyon.

I told *Crossfire* no, but the producer called back and made a hard case that I should be the person to come on the show. So I prayed. I prayed, *Lord, if you want me to do this, I will, but I really don't want to. So can you please help me walk around the landmines and honestly portray the Christian belief regarding marriage, that I might be thought provoking instead of displaying the kind of emotion-baiting that makes for good TV?*

Still nervous, but walking in obedience, I agreed to go on CNN for the segment, titled "Bigotry vs. Belief." That evening I walked into the greenroom with CWA's communications director, Alison Howard, who had come along to pray for me. As I sat down, all I could think was, *How can I possibly take a biblical principle and explain it to people who don't believe the Bible?* But I sensed that God wanted me to do the segment, so I continued to silently pray until the producer came and brought me to the set.

Representing the left that night was Van Jones—the same Van Jones who President Obama appointed as Special Advisor for Green Jobs, Enterprise, and Innovation at the White House Council on Environmental Quality. To say Van is to the left of me politically is a huge understatement. We might be polar opposites. Van was roundly pilloried by the right for his political activities prior to joining the Obama administration, which included signing a petition suggesting that the Bush Administration had deliberately allowed 9/11 to happen, and he had resigned from his post after a video surfaced in which Van used offensive language to refer to the Republican Senate.

Accompanying Van on the left was LZ Granderson, a commentator for CNN and ESPN. LZ is an African American gay activist, who is very smart and used to TV brawls. *Dang,* I thought, *I am toast.*

The opening credits ran along with pictures of angry-looking Christian protesters, and Van kicked off the segment by quoting Phil in the most indelicate part of his interview in which he mentioned part of the female anatomy. Immediately, of course, Van went to me for response. And that's when it happened. God showed up. I was amazingly calm and confident. In fact, I was having fun. So much fun that instead of jumping right into the debate, I made a joke about Van's vulgar opening and fake-apologized to my parents, watching on TV, in a sulky teenage voice: "Sooorry Mom and Dad." And we all laughed.

That was it. The ice was broken. Suddenly, we were four human beings talking about a tough issue. No one was nasty. I was able to speak to the fact that the Scripture Robertson had quoted has something in it to offend everyone—it condemns drunkenness, lying, slander, greed, adultery, idolatry, and more. When it comes to marriage, the Bible doesn't just deal with homosexuality but also divorce and sex outside of the sanctity of marriage. The Bible offends because it calls us to account, *all* of us. We are all guilty and all in need of redemption.

Early in the show LZ essentially called Christians bigots, and I interrupted him. "Hang on," I said, "could we not agree that not everyone who believes the Bible is a bigot? And what about the other religions?" I asked him. "Orthodox Jews, Muslims, even the Dalai Lama—are they all just bigots?" *Uh-oh,* his face said, *I can't insult minority religions.* No, he backed down. He knew that it wasn't true. All major religions and every civilization throughout history that has disagreed with homosexuality could not have been basing their beliefs on spite.

By the end of the segment I was reminded that God never sends us into a situation without giving us everything we need to fight the battle for truth. The producers may have been disappointed, but they seemed supportive and I was thrilled. I learned a lesson too: Van Jones is a gentleman. He grew up in a Christian home and knows the Bible even if he doesn't believe it all to be inspired. He has loved ones who are sincere believers. On another occasion on *Crossfire* I talked about redemption of our broken lives through Christ. On that segment, off air, he told me he loved what I said and that he loves the message of redemption in Christ. He is a family man and a nice guy. Turns out I had prejudged someone too. Shame on me.

My experience on *Crossfire* underscored an obvious truth: The issue of marriage is complicated. It encompasses many different questions and can be approached from a wide variety of angles. We live in an era when any discussion on this topic is dominated by the question of gay marriage. And yet a biblical view of marriage is so much bigger than sexuality. By narrowing the scope of the conversation to consider only this single aspect, we are losing sight of the whole picture.

Marriage in America Today

Marriage in America is a mess. The Supreme Court decision in *Obergefell v. Hodges* to legalize gay marriage in June 2015 made this blatantly clear, but marriage has been flailing in our country for a long time. Despite decades of social science warning us of the negative consequences, divorce rates are continuing to rise, with almost half of all married Americans divorced or separated by their fifties.[4] Cohabitation, too, is on the rise, with 7.8 million couples declining to walk down the aisle in 2012 compared to 2.9 million in 1996.[5] In fact, one quarter of all unmarried people between twenty-five and thirty-five are currently living with a partner.[6]

Young people are waiting longer to marry, if they do at all. Out-of-wedlock births are at 41 percent, accompanied by well-documented social problems, including a greater likelihood of children being raised in poverty, convicted of juvenile crime, dropping out of school, and being treated for emotional and behavioral problems.[7] Liberals like to talk about income inequality but refuse to acknowledge that much can be traced directly to family inequality—missing dads.

And, while it shouldn't be the only aspect of the debate we focus on, there is no doubt that redefining marriage to include gay couples is also playing a substantial role in diminishing the elite status of marriage in America. If it's an arrangement based on affection, then what about other kinds of love? What about polygamy or throuples? (Yep, throuples is a thing—three people who love each other and live in "more or less a permanent domestic arrangement.")[8] Why shouldn't they be able to marry? It's just another kind of love, right? Who are we to judge? Chief Justice John Roberts acknowledged as much in his dissent of *Obergefell v. Hodges*, noting that under the Court's logic, there will be no way of stopping it:

> One immediate question invited by the majority's position is whether States may retain the definition of marriage as a union of two people. . . . Although the majority randomly inserts the adjective "two" in various places, it offers no reason at all why the two-person element of the core definition of marriage may be preserved while the man-woman element may not. Indeed, from the standpoint of history and tradition, a leap from opposite-sex marriage to same-sex marriage is much greater than one from a two-person union to plural unions, which have deep roots in some cultures around the world. If the majority is willing to take the big leap, it is hard to see how it can say no to the shorter one.[9]

Marriage is not just an arrangement of people who love each other. As we'll discuss below when we get into the biblical view of marriage, it's something special. It's a divine covenant. Even people who don't view marriage as a spiritual union can recognize that there is something elevated about the institution—that for all of history, marriage has been defined as between one man and one woman. Today, however, this universal truth is under siege.

With the *Obergefell v. Hodges* ruling in favor of gay marriage, five unelected judges redefined marriage for an entire country in one fell swoop. They overturned laws in fifteen states, imposing the will of the courts over the desires of the people. The justices would like to argue that they are on the right side of history and that this is the direction our country was inevitably headed, but in reality people are still deeply divided on this issue.

The tension between people who hold a traditional view of faith, specifically small business owners, and activists has reached a fevered pitch. On one side you have those who believe that traditional marriage is the preeminent and necessary building block of society and that its redefinition has moral, cultural, and economic consequences. On the other, you have activists and those of more liberal views who believe that marriage should be redefined and manipulated to fit our own desires and whims.

Marriage is under attack from those who wish to redefine it, from those who fail to uphold marriage vows once they've taken them, and from those who choose cohabitation or sexual relationships outside of marriage. However, the most stunning and worrisome indicator to me of the fragile state of marriage in our country today is that, according to a Pew Research survey in 2010, almost 40 percent of people who responded said that the institution of marriage is becoming obsolete—they just don't think it matters.[10]

An article by Brigid Schulte in the *Washington Post* about the decline of marriage highlighted this attitude. Schulte recounted an interview with one young woman who was in a committed relationship but had no plans to ever marry: "'But what's the point of spending all that money on a wedding?' she asked. She doesn't like the idea of women changing their names or the 'ownership' qualities associated with marriage. 'My boyfriend and I are committed to each other. We just don't feel the need to get married.'"[11]

Sadly, this is all too typical of the way our society views marriage today: antiquated, unnecessary, limiting. As Christians, we know that marriage is a divine gift that joins a man and woman to provide love, stability, healthy families, and spiritually rich lives for the couple and their children. But our culture is trading it in favor of playing the field, retaining independence, or redefining marriage to fit any opinion, lifestyle, or personal preference.

Take, for instance, the recent scandal in which hackers published the client list of the website Ashley Madison, which bills itself as the premiere destination for individuals seeking "married dating, discreet encounters and extramarital affairs."[12] The revelation of the site's customers should have rocked us to our core. Almost forty million men—and I say men because 99 percent of those who had signed up for an affair were men—were revealed to be seeking extramarital affairs.[13] Every zip code in the nation had married men involved except for *three*.[14] And the Christian community was not immune: a few top Christian leaders were outed, and Ed Stetzer, executive director of LifeWay Research, estimated that as many as four hundred church leaders, deacons, and staff members would end up stepping down as a result.[15]

Families all over the country were devastated by this turn of events, but the really sad part is that this was only the tip of the iceberg. Christians have not held themselves to a higher standard; instead, men and women have made a mockery of God's holy institution through illicit affairs and pornography. While we were busy worrying about homosexual sin, our own homes were falling apart around us, and we never even looked up. We are at a point in which hard truths must be faced and steps have to be taken to restore the credibility of the church on the issue of marriage. Pastors must deal with the fact that the church is in crisis. I cannot express this strongly enough. The church must understand, "Thou art the man" (2 Sam. 12:7 ASV), and our day of reckoning has come.

As conservative Christian women, we have work to do. It is now even more important than before that we stand up, clear our throats, and give a spirited defense for the gift of marriage as God intended it.

But first, let's get our bearings straight. There is a lot of misinformation and confusion out there, and we need to be sure we're standing on firm ground before we wade in. To be able to address this topic in the public square, we must have a clear understanding of the biblical view of marriage.

A Holy Institution

First, from the beginning, God intended marriage to be a unique union between a man and a woman. In Genesis, God's intention is clear when he makes Eve as a partner for Adam, as one who perfectly complements him. She is "bone of [his] bones and flesh of [his] flesh," completely distinct from Adam and yet also his perfect complement (Gen. 2:23). Together, they reflect the image of God: "In the image of God he created them; male and female he created them" (Gen. 1:27). And their completion is found in marriage, which joins man and woman together in a kind of perfect harmony: "Therefore a man shall leave his father and mother and be joined to his wife, and they shall become one flesh" (Gen. 2:24 NKJV). In Ephesians 5:32, Paul calls this a "great mystery"—something profound and beyond our understanding, something more than the merging of two physical bodies.

This points us to the second key truth of the biblical view of marriage: marriage is a holy institution, not an earthly one. In fact, the "great mystery" of marriage, as Paul explains in the same Ephesians passage, is that it is the earthly reflection of Christ and his church. Marriage is a covenant between husband and wife that reflects the covenant between God and his people—as Christ and his people are one body, so a husband and wife are one flesh. Paul elaborates: "Husbands, love your wives, just as Christ also loved the church and gave Himself for her, that He might sanctify and cleanse her with the washing of water by the word, that He might present her to Himself a glorious church, not having spot or wrinkle or any such thing, but that she should be holy and without blemish" (Eph. 5:25–27 NKJV).

Marriage, then, is not just a legal contract or a public expression of love for our spouse; it is the very image of God's love for and oneness with the church. As John Piper has preached, God "patterned marriage very purposefully after the relationship between his Son and the church, which he planned from eternity. And therefore marriage is a mystery—it contains and conceals a meaning far greater than what we see on the outside."[16] It is far greater than a mere human institution; it is God-given and God-reflecting. As a covenant, it supersedes any human arrangement.

This means that we are not free to redefine or renegotiate marriage as we see fit; marriage was given to us by God, and we have a responsibility to protect it as a divine institution. When we move away from an understanding of marriage as God intended it, we move away from the truth of Christ and the church—the very essence of who we are as Christians.

Not that every Christian has to marry, of course. While God gave us the institution of marriage as a means of flourishing, we do not have to marry to be complete. We are already complete in Christ, who fulfills us

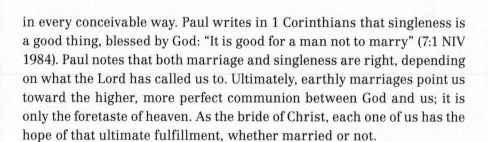

in every conceivable way. Paul writes in 1 Corinthians that singleness is a good thing, blessed by God: "It is good for a man not to marry" (7:1 NIV 1984). Paul notes that both marriage and singleness are right, depending on what the Lord has called us to. Ultimately, earthly marriages point us toward the higher, more perfect communion between God and us; it is only the foretaste of heaven. As the bride of Christ, each one of us has the hope of that ultimate fulfillment, whether married or not.

A Universal Institution

There is so much more we could say about the importance of this institution to God and to human flourishing, but I also want to point out that every other major religion also believes that traditional marriage is central to human life. Orthodox Judaism and the Muslim faith both believe that marriage is between a man and a woman and that such unions are the bedrock of society. Like Christianity, these religions encourage marriage as a benefit to spiritual growth, human relationships, and society through the gift of children.

And it's not just major religions that view traditional marriage as central to human life; it has been the foundation of every major civil society and culture throughout history. As Tim Keller writes, "marriage had its origins in 'prehistory'—in other words, the human race cannot remember a time in which marriage did not exist."[17] Traditional marriage is not particular to any religion or tradition; it has instead been embraced separately and organically by every flourishing society around the world.

The ancient Greeks and Romans believed in the institution of marriage, as did early Asian and African civilizations. More modern societies, too, have taken this view; from Enlightenment thinkers like John Locke and Immanuel Kant to Eastern thinkers like Ghandi—all have viewed marriage as a union between a man and a woman for the primary purpose of creating and maintaining a family. Civil societies have legally recognized the institution, protecting and encouraging it through laws and policies.

The Cornerstone of the Family

Why has marriage been viewed as so fundamental to human societies? One primary reason is because of its centrality to procreation. Societies have always recognized that men and women are distinct and complementary and that there is no way to perpetuate the human race without the union of the two. It is this God-ordained orientation toward children that makes man-woman marriage supreme in the order of human relationships.

Beyond biology, though, marriage leads to the institution of families, without which society could not flourish. Families allow us to raise and nurture children, develop values and traditions, and create relationships. And marriage, as Heritage Foundation scholar Matthew Spalding has eloquently argued, is the cornerstone of the family: "It produces children, provides them with mothers and fathers, and is the framework through which relationships among mothers, fathers, and children are established and maintained."[18] Of course, not every marriage has to bring forth children, and in some cases, sadly, infertility or medical conditions make procreation impossible. In general, though, God's plan in marriage will most often lead to children.

Once we bring children into the world, two-parent, mother-father families are crucial to their well-being—and to society's more broadly. Married parents are the most likely to stay together for the next eighteen-plus years it takes to raise a child. While there are many wonderful and heroic single parents out there, children unequivocally do better with a mom and dad in the home. We have years of data to back this up. Fatherless or single-parent homes produce children more likely to drop out of school, end up in jail, and not participate in the workforce.[19] Childhood poverty, in particular, is exacerbated without two-parent households; marriage reduces the probability of child poverty by 82 percent.[20] Even President Obama has emphasized this reality; a few months after taking office in 2008, he noted that children who grow up without a father "are more likely to have behavioral problems, or run away from home, or become teenage parents themselves. And the foundations of our community are weaker because of it."[21]

Families create shared sets of beliefs, values, and responsibilities. The values established in intact homes have long-lasting effects on the children raised in them; for instance, teens who frequently have dinner with their families are at a lower risk for substance abuse, are less likely to be sexually active, and are more likely to have stable and healthy romantic relationships as adults.[22]

Put simply, children need a mom and dad at home. And while some have claimed that same-sex parents can meet the same needs for children as heterosexual parents, recent research suggests that this is not true. As the Heritage Foundation has reported, the prevalence of emotional problems among children living with same-sex parents is 4.5 times as high as among children living with their married biological parents, and three times as high as children with a single parent.[23] At the end of the day, however, these kinds of parental arrangements are relatively new, and there is not a lot of data to make this case. Unfortunately, by the time the longitudinal studies proving this point have been completed, children will have had to do without either a mother or a father for their entire childhood.

We saw this happen with divorce in the 1960s. Everyone swore it didn't hurt kids until twenty years later when we had the data to prove they were wrong. Judith Wallerstein was widely credited with research in this area and the slogan "if you're not happy, your kids won't be." But then, as an honest social scientist, she had to refute her own work a couple of decades later. After following the children of divorced parents over a period of more than twenty years, she concluded that divorce was a wrenching experience for children that only continued to get worse as they moved into adulthood. "Contrary to what we have long thought, the major impact of divorce does not occur during childhood or adolescence. Rather, it rises in adulthood. . . . Anxiety leads many [adult children of divorce] into making bad choices in relationships, giving up hastily when problems arise, or avoiding relationships altogether," she found.[24] Parents, guard your marriages.

Recently, in the lead-up to the *Obergefell vs. Hodges* arguments, children who were raised by gay parents came forward to admit that they did not feel their upbringing was as positive as it would have been in a heterosexual-parented household. One woman who was raised by her gay mother and her partner wrote an open letter to the gay community, published in *The Federalist*, in which she stated the following: "Same-sex marriage and parenting withholds either a mother or father from a child while telling him or her that it doesn't matter. That it's all the same. But it's not. A lot of us, a lot of your kids, are hurting. My father's absence created a huge hole in me, and I ached every day for a dad. I loved my mom's partner, but another mom could never have replaced the father I lost."[25] This is the same story we hear from children of heterosexual parents where one of the parents is not present. Kids need and deserve a mom and dad.

This is where the other side brings up the hard cases. Hard cases are helpful in politics. The left uses them—and I do mean *uses* them—to persuade, but good law is never based on the outliers. In this case the left wants to talk about kids stuck in foster care—particularly, as in the Supreme Court case *DeBoer v. Snyder*, children with special needs.[26] Wouldn't they be better off adopted by same-sex couples than languishing in foster care? There is a problem with this scenario, however: there is no proof that the legalization of same-sex marriage and subsequent adoption reform will change the rate of special-needs kids being adopted. Sure, some gay couples would adopt special-needs children, as would some heterosexual couples, but this is a minority position that will not be dramatically affected by changing the definition of marriage.

Anthropology, biology, and sociology all tell us that men and women complement each other, and it only goes to follow that children benefit from having both parents in the household. A woman can be a good mom, but she can never be a dad. A man can be a good dad, but he can never be a mom. A mother and father provide unique gifts and meet different needs for their children. To deprive children of that is unfair and ultimately harmful to their own development and happiness.

Same Sex Marriage Laws and First Amendment Rights

As these recent court cases show, we are at a cultural tipping point when it comes to the issue of same-sex marriage in the United States. Same-sex marriage is now the law of the land, despite the fact that the country remains deeply divided. And with the Supreme Court decision to legalize gay marriage has come a host of other concerns that are going to impact all of us, whether we like it or not.

On the day *Obergefell vs. Hodges* was argued before the justices, I prayed outside the court with others. It's so important for Christians to understand what this all means for us. Even if you are not interested in the sociological issues, this decision isn't something you're going to be able to ignore. The most adamant proponents will not be happy unless we are forced to submit and embrace their views at the violation of our consciences. For this reason, it's critical that we consider how same-sex marriage laws affect our First Amendment religious freedoms as business owners, nonprofits, and individuals.

Consider the case of Elane Photography in New Mexico. In 2006, Elaine Huguenin declined to photograph the wedding of a lesbian couple, explaining that the photographs would communicate a message that went against her personal beliefs. The couple easily found another photographer. Nonetheless, they took Huguenin to court, where she was forced to pay $7,000 in damages. The ruling was upheld by the New Mexico Supreme Court. One of the justices, Justice Richard Bosson, went so far as to tell the Huguenins that compromising their religious views was "the price of citizenship" in civic life.[27]

Elane Photography is not an anomaly; there are many small businesses that have chosen not to provide gay-marriage-related services and are now being pilloried, vilified, and even prosecuted by the law. A seventy-year-old florist in Washington State had a case brought against her last year by the state's attorney general after she declined to provide flowers for a same-sex wedding. Bakers in Colorado and Oregon have faced similar prosecution for declining to bake wedding cakes for same-sex ceremonies, and a New York couple who refused to host a same-sex wedding in their back yard were fined $13,000.[28]

With the ruling in *Obergefell*, this is only going to get worse. Christians should steel themselves for the predicted onslaught of viewpoint discrimination that will affect our businesses, employment, and educational opportunities. It's not just bakers, photographers, and florists losing their businesses anymore; now the battle includes military officials, judges, clerks, other public and private employees, and school accreditations. When a county clerk in Kentucky, Kim Davis, refused to sign marriage licenses for same-sex couples in August 2015, she was thrown into jail. That's right; she was put into jail for attempting to exercise her firm religious convictions. We are moving toward a society in which anyone who holds traditional Christian beliefs is not going to be able to serve as a county official, a judge, or any number of other public positions. Basically anyone who can't find a way to dismiss the Bible's teaching on homosexuality is in for a rough ride.

Take the case of Gordon College, a small Christian college outside of Boston. Like many Christian schools, Gordon has a policy for students and employees prohibiting sex outside of marriage, which they define as the union between one man and one woman. Activists began screaming that this was discriminatory, and in September 2014, the school was told that labeling "'homosexual practice' as a 'forbidden activity'" violated their standards for accreditation.[29] Gordon was given one year to adjust its policy or lose accreditation. This is a school with a tradition of impeccable academics and a sterling reputation. It now stands to lose everything.

Similarly, Christian adoption agencies are feeling the effects of the crusade against religious liberties. Private, faith-based organizations play an instrumental role in placing thousands of children with adoptive families every year. Now, these agencies are being forced to choose between their deeply held beliefs and their ability to continue to serve these vulnerable populations. In 2003, Catholic Charities in Boston, Massachusetts, was placing more children in adoptive homes than any other state-licensed agency. But the decision by the Massachusetts Supreme Court that year to recognize same-sex marriages meant that all state-licensed adoption providers now had to agree to place children with same-sex couples—which directly conflicted with Catholic Charities' beliefs. Rather than forsake their conscience, the organization was forced to end their adoption and foster care programs, leaving hundreds of children each year to have to find other means of connecting with loving families.[30] Other agencies around the country now face similar choices. Ultimately, the group that is hurt the most is the one in greatest need: vulnerable infants and children who wait for permanent, loving homes.

The most worrisome part of this trend of religious intolerance sweeping through our country is that when those who want to defend religious liberties try to fight back, they are cast as bigots and are torn to shreds by the media and the left. In April 2014, Brendan Eich, the CEO of the software company Mozilla, was forced from his position for donating $1,000 to support Proposition 8, California's 2008 initiative opposing the legalization of same-sex marriage. Despite the fact that the donation, made six years earlier, reflected Eich's personal and religious convictions and had nothing to do with his role at Mozilla, a furor erupted after he was promoted to CEO, and after just a week Mozilla caved to pressure and forced Eich to resign.

More recently, in the spring of 2015, the states of Indiana and Arkansas attempted to pass religious freedom acts to protect businesses and individuals who seek to secure exemptions from certain government mandates based on religious beliefs. The bills in both states were modeled on the federal Religious Freedom Restoration Act, which Bill Clinton signed into law in 1993. When these two states attempted to pass their bills last year, however, a national uproar emerged. The media pounced on what it called anti-gay legislation, and Indiana Governor Mike Pence and Arkansas Governor Asa Hutchinson found themselves on the receiving end of a wave of intolerance and vitriol.

Despite the assertions of the left, the bills did not give anyone the right to discriminate against gays or lesbians; they simply made it clear that government cannot interfere with a person or company who wants to exert their individual religious liberties unless there is a compelling governmental interest, i.e. a really good reason. But that didn't stop the left from waging an all-out crusade against the bill's passage and those who supported it.

Businesses like Apple, Google, and Angie's List came out in force against the bill, as did the NCAA. Pence gave in to the threats of the liberal media and big business, agreeing to amend the Indiana bill as they required. Republican State Senator Scott Schneider told the *New York Times* that he felt he had to agree to the revisions for "the economic viability of the state."[31] Shortly after, lawmakers in Arkansas followed suit and changed that state's bill as well, although not in as damaging a manner.

Does any of this sound like tolerance to you? The problem with the marriage debate in our country is that the left is now shutting down any alternative opinions by bludgeoning opponents with the labels of bigot and ignorant. In Indiana, after the owners of a pizza shop expressed support for the religious freedom bill and stated that while they would serve gay customers, they did not support gay marriage, their words went viral and the family-owned shop received death threats and hate mail that forced them to shut down their store.[32] That's the kind of "tolerance" the left has for conservative viewpoints.

As Louisiana Governor Bobby Jindal wrote in the *New York Times* shortly after the uproar in Indiana and Arkansas, "A pluralistic and diverse society like ours can exist only if we all tolerate people who disagree with us. That's why religious freedom laws matter."[33] Christians need to tolerate and treat non-Christians and those who don't share our viewpoints with respect, and in return, we deserve the same treatment from others. The heightened animosity and hateful rhetoric being bandied about in the public square today is unacceptable.

What Can Esther Women Do?

We've got some work to do in order to reintroduce civility into the conversation while also attempting to win over hearts and minds. We want to see tolerance emerge in our society today, yet we also need to stand firm on our values and beliefs. There are many ways to speak into this space, but I think we need to start with saying no to arrogance and unkindness, holding up Christian marriages as examples while also acknowledging where we and others have fallen short, fighting for the rights to sacred religious liberties, and continuing to speak truth about the beauty of God's intention for marriage.

REINTRODUCE CIVILITY

We must affirm the right of all people to live and worship as they choose, and we need others to join with us on this front. Condemning unkindness is not a religious or political stance; it is a human one, and our message transcends those divisions. This means that we condemn liberal attacks against Christian and conservative views; but it also means that we must take a stand against nastiness toward gay people or any group for that matter. We absolutely must condemn countries operating under sharia law where homosexuality is a crime punishable by death.

In Nigeria in early 2015, fourteen men were dragged from their beds and attacked by men with clubs and iron bars who said they wanted to "cleanse" their neighborhood of gay people.[34] And who could forget the video of ISIS pushing a gay man off of a roof to his death in Mosul, Iraq?[35] We have to speak out against these kinds of atrocities, and against governments that condone them. Violence of any kind has no place among those who seek peace, and as followers of Christ, it is our duty to stand up against this kind of injustice.

We need to condemn violence abroad as well as here in the United States. But even short of violence, we need to consider whether we do what's right when people say something unkind about gay or transgender people and those who don't share our opinions or lifestyles. Because here's the problem: people practicing these lifestyles can't hear our words of love and hope when we are allowing other people to define us.

When I spoke at the Supreme Court regarding the *Obergefell v. Hodges* case in April 2015, I passed a group of people rallying outside the steps of the court with signs conveying messages of hate toward the gay community. They shouted words that were offensive, vitriolic, and ignorant, and which Jesus would never condone. I was unable to simply walk by. When it was my turn to speak at the podium, I called them out. One sign said that homosexuals are perverts. I said, "We are all perverts." And we are. We are broken and perverted from God's perfection by the perversion of sin. Our sin might not be homosexual sex or heterosexual sex outside of marriage. But we all have sin in our lives and hearts, and to pretend otherwise is a lie.

The group I called out may have been the Westboro Baptists, but there was nothing remotely Christian about their behavior, and we can't let them get away with it. It is more in line with radical Islam. We are all broken, and the hatred they were spewing that day was embarrassing to me and to the God they pretend to represent. I said to them, "You embarrass me and you embarrass God." We are to be champions of the weak. Clearly the homosexual community feels unloved and unaccepted.

We do not in any way have to accept someone's sin in order to love him or her. However, while we must treat the homosexual community with love and respect, we should not embrace their lifestyle. We cannot support their sin as a positive choice, regardless of whether the government condones it. As I'll discuss in a moment, we are still called to be salt and light in this world, both in our personal relationships and in the public square.

I think Jesus' actions toward the woman caught in adultery by the Westboro Baptists (I mean Pharisees) are instructive when it comes to loving those caught in sin. In John 8, the Pharisees parade this woman before Jesus demanding, "In the Law Moses commanded us to stone such women. Now what do you say?" (v. 5). Jesus, of course, responds by suggesting that any of the men without sin go ahead and throw the first stone. None of them is able to. With compassion, Jesus says to the woman, "Then neither do I condemn you . . . Go now and leave your life of sin" (v. 11).

Note that he forgave this woman completely but also instructed her to leave her sinful lifestyle. We are all that woman. If we are rightly thinking about our own hearts, we come before Jesus with shame, but he forgives and then calls us to redemption.

Christ loved sinners of all stripes. Prostitutes, tax collectors, adulterers—all are welcome in his presence and at his table. We need to encourage this kind of welcoming and loving attitude toward the gay community. You cannot minister and share the gospel unless you first love. We need to remind each other of Jesus' words in Matthew 9:13: "For I have not come to call the righteous, but sinners." God's heart is for *all* sinners, and so should ours be.

When speaking to those who support same-sex marriage or who are themselves gay, we must show the compassion that we preach. By treating them with kindness and by speaking words of grace and redemption, we are better able to express the love of God and perhaps point them toward him. Let me be clear: I am not advocating the kind of biblical dishonesty that we are seeing among many mainline Protestant churches.

"Open minds and open hearts" is a good slogan, but what it really means is that, sadly, some of these churches no longer believe in the Bible's message on holiness or anything else they want to ignore. They don't believe in sin and redemption—just feel-good religion. That's not what Jesus calls us to.

Nor am I advocating a truce on public policy, because truth is truth and bad public policy hurts everyone. But when we speak about the issue of marriage, we must approach it from the perspective of the gospel: we are sinful, and Christ redeems all sin. Gay or straight, liberal or conservative, we all need to hear the truth of the gospel. Love should be the driving force behind our approach to this topic, and we must be careful not to lose sight of that.

I know this isn't easy. During the *Crossfire* interview I mentioned earlier, I had an opportunity where I blew it. Van Jones asked me a question about what I would say to a lesbian couple regarding their lifestyle. I took him on for trying to use emotion to cloud the issue, but instead I should have said something else. I should have said that my answer to all gay people is this: Please join me in seeking after Christ and his holiness. Join me and all the other sinners in my church on Sunday morning, and let's work out our salvation together as broken human beings in need of God's forgiveness and healing.

Grace is not always the easiest or immediate response, especially when you feel you're being baited, but it's the right one. This is where Esther Women have to start. And even if you don't feel like you can specifically articulate the gospel message, you can preach it with your actions.

REPRESENT MARRIAGE WELL

As Christians speaking to this issue, we also need to take a good look at our own marriages and the examples we set before the world. Uh-oh, now I'm stepping on your toes. I can't pretend to have this all down perfectly, but here's the truth: Marriage is a precious and beautiful gift from God, and we want everyone to see it that way—but that means we have to represent it well ourselves. If our Christian marriages don't reflect the truth of God's glory, then we aren't doing our jobs.

Tim Keller perfectly highlights the importance of our marriages: "Through Christian marriages, the story of the gospel—of sin, grace, and restoration—can be seen and heard both inside the church and out in the world. Christian marriages proclaim the gospel."[36] Our marriages are intended to show the beauty of marriage and, by extension, the gospel, to the world, and it's important that we put in the work to make them strong, glorifying to God, and representative of his grace.

What does this look like? I think it means we need to ensure that we're living out marriages that fulfill God's commands. Are we serving our husbands in love? Do we build them up, or do we complain too much? I'll admit it, I complain sometimes. I hate it when my husband leaves the bathroom sink dirty or his clothes in the floor. (No, I don't pick them up for him.) It's stupid, but I sometimes grouse about silly stuff instead of focusing on the amazing gift God gave me in my husband.

Do you publicly take your husband's side, or do you tear him down? Have you ever been in a crowd of couples and observed a spouse making jokes at the other's expense? I don't mean the verbal volleys that are safe and funny, but ones that, if you look behind the humor, really sting, like jokes about the other's weight. I have, and when I see it, I know that things are going south at home. Husbands and wives are to be on each other's team, to be the other's best cheerleader. If you can't do that, then I exhort you to get help. It's not too late. Divorce will not solve your problems; it just creates different ones.

As parents, are we raising children who are respectful, love the Lord, and are contributing to society? Are we emphasizing the values of a Christian home when we sit around the dinner table or spend time together? Are you putting your kids before yourself? Are you calling the sulky, smart-mouthed teenager to repentance through love or just blowing your top? Are the little ones so hard—and they *are* so hard—that you are self-medicating into numbness instead of looking to God, your spouse, and your community for help?

If you're not married, does your life still reflect God's desires, meaning that you're not engaged in sexual activity or cohabitation outside of marriage? Does your dating life magnify the Lord? Are you kind when you break up with someone or turn him down for a date? How about when he breaks up with you? I was single until I was twenty-nine, and yes, I sent back gifts and tore up pictures after breakups. But it never made me feel better. Time and God's provision took care of healing from rejection. This is part of the process that leads to marriage, and even when we're not there yet, we need to make sure that our actions glorify God's vision of marriage in the world.

Proclaiming the gospel through our marriages also means that we create spaces and lives that are welcoming and draw others to us. One of the gifts of marriage is that it creates stable homes and families. We should welcome people into our homes to witness and also benefit from the joy and peace Christ gives us, in part, through the gift of marriage. And as we open our homes, we should also open our lives, offering transparency and speaking openly and honestly about our marital struggles and the ways we work with our husbands to strengthen our marriages. In this way we create stronger communities and also gain opportunities to give counsel and advice to others.

Of course, this means that we also have to acknowledge where we have fallen short—perhaps we have been through divorce, adultery, or other sins that have marred current or previous marriages. Rather than being silent on the issue, we ought to use such experiences to proclaim the work of God—we are sinners too, and in him we find forgiveness and the ability to start fresh. As Lamentations 3:22–23 tells us, "Because of the LORD's great love, we are not consumed, for his compassions never fail. They are new every morning." Homosexual relations are not the only way in which people fall short of God's intention for marriage, and by acknowledging our own failings in this area, we can share the truth of the gospel and Christ's redemption.

STAND FIRM

We must love others and set a good example, but that does not mean shrinking back or standing silently by when God's institution is besmirched. We must exhort our Christian sisters to stand firm in our position and our belief in the biblical view of marriage. We need to be the moral ballasts in an area where there is so much confusion and grayness. We are on the side of ultimate, divine truth, and we can't shirk our responsibilities. As I've said repeatedly, the institution of marriage reflects Christ and the church. It is not for us to change or manipulate this definition; it is given to us by God. This is something nonnegotiable, and we can't give it up or look the other way. At the end of the day, as the apostle Peter declared in Acts 5:29, "We ought to obey God rather than men" (NKJV).

This is a time for boldness. While we can also emphasize God's love for all people and the need for tolerance, we cannot accept the state of marriage in our country today. This topic strikes at the root of our theology, and while we don't have to convince all nonbelievers to view these issues the same way we do, we must still affirm our right to hold these beliefs and civilly express our opinions.

The First Amendment offers us this protection, as it does for everyone else of every other view. Honest debate in the public sphere is a good thing, and we want to encourage debate from all sides. Unfortunately, the debate over redefining marriage has curtailed free speech and religious freedom, and this will get worse unless we stand up and speak out for the right to hold opposing and conservative points of view. We cannot be bullied into being silent or accepting opinions that clearly go against our religious convictions. We must treat the other side with civility and respect, but we can't allow ourselves to be forced into submission and complicity.

FIGHT BACK

Speaking up is a start, but we must also move beyond words and into action. We must lead. Owen Strachan of the Council on Biblical Manhood and Womanhood has noted that the gospel "creates activists."[37] Jesus' stance was clear, and his commitment to truth was unflinching. He wasn't afraid of ruffling feathers, and he did not keep silent when it came to matters of the kingdom. We must be the same. We cannot be timid when it comes to this question.

We must push ahead and take proactive stances to protect a sacred institution under siege today. As Esther Women, we need to be speaking out on this topic, supporting legislation that protects religious liberty. People should not be forced to choose between violating their consciences and losing their jobs. We must insist that Christians be given the same opportunity as others to practice their religious beliefs. Accommodations are made in order to protect religious rights all the time—doctors licensed by the state don't have to do abortions, pacifists are allowed alternative military duty, the Transportation Security Administration takes special care with Muslim women. All of this inconveniences someone. A free society doesn't mean you can force others to participate in your choices when it conflicts with their deeply held religious beliefs.

Looking ahead to more long-term goals, we must join together to address the judicial activism that has brought us to this point on many issues, not just marriage. We must insist that the Supreme Court and other judicial appointees seek to uphold the US Constitution instead of working to create social change by finding new rights never intended by the founders. We must carefully consider the leaders we elect and use our votes to bring into power men and women who embrace godly values and judicial restraint. Overturning *Obergefell*, just like *Roe v. Wade*, will take either a reordering of the Supreme Court or a constitutional amendment on marriage. Both the abortion and marriage court decisions can be readdressed and made to reflect the inhabitants of individual states and the overall nation if and when we vote our values.

Ultimately, this is a very complex topic with roiling emotions on both sides. At the end of the day, as Esther Women, our job is to speak truth in a way that points back toward our heavenly Father. We may not have all the answers when it comes to the marriage debate, and we may not be able to change the tide of public opinion or the decisions of the courts. We can, however, stand on the biblical principles that undergird our understanding of marriage as a divine covenant and a great mystery. We have been entrusted with that covenant by God, and we must uphold it as our sacred duty.

Crystal Macias

YWA CHAPTER PRESIDENT, UNIVERSITY OF TEXAS AT EL PASO

Crystal Macias, the president of the YWA chapter at the University of Texas at El Paso, is leading the way for young female conservative voices today. In the wake of the Supreme Court decision legalizing gay marriage in 2015, she wrote a letter to local pastors in El Paso, encouraging them to come together for a season of fasting and prayer to reverse the direction our country is headed. Showing great courage, she refused to back down in the face of a culture and society that seemed to disregard everything she believed. "Inaction is no longer an opinion. We must stand boldly on the Word of God and not be intimidated," she wrote. "A revival in our churches is the key to restoring our country."[38]

Crystal, the daughter of a Mexican immigrant, knows that changing culture takes perseverance and determination. Today, she is a leading voice on the UTEP campus, where she urges other young women to join her in speaking up. "The main problem conservative women face on college campuses is silence," she says. "Many conservative women are afraid to speak about abortion and

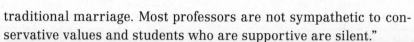

traditional marriage. Most professors are not sympathetic to conservative values and students who are supportive are silent."

Crystal believes that the best action conservative women can take to begin to find their voices is to pray. "It is difficult to take action without prayer," she says. But "God has a plan for every individual life and will guide anyone who is willing to listen."[39] I hope Crystal's faith, boldness, and passion to speak the truth help inspire a new generation of Esther Women to follow her lead.

CHAPTER 5

Abortion and the Sanctity of Life

his might come as a surprise, but despite working for years as a lobbyist for a pro-family women's organization, initially I wasn't interested in having kids. Don't get me wrong—I liked kids. I believed that they are a gift from God, his reward (Ps. 127:3). I just wasn't that excited about the idea of years without a solid night's sleep and spit-up on my perfectly tailored suit.

So when, three months after I got married, I hid in the stall of the ladies' room at work to take a pregnancy test (just to reassure myself), I was shocked to see two lines show up, indicating a positive result. I was so shocked that I called an OB/GYN for an appointment that day to take a real test. I was pretty sure that the one I had taken earlier had to be wrong.

Nope. The doctor patiently explained that yes, indeed, I was pregnant. Apparently those over-the-counter-pregnancy-test makers are serious when they say the tests are 99.9 percent accurate.

What?! was my first thought. *How could this happen?* I mean, I knew *how* it happened, but I certainly had not planned it. All I could think was that my life was going to change, and I was scared. What if I was a bad parent? What if I messed everything up? I was in panic mode.

By the grace of God, my husband was thrilled. At the time, we were both working for ministries. Will worked for Prison Fellowship and I worked for CWA; we were basically broke, but he was thrilled. His boss at the time, the late Chuck Colson, joked with me that Will came into his office and said the same thing I did: "I'm not sure how this happened!" I asked Chuck if he wouldn't mind taking the time to explain it. He was very sweet and supportive of two kids clearly in over their heads.

For the first two months I couldn't discuss my pregnancy without tears. Hormones and constant nausea did not help matters. Will once said the words pasta salad and I had to run to the bathroom to get sick.

Even worse, the only thing that kept me from throwing up in those early weeks was inexplicably a plethora of McDonald's cheeseburgers—and Lord knows I hate gaining weight. The people at the drive-thru got to know me well, and as a result, I packed on the pounds immediately. I felt out of control of my own body—and I was.

We went to a church event a couple of weeks after I found out about my pregnancy, and I was unlucky enough to be caught in the middle of a group of moms trading varicose-vein and childbirth horror stories. (Why *do* we try to one-up each other on that?) None of them knew I was pregnant, but I was so upset that I had to leave. I couldn't even talk to Will on the way home. All I could think was darn him for being so happy. I was glad he was happy, of course, but I wanted him to freak out a little with me too. Well, that wasn't going to happen. He's an unwavering optimist.

It wasn't until I was around twenty weeks and saw my sonogram that I was able to come to terms with my pregnancy. I had known it on an intellectual level, of course, but I couldn't get my head around the fact that this was my baby, not just a part of me but a separate and important person made in God's image. Will and I both cried when we saw the screen and the doctor announced that we were going to have a daughter. This time it was tears of joy—for both of us.

We began to prepare. Her room was painted pink. We found inexpensive furniture. My sister-in-law sent me boxes of beautifully smocked baby clothes, and I ironed and hung them on little hangers. I read several parenting books and, finally, I felt ready. I got bigger and bigger and waited and waited, but I was sure I was prepared.

When my due date rolled around, we checked in to the hospital for me to be induced. At last, after twenty-two hours of labor, I gave birth to our beautiful Claire—and let me tell you that *nothing* could have prepared me for how she changed me.

Suddenly, everything I knew about love changed. I can only describe it as feeling like that scene in *How the Grinch Stole Christmas:* my heart grew three times its normal size. My very capacity for love in the past seemed trite and miniscule by comparison. I didn't care anymore about my comfort and convenience. My heart was a vast, open, tender wound for this little person God had rewarded me with, even though I didn't know I wanted her.

What a gift. What an amazing, spectacular gift that God allowed me to parent this beautiful and sometimes willful but always fascinating creature. In his divine mercy he chose me out of all the other women in the world to be Claire's mom. I weep now with gratitude as I write this with the bittersweet knowledge of how fast eighteen years have gone. I recently dropped her off for her freshman year of college. I am so proud of the woman she has become. How did it go by so quickly?

Unwanted Pregnancy, Not Unwanted Child

Without a doubt, the circumstances of my life were better than those of many women facing an unplanned pregnancy, but I still think my story is representative in some important ways. Lots of women struggle with feelings about being pregnant or about parenting. Yet what too many folks on the left don't understand today is this: an unwanted pregnancy doesn't mean an unwanted child. Sadly, we live in a self-centered society that claims the answer to unplanned pregnancy is abortion. But there are so many alternatives. And the truth is, as we'll see, abortion is not what most women want.

We are far more capable of parenting than we realize, and after the initial shock of "I can't do this!" wears off, women often find a strength they didn't know they had. Our bodies prepare us for childbirth, and nature prepares us to raise our children. I don't say this to diminish the difficulty of raising a child—particularly for single mothers or women in poverty, struggling to make ends meet—but it can be done, and there are resources within our churches and communities to help us along the way.

For any woman reading this who has had that moment in the restroom as I did, staring at a pregnancy test stick and scared out of her mind, know that you are not alone. Before you panic any further, look online to find the closest pregnancy care center. There are nearly three thousand around the nation. They can help with everything from obtaining health care to providing resources once the baby is born, and they are staffed by compassionate, caring people who are there to love you, not to judge.

Pregnancy centers can also help to facilitate a selfless and courageous choice: adoption. Millions of amazing women have coped with the temporary state of pregnancy in order to give life instead of death. In the process they are able to bless another family. There are currently an estimated two million couples waiting and hoping to parent someone else's child.[1] More than 135,000 children are adopted in the United States each year, and more than 90 percent of adopted children ages five and older have positive feelings about their adoptions.[2] The courageous women who choose adoption over abortion are heroes.

Here's an important point: choices have consequences. In the case of choosing abortion or adoption, those consequences have a generational impact.

I know this firsthand because my parents are one of those families blessed with the opportunity to parent someone else's biological child. It's funny, but I forget sometimes that my own brother, Jim, was adopted. He is such a vital and cherished member of our family that I don't ever think about his being originally born to another one.

Sadly, not everyone makes the same selfless choice that Jim's birth mother made. I was reminded of this a few years ago when eighty-year-old Gloria Steinem was featured at the same Nick News event as my daughter, then fifteen. Gloria was annoyed when Claire and a couple of other pro-life teenagers stated in her presence that Lila Rose of the pro-life organization Live Action was their hero. Gloria took the opportunity while parents were out of the room to go up and tell these kids that she was happy she had an abortion. When Claire told me what Gloria had said, I asked her, "Did you ask her how many kids she ended up having?" Claire said that she hadn't, and I continued, "She would have told you none. She sadly aborted all of her kids." I have to wonder if the woman famous for her support for abortion would trade it all to have progeny to carry on her name, to love her in her old age. She is not the only woman I know who never had children because when she was presented with the option, it didn't seem like the perfect time. It's really so sad.

Today, the left unrelentingly promotes the idea that unwanted pregnancies do in fact mean unwanted babies, a message that has led us deeper into a culture of abortion that shames this great nation. More than 56 million babies have been aborted in this country since 1973, when the Supreme Court took an issue being worked out in the states into its own hands in the *Roe v. Wade* decision.[3] As a mother, a woman, and a Christian, I can't bear to see the place to which we've come. "Safe, legal, and rare," the mantra of the Clinton Administration in the '90s, is a joke. Abortion ends one life and wounds another, or several others. It's certainly legal in the United States, but rare, not so much. According to the Guttmacher Institute, one in four American women will have an abortion by age thirty.[4]

Unfortunately, the conversation about abortion has become clouded with misinformation and politics. And there is an entire industry making bank off of scared women and dead babies. We are told that abortion is not a big deal; that it's a humane choice for the unborn baby; and that to be anti-abortion is to be anti-women. Guess what? None of this is true. And it's time we got the facts straight.

The Truth about Fetal Development

One of the biggest questions surrounding the issue of abortion used to be, when does life begin? For years, the pro-abortion movement argued that a fetus was just a bunch of tissue, not a life. But medical and scientific advances have proven definitively that life starts at conception. The moment a sperm penetrates an egg, a new entity comes into existence: a zygote, the first cell formed at conception, which is composed of DNA and other molecules.[5] That's right; from the moment of that divine spark of conception a person contains all the same DNA he or she will die with. The zygote quickly develops into a human embryo, and then, after eight weeks, is termed a fetus.

This might all sound a bit technical, but consider this: After eighteen days, a baby's heart begins occasional pulsation, and at twenty-one days is beating rhythmically. After twenty days, the foundation for the baby's entire nervous system exists. By thirty days—just one month of gestation—the baby has eyes, ears, a mouth, and kidneys. And after only forty-two days, the baby has his or her own brain waves and reflexes.[6] There is never a blob of tissue, just a living, growing, responsive human being, a member of our human family.

Unable to avoid these truths, the left has often tried to focus the debate about abortion on the idea of viability, or whether a baby can live outside the womb. Abortion advocates have claimed that before twenty-four weeks, a fetus cannot survive on its own, and therefore is not a person and not deserving of protection. But this argument too is being demolished by medical advances. As the *New York Times* reported last year, viability is a moving target, and premature babies can survive outside the womb at just twenty-two weeks.[7] Even Supreme Court Justice Sandra Day O'Connor, a staunch supporter of abortion, has admitted that as technology gets better, it "continues to improve the chance for immature fetuses to survive outside the womb. That strengthens the appeal of arguments that . . . abortions are the taking of viable life."[8]

The idea of viability is problematic in and of itself; while the left wants to claim that a fetus dependent on its mother or on artificial support isn't a person, the embryo is in fact an entirely different life with its own heartbeat and DNA, and sometimes even has a blood type different than the mother's. The DNA is unique and specific to that baby, an entire genetic design that will determine everything from eye color to personality traits. The person that little baby will become is already established. To argue that something dependent on outside support to survive isn't a life is ridiculous—that would mean that people who rely on kidney dialysis or pacemakers aren't really people. Science and medicine back up the claims of the pro-life movement. Abortion proponents are today's flat-earthers and science deniers.

Abortion Procedures

When we ignore the truth about the humanity of unborn children, we allow ourselves to look past the cruelty embedded in the act of abortion. It is important not to allow ourselves to be desensitized to this extremely violent act. There are several ways abortions are performed, and it's important that you familiarize yourself with some of them.

The most common type is a suction abortion, used during the first three months of pregnancy, when a baby is sucked from the womb and the placenta torn away. Despite its frequent use, suction abortion carries risks of hemorrhage, uterine puncture, and infection from placental or fetal tissue left in the uterus. Another option during the first trimester is a chemical abortion. This involves abortifacient drugs that starve the baby in the womb, then induce contractions and expel the dead body. It is often accompanied by severe bleeding, nausea, vomiting, and pain.

In the second trimester, the most common procedure is D&E (dilation and evacuation), where the cervix is dilated and the baby grabbed with forceps, dismembered and removed from the womb. This dismemberment technique is particularly brutal, especially as the baby's skull has often developed by this time and sometimes must be crushed in order to be extracted. The risks associated with D&E include cervical lacerations and hemorrhage.

In later second- and third-trimester abortions, instillation techniques are often used—usually requiring the injection of lethal chemicals. A typical installation technique is saline amniocentesis, or salt poisoning. The amniotic fluid is injected with a solution that poisons the baby and often burns its developing body. The following day, the mother gives birth to the dead child. Risks with this procedure include severe hemorrhaging, seizures, and central nervous system damage.

Finally, there is partial-birth abortion, which was made illegal in 2003 with the Partial-Birth Abortion Ban Act, but is, perhaps, still being used. In such cases, the abortionist delivers all of the baby's body except for the head, which is left in the birth canal until the doctor punctures it with scissors and evacuates the brain matter, thus deflating the head.

These methods are uncomfortable to read about, but we have to realize what we're facing. I also think they make a strong case to dissuade women from choosing to have an abortion by alerting them to what these procedures entail and to the risks, which I'll discuss more fully below. Regardless of which method is used, each is cruel, painful, and sometimes dangerous for the mother, and causes the death of a living baby boy or girl.

The Risks of Abortion

Pro-abortion activists claim that abortions are safe, easy, and can save women's lives. Yet abortions take a terrible physical, emotional, and psychological toll on women. Many women today are still struggling to come to terms with the pain they've suffered since choosing to abort a baby.

From a physical-health standpoint, abortions are undeniably dangerous. Because the abortion industry is largely unregulated, abortion clinics operate outside of normal health care standards. In 2013, only five states regulated abortion clinics in the same manner as they do facilities performing other outpatient surgeries.[9] Clinics have been known to operate without properly sterilizing equipment, without properly trained staff, and without functioning emergency equipment.[10] These clinics often provide substandard care that puts women at risk and has even resulted in their deaths.[11] Americans United for Life (AUL) reported that since 2009, "at least 86 abortion providers in 29 states have faced investigations, criminal charges, civil lawsuits, and administrative complaints for substandard treatment [or] for violating state abortion laws."[12]

Such realities came to the forefront in the spring of 2013 when Dr. Kermit Gosnell, a late-term abortion doctor in Philadelphia, was put on trial for killing babies born alive by cutting their spinal cords, killing a woman during a botched abortion, and running an unsanitary clinic that injured women and violated state laws. Gosnell was found guilty of first-degree murder of three babies and involuntary manslaughter of the woman who died during the abortion procedure, as well as twenty-one counts of abortions after Pennsylvania's twenty-four-week limit and more than two hundred counts of violating the twenty-four-hour informed consent law.[13]

Other abortion providers clamored to distance themselves from Gosnell and his practices, despite the fact that some, including the local Planned Parenthood and the National Abortion Federation, had been aware of the clinic's horrifying conditions and procedures.[14] But Gosnell is not an anomaly. According to the organization Life Dynamics, as of April 2013, at least 347 women have died from complications due to legalized abortion, and far too many clinics provide unregulated services and substandard care.[15]

Chemical abortions also pose a physical threat to women. Chemical or medical abortions have become more common, particularly in the early stages of a pregnancy, and represent a cash cow to the industry because they require less oversight and patient care. These abortion-inducing drugs are often prescribed in an off-label manner, with clinics sending women home with the drugs to self-administer outside the FDA's approved time limit.[16] Some providers even practice telemed or webcam abortions, where no doctor is present in the room and the patient never receives a physical examination. Instead, the doctor explains the procedure via webcam and dispenses the abortion chemicals by a remotely activated drawer.[17] This is a traumatizing experience for women, who are left to deal with any hemorrhaging and the remains of their unborn children. It also poses a significant threat to their health because a physical exam would reveal if a woman has an ectopic pregnancy (which can cause rupturing when abortion-inducing drugs are used), and would also ensure that such drugs are not being administered too late in the pregnancy, which can increase risks.[18]

Finally, many studies have found a link between abortion and breast cancer (the ABC link). Although pro-abortion advocates vehemently deny this link, thirteen of fourteen American studies have shown that abortion increases a woman's risk of breast cancer.[19] Because estrogen levels increase during the first trimester of the pregnancy to prepare a woman for breast-feeding, milk-producing cells reproduce rapidly. If a pregnancy is terminated before thirty-two weeks, these cells are left behind. Such immature cells are more susceptible to carcinogens and more likely to develop cancer. This risk decreases if a woman carries her pregnancy to term, as the cells mature and become more resistant to cancer.[20] (This is not true in the case of miscarriage, as these pregnancies typically don't produce enough estrogen, which plays a central role in the proliferation of cells vulnerable to cancer.)[21]

The physical risks are startling enough. Yet abortion also poses a terrible threat to the emotional and psychological health of women. Despite what pro-abortion activists claim, abortion has repeatedly been tied to higher rates of depression, anxiety, suicide, and substance use. According to a study by the *British Journal of Psychiatry* in 2011, women face a startling 81 percent increased risk of mental health problems following abortions.[22] The effects of such psychological distress can range from insomnia and mild depression to infertility, failed relationships, eating disorders, PTSD, and a host of other negative outcomes.[23]

And while many women do report feeling depression, grief, guilt, and anxiety after an abortion, researchers believe that the prevalence of such experiences is much higher than actually reported. In fact, women who experience the most devastating emotional and psychological effects are the least likely to report it.[24] Society offers women no acknowledgment or support for the pain and grief they experience in the wake of an abortion, and sadly, many suffer in silence.

Roe v. Wade and *Doe v. Bolton*

If the medical facts of fetal life and the devastating physical and emotional effects of abortion are clear, how did we get so far off course? The twentieth century saw an almost unthinkable shift in the way abortion was viewed and regulated by the government, and sadly, it happened not by the will of the people, but through the courts. In 1973, the Supreme Court ruled on two companion cases, *Roe v. Wade* and the lesser-known *Doe v. Bolton*. Taken together, these cases legalized abortion for any reason at any time during a pregnancy. Abortion had been present in society prior to this, and throughout the 1960s and '70s pro-abortion groups had been making ground, with many states legalizing abortion in extreme cases only. With the *Roe* and *Doe* decisions, however, abortion-on-demand was imposed nationwide. Stepping far beyond the will of the people or general public opinion, these cases established a culture of death in our nation.

In *Roe v. Wade*, the 7–2 decision argued that the Fourteenth Amendment's due process clause guarantees a woman's right to abortion. Basically, the justices argued that the "right to privacy"—a phrase which exists nowhere in the text of the Constitution—permits a woman to have an abortion for any reason during the first trimester, and that after viability, the state may allow for abortions if necessary for the health of the mother. *Doe v. Bolton* took this one step farther, expanding the health exception to include almost anything. As Justice Harry Blackmun wrote in the opinion, the justification for a late-term abortion should be considered "in the light of all factors—physical, emotional, psychological, familial, and the woman's age—relevant to the wellbeing of the patient."[25] As the Heritage Foundation has noted, the inclusion of any psychological or emotional factor as defined by *Doe v. Bolton* is so wide as to have "applicability to virtually every unwanted pregnancy."[26]

In some states, if a woman can find a doctor willing to perform a third-trimester abortion, she can get one. And many women have. Since 1973, there have been more than 56 million abortions performed in the United States, and at least 40 percent of unintended pregnancies end in abortion.[27] Incredibly, our abortion policy is one of the most liberal in the world: only six other nations allow for abortions after twenty weeks, among them, China, Vietnam, and North Korea.[28] The overreach of *Roe v. Wade* and *Doe v. Bolton* was shocking, overturning abortion bans in all fifty states and ultimately aligning our nation with countries who show no concern for human rights. Our permissive abortion laws do not reflect the broader humanitarian standards of the international community—or even, as we will see, the opinion of most Americans.

Women and Public Opinion

Last year, a Gallup poll was released which suggested that for the first time since 2008, more Americans were pro-choice than pro-life.[29] This is a convenient narrative for the left, and pro-abortion activists were quick to run with it, but the reality is much more complicated.

In fact, most Americans do not support abortion. A careful look at the Gallup poll makes it obvious that such claims don't hold water; while more Americans said they would label themselves as pro-choice, the numbers show that 55 percent of Americans oppose all abortions or say abortion should only be legal in a "few circumstances." Only 29 percent of Americans support abortion in all circumstances.[30] Clearly, the country is not aligned on this issue, and to claim that most Americans are pro-choice is blatantly false.

Even so, the left continues to push this notion. They make sweeping claims about the country's stance on abortion and back them up with skewed data. In particular, they distract from the central issue by using rape victims for their political fodder. Rape and incest are the exceptions for which most Americans statistically accept abortion as an option, but these rarely occur. Hear me when I say that even one abortion is too many, but the pro-abortion Guttmacher Institute itself has acknowledged that women seeking an abortion because they were victims of rape is less than 1 percent, and women who say they became pregnant from incest is less than half a percent.[31] This argument is a red herring used by the left to obfuscate the issue.

For this reason federal law and many state laws allow for rape and incest exceptions in abortion funding and other prohibitions. This concession remains rightfully controversial within the pro-life community due to the fact that the unborn child is innocent of its biological father's actions. I, like many pro-life Americans, do not believe that even such tragic circumstances during conception justify taking a baby's life. Many of us have friends or know someone who was conceived in rape. This is unequivocally a horrible experience for any mother, but abortion only compounds her pain by adding guilt to trauma. We must minister to her and work hard to give her healing and other options, such as adoption. We know that statistically three-fourths of rape victims do not choose abortion.[32] Clearly many of them agree on this point. I should add however that I have and do support legislation that contains a rape incest exception if it is essential to protect the vast majority of babies. Public policy is downstream of public opinion, and we still have work to do.

Most of us support life of the mother exceptions, however, because it is the question of one life or the other, and sometimes both are at risk. This is completely different from a health exception, which is a legal loophole defined by *Doe* and used to promote late-term abortion. Life exceptions are so rare, due to the great strides made in obstetric medical care, that many health professionals no longer believe it to be a relevant issue. However, it is precisely these hard and rare issues that the left uses to distract from the fact that their radical view and our current laws are out of touch with the vast majority of Americans.

Yes, the hard cases are where we lose some public opinion, but outside of this, the majority of our nation's citizens believe that abortion is morally wrong. Young people are the most adamant on this point: 58 percent of millennials believe that abortion is a moral wrong.[33] And 80 percent of Americans say that they support stricter abortion laws.[34]

Even more firmly, Americans do not believe that we should have to fund other's right to choose—according to the most recent data, 68 percent of Americans don't think that abortions should be funded by taxpayer money.[35]

However, the left doesn't want to have this discussion. Here's a case in point. A couple of years ago I was on a panel on Sean Hannity's show on Fox to discuss Obamacare. Sean, a strong pro-life voice and great American, has been kind to me and to CWA over the years by welcoming our perspective. I was happy to appear once again on his smart and successful show. The rest of the panel was made up mainly of economic groups, but Sean called on me at the beginning, and I began to talk about the fact that Obamacare violates the rights of people of faith by forcing us to subsidize other people's abortions.

In the middle of my sentence, liberal commentator Tamara Holder started yelling, "This is bananas!" She tried to cut me off and change the subject until I finally said, "Tamara, what about my rights? Why should I have to pay for your abortion or your birth control?" That's an important question, isn't it? Why do pro-abortion advocates fight for what they whitewash as the right to choose when it's not really about choice? Pro-abortion advocates don't support choice; they support abortion, in any number, for any reason, at any point in pregnancy, and all paid for by the taxpayer. This is the position of President Obama, Hilary Clinton, Planned Parenthood, and the abortion advocacy machine.

And they don't care who the taxpayer is—not even if it's a group of nuns who have taken vows of celibacy and poverty. This was the case in 2014, when the Little Sisters of the Poor, a Roman Catholic congregation of religious sisters, were forced to file a lawsuit to request that they not be required to adhere to the federal government's contraception and abortion mandate, which violated their beliefs about the sanctity of life.[36]

At the 2015 Women in the World Summit, Hillary Clinton summarized the left's view on religious liberty when she told listeners that "deep-seated cultural codes, religious beliefs and structural biases have to be changed" for the sake of giving women access to "reproductive health care and safe childbirth."[37] Those words should outrage every woman of faith in this country, whether you are Christian, Jewish, Muslim, or any other religion. Apparently, we don't deserve the right to hold our religious beliefs if they conflict with the right to choose. That kind of mentality is not advocating freedom; it's seeking tyranny.

The Facts about Taxpayer Money

While the debate about funding abortions and contraception can get bogged down with partisan rhetoric, the federal government spends billions of dollars every year funding abortion providers. In 2010, the most recent year available from Guttmacher Institute data, government expenditures for family planning services totaled $2.37 billion.[38]

Planned Parenthood is the largest recipient of government funding, receiving more than half a billion dollars a year from taxpayers.[39] Seventy-five percent of those funds come from Medicaid—between 2010 and 2012, Planned Parenthood received $1.18 billion in state and federal Medicaid dollars.[40] They are the nation's largest abortion provider (one out of every four abortions takes place in one of their clinics), and from 2013 to 2014 alone, they performed 324,653 abortions.[41] They downplay the centrality of abortion to their organization, claiming that it only makes up 3 percent of their services, but as National Right to Life has explained, this is disingenuous: "the gist of this accounting gimmick is to count every packet of birth control pills, every pregnancy test, every box of condoms, etc., as a separate service, regardless of their relative cost."[42] In other words, if a woman comes to Planned Parenthood and receives an abortion, it is counted with the same weight as if they were handing out individual condoms at a frat house.

Planned Parenthood has enjoyed a thin veneer of respectability by hiding its core mission—although even that came crashing down in the summer of 2015 when a series of videos was released showing the organization's medical director and employees discussing the harvesting of aborted babies' body parts to sell, and admitting to altering abortion procedures in order to preserve the organs.[43] They also discussed partial-birth abortions, which, as I mentioned, was outlawed in 2003. The videos exposed what we have long known: Planned Parenthood is not a guardian of women's health. They don't do mammograms as often as they have claimed.[44] They don't help women choose from a range of options. When a pregnant woman comes to Planned Parenthood for help, 98 percent of the time she aborts her baby, and they make a profit.[45]

Lila Rose of Live Action has documented the many nefarious activities of the organization, which include aiding and abetting sex trafficking (seven Planned Parenthood clinics in four states supplied confidential birth control, STD testing, and secret abortions to underage girls and their traffickers), and refusing to comply with the law by providing abortions to underage girls without parental notification.[46]

Planned Parenthood also has a long history of racism and mistreatment of minorities. When Live Action conducted an investigation last year by calling a Planned Parenthood clinic and requesting to donate money to go specifically toward the abortion of black babies, the caller was told that request was completely "understandable." More than 79 percent of Planned Parenthood clinics are near minority neighborhoods, and many of them set up so-called women in need funds that designate money specifically for minority abortions.[47] With more than 850 abortions performed on African American women daily, according to Live Action, "Planned Parenthood is (intentionally or not) exterminating the black community."[48]

Sadly, they are right in line with their founder Margaret Sanger and her original plan for Planned Parenthood. In 1939, Sanger wrote about her plan to eliminate the black community: "The most successful, educational appeal to the Negro is through a religious appeal. We do not want word to go out that we want to exterminate the Negro population, and the minister is the man who can straighten out that idea if it ever occurs to any of their rebellious members."[49] Apparently, that thinking has stuck.

Despite these despicable roots, Planned Parenthood is dependent on taxpayer money for their abortion services; government funding makes up 41 percent of their revenue.[50] (While the federal government cannot directly fund abortions because of the Hyde Amendment, we all know that money is fungible.) And the organization is keenly aware of this reality: they spent more than $12 million in the 2012 presidential election to ensure that Barack Obama and other pro-abortion candidates were elected and would continue to fund their abortion services.[51] They use the federal government to prop up their abortion business, despite the fact that most Americans don't want to financially support them.

Because it is not subject to the restrictions of the Hyde Amendment, Obamacare has only exacerbated the issues. Obamacare authorized a tax credit to subsidize the purchase of private health care plans by millions of low- and middle-income families—private plans that often cover abortion on demand, yet still receive federal funding. As Virginia Foxx (R-NC) noted before Congress last year, "In other words, hard-earned taxpayer dollars are now being used to pay for elective abortions."[52] In an attempt to combat this, Concerned Women for America worked with the House of Representatives to pass the No Taxpayer Funding for Abortion Act in January 2015 to prevent insurers that accept federal funding from covering elective abortions, but without a pro-life president, the bill will be vetoed.

So the gravy train continues for Planned Parenthood. Ten brave governors have at least partially defunded the organization in their states, including Scott Walker (R-WI) and Chris Christie (R-NJ).[53] We need that replicated in every other state and on the national level as well. CWA and other pro-life organizations are leading the fight to defund Planned Parenthood and to instead use the money to fund the more than nine-thousand community health centers in the nation. These centers can better care for poor women in need of gynecological care or any other medical care.[54] They have no abortion incentive and they treat the whole woman. The left presents a self-serving and false narrative that without Planned Parenthood poor women would not receive care.

There are also an estimated 2,500 to 3,000 nonprofit pregnancy care centers around the country that provide alternative options for women and that receive the majority or entirety of their support from private funding.[55] Rather than leeching off the American taxpayer, these organizations, often led by people of faith, use private donations to provide women with pregnancy tests and sonograms, counseling, post-abortion support, adoption information and referrals, medical care referrals, and financial and legal assistance at no cost.[56] Offering women compassion and meeting the physical, emotional, and spiritual needs that come with unwanted pregnancies and difficult decisions, pregnancy care centers are critical in broadening the conversation and enabling women to find meaningful alternatives to abortion.

The Fight on Capitol Hill: The Twenty-Week Ban

The pro-life movement has had major success in legislation and in winning hearts and minds on the issues of sex-selective abortions (yes, they do happen in this country),[57] five-month bans, and clinic regulation. We are fighting those battles and winning both in the states and on the federal level. But there is still a lot of work to be done.

The Pain-Capable Unborn Child Protection Act sponsored by Representative Trent Franks (R-AZ) and Senator Lindsey Graham (R-SC) is the most important piece of pro-life legislation in the past decade because it not only limits abortion but also explains to a distracted public what's at stake. Public policy is downstream of public opinion. We must change hearts and minds in order to change law. The Pain-Capable

Act, for which Concerned Women for America members had been campaigning since 2012, does both. It gives legal protection to unborn babies beginning at twenty weeks or five months. At twenty weeks, babies in the womb have a heartbeat, can hear and respond to their mothers' voices, and can already, according to scientists, feel excruciating pain.[58] The idea that such a life could be killed in the womb is horrifying, not just to the hard-core pro-life movement but to the majority of Americans (75 percent, according to one recent poll).[59] This bill also protects women, who are at a much greater risk with later-term abortions. At twenty weeks of pregnancy, a woman is thirty-five times more likely to die from an abortion than she was in the first trimester, according to AUL.[60]

The passage of the bill by the House in May 2015 was an encouraging victory after a heartbreaking setback on the March for Life day that January. After we had worked for two years to bring the bill to a vote with the help of the House leadership, the bill was stalled by two women legislators we believed were on our team, Renee Ellmers (R-NC) and Jackie Walorski (R-IN).[61] As *World Magazine* reported, Ellmers and Walorski "withdrew their support and advocated for others to do the same. Leadership pulled the bill the night before the March for Life, leaving pro-lifers feeling betrayed and conservatives of all stripes wondering whether the new Republican majority is doomed to fail."[62]

Ellmers and Walorski's actions were not the only reason for the bill's setback in January 2015, but they created the chaos that helped it spin out of the control of the House leadership. House Majority Leader Kevin McCarthy came with a broken heart to give the news to pro-life leaders as we gathered to celebrate our two years of effort the night before the March for Life. He told me that he was sorry but assured us, "You have my word we will get this done." I was distraught. How could I explain to our members that a handful of rogue Republicans could sidetrack a bill that was so important?

The next day I stood next to the stage at the March for Life alongside my friend and colleague, Jeanne Monahan. I was exhausted from my inability to sleep the night before. I had spent it tossing and turning, thinking about how to get the bill's coalition back together. That morning I had been on Capitol Hill with about a hundred of CWA's Young Women for America college chapter members. They had been lobbying the Senate office on the same bill that had just blown up in the House. They were undeterred by the House setback, buoyed by the firm belief in their cause.

As I waited to walk onstage, the fourth most senior member of the House of Representatives, Cathy McMorris Rodgers (R-WA), walked by. When she saw me, she stopped. She grabbed my hand and, standing inches from my face, looked me in the eye with a steely determination that I had never seen before. She said, "Penny, I am sorry about what happened, but hear me when I say this: I promise you that we will pass this bill."

Wow. I was almost knocked over by her intensity. I knew she meant it. Cathy is a strong proponent for life. Her first child, Cole, was born with Down syndrome, and she formed the Congressional Down Syndrome Caucus on Capitol Hill. She speaks for the least of these and personally lives out those values, but at the moment I couldn't see how she was going to succeed. Even with the support of Speaker John Boehner and his team it looked bleak because rogue members had given our enemies new arguments and an opening to exploit.

But, incredibly, things came together because Kevin, Cathy, and the leadership staff were true to their word, because CWA members and other organizations continued to fight, and because God is sovereign even when my faith is weak. In May 2015 I was thrilled to watch in the Capitol Gallery as members of the House of Representatives, mostly women, spoke passionately and voted overwhelmingly to pass the bill to stop abortions after a baby can feel pain. The final vote was 242–184. At publication CWA is working with Senator Lindsey Graham to pass the bill in the Senate. We will need either a pro-life president or a veto-proof majority in the House and Senate before it becomes law, but I know it will happen soon.

We must work tirelessly to incrementally peel back the tentacles of *Roe v. Wade* and educate people that abortion harms women and children. This bill is one step in a long but worthy fight.

Concerned Women for America is dedicated to this battle in the national media and with our grassroots members actively engaging their elected representatives on the bill. We will continue to work with our Young Women for America chapters to educate other students and work with them, using social media to engage others in the debate.

What Can Esther Women Do?

Pro-life advocate Frederica Mathewes-Green rightly said, "No one wants an abortion as she wants an ice-cream cone or a Porsche. She wants

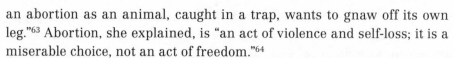

an abortion as an animal, caught in a trap, wants to gnaw off its own leg."[63] Abortion, she explained, is "an act of violence and self-loss; it is a miserable choice, not an act of freedom."[64]

We should consider the issue of abortion in America with this in mind. It is with compassion that we must share the facts and speak our minds. This is not about winning a theoretical argument; it is about the suffering of women, the loss of children, and the need to find compassionate, effective answers to a terrible national stain.

STAND ON SOLID BIBLICAL GROUND

When we talk about abortion, we must emphasize that we are talking about human lives—that each unborn baby is a beautiful, living, growing human being, and that we can't allow any baby to be dehumanized in order to justify our right to choose. Among our Christian sisters, we can emphasize the biblical basis for the sanctity of each life. God gives us children as a gift, and to scorn that gift is to scorn him. God cares about each of us from *before* we are born—before we are even conceived. "For you created my inmost being; you knit me together in my mother's womb. I praise you because I am fearfully and wonderfully made . . . My frame was not hidden from you when I was made in the secret place, when I was woven together in the depths of the earth. Your eyes saw my unformed body" (Ps. 139:13–16).

God creates us perfectly, with skill and care, and we must honor his handiwork. He also has a plan for each of us from before our birth; as he told the prophet Jeremiah, "Before I formed you in the womb I knew you, before you were born I set you apart" (Jer. 1:5). No matter what the circumstances of a baby's conception or a mother's readiness to be a parent, God is intimately involved from the beginning, and the future of that child is already in his hands. We are merely stewards of God's creation, and the choice to give and take life doesn't belong to us.

KNOW THE FACTS

Of course, there are many for whom the biblical foundation for the sanctity of life is not a persuasive argument, and when we raise the issue of abortion with them, we should rely instead on scientific facts. Pro-abortion advocates want to say that a woman's body belongs to her, and she should be able to choose to use it as she wants; but we know that a baby isn't merely part of her body—it's a separate life with a separate heart, brain, and genetic makeup. Arming yourself with facts such as when a baby's heartbeat is detectable (eighteen days) or when a baby shows brain activity (six weeks) is important, not to prove a point, but to encourage others to see these unborn babies as the human children they are.

We also need to know the facts about the many types of abortion. If you are able to have the conversation with a woman contemplating an abortion, you need to be able to tell her why it is a brutal procedure for both her and the baby. We should not, of course, discuss this with a woman who has already had an abortion, unless she is considering another one. She needs our compassion, not our condemnation.

Equally as important, we need to be able to articulate the facts about the emotional pain abortion inflicts upon women. Society tells us that an abortion is an empowering choice. But the truth is that abortion harms women, both physically and emotionally, and we need to be the ones to speak up about it. Pro-abortion groups have no interest in admitting that women suffer after abortions or in offering any kind of compassion or help, because it would undermine their argument that abortion is a positive good for everyone. We must combat this with facts about how women suffer and by providing compassion and care to women who have gone through this trauma.

OFFER COMPASSION

Do you know women who have gone through an abortion? I do. Talk to them. Let them share their stories, and offer both a listening ear and a compassionate response. Point them to places where they can find help. Groups like Project Rachel (the post-abortion ministry of the Catholic Church and the founder of HopeAfterAbortion.com) and Silent No More offer resources and information for women who seek to heal from the pain of abortion. Encourage your churches and pastors to familiarize themselves with such resources as well. We need churches to be equipped to offer support for women who have gone through this experience. The more we can speak up about the ways women suffer after abortion, and the more light we can shine on resources available to them, the better we will be able both to minister to these women and to encourage others to find alternatives.

We also can't be afraid to speak out about how abortion affects men and families too. Although society never acknowledges it, abortion forces men to give up their role as provider and protector, and it can have long-lasting, detrimental consequences. Wayne Brauning, the founder of MARC (Men's Abortion ReCovery) Ministries, has stated, "Men everywhere report that abortion is a horrendous and heartbreaking experience, whether they oppose or support [their partner's] decision to abort." Such men feel "angry . . . guilty and powerless."[65] The ramifications of abortion on a relationship can be devastating too.

The children of mothers or parents who have gone through abortion suffer as well. One study showed that children whose mothers had abortions had less supportive home environments and more behavioral problems.[66] Given that many of these mothers are struggling with depression, grief, and in some cases substance abuse, this is unsurprising. We must be willing to speak up about these realities, because the longer they go unnoticed, the more men, women, and children will suffer in silence.

PROMOTE AWARENESS FOR ALTERNATIVES

On the other side of the coin, when it comes to women who are pregnant and are considering abortions, we need to promote awareness about alternatives. Despite the pro-choice misnomer, women in crisis pregnancies often feel as if they have no choice. They need to know that they are not alone and that they have other options, aside from abortion.

As I've mentioned, the many pregnancy care centers in this country provide incredible resources, from financial and emotional support to referrals for adoption, social services, and medical treatment. They also provide resources and counseling for husbands and partners, who need to be a part of this conversation. Women who feel that they have practical and emotional support from their partners are far more likely to choose life, and pregnancy care centers are working to help men speak into this space.[67]

We need to support the work of such organizations and to increase their visibility to women facing difficult situations. Among your Christian friends, consider committing to pray for pregnancy care centers, volunteer there, or even support them financially. The best way to combat abortion is to spread awareness that other options exist.

For those of you who feel called to do more, let me say a word about sidewalk counseling. Outside abortion clinics all over this nation, kind-hearted volunteers stand with warm smiles, coffee, and balloons offering to help women in distress. The media's image of angry people yelling is false and ridiculous. It's just the opposite, in my experience. I recently went to pray outside Planned Parenthood's flagship clinic in Houston,

Texas. This $26 million building is their showcase facility, the largest in the nation.[68] Joining me on the sidewalk were a handful of volunteers who faithfully take turns with others in their community to offer women alternatives. Some stand in silent prayer, but others flag down the cars entering the lot. If a car stops, the volunteer smiles and offers them the opportunity to go across the street to a state-of-the-art mobile health clinic where women can receive a free sonogram from qualified health professionals as well as counseling.

These folks are nonthreatening people of faith offering another choice, and guess what? It works. As I stood with these volunteers, I watched as young women and their husbands or boyfriends walked across the street to investigate other options available to them. Consequently, just as in my own experience, when those women see their babies for the first time, they will often come to terms with their pregnancies and welcome life. Consider joining local CWA ladies and others who go to ground zero in the abortion battle in order to share the love of Christ, or even donating to purchase more state-of-the-art mobile clinics.

Sharing the love of God with women in need isn't just the right thing to do; it's biblical. God asks us to care for women and children and to support those who find themselves in difficult circumstances. In Matthew 18:5 Jesus tells his disciples, "Whoever receives a little child like this in My name receives Me" (NKJV), and again, "Whatever you did for one of the least of these brothers and sisters of mine, you did for me" (Matt. 25:40). We are called to care for women who are struggling and to help promote adoption and other resources for their children.

ADVOCATE FOR LIFE

This is an issue for which advocacy is critical. The courts pushed abortion laws far beyond the pale in 1973, and we have to combat that with new laws that protect our citizens and value the dignity of human life. As Esther Women, we need to vocally support such work. As important legislative votes come up, we should write to our state and federal representatives urging them to act. Sign up at www.concernedwomen.org to receive emails alerting you to important opportunities to advocate for life. And consider participating in rallies and events that promote the sanctity of human life, such as the March for Life.

Every year on the anniversary of *Roe v. Wade*, CWA joins with hundreds of thousands of other people in Washington, DC, to march from the White House to the Supreme Court in support of life. Families, school groups, and churches join together with one voice to cry out for the least of these. If a trip to DC is not a possiblity for you, think about organizing a group to march in your own town. It's an amazing testimony to both your elected officials and to the media.

Let me also give a shout-out to those who participate in peaceful demonstrations. Just as in the civil rights battle, there is a place for civil disobedience in the battle against abortion. Although I have never participated, I can't say that I never will. Recently a group of pro-lifers got tired of waiting for the twenty-week ban to come to the House floor and held a sit-in outside Speaker John Boehner's office, asking him to bring up the bill. Although I believe that the Speaker wanted to pass the bill, I also believe that this activity helped to focus the attention of the House leadership. Such actions remind me of the importance of every level of activism.

Finally, vote your values. Concerned Women for America Legislative Action Committee and others work tirelessly to provide voter education. Take the time to question candidates. If someone running for public office does not understand or believe in the necessity of respecting life from conception to natural death, then he or she does not possess the judgment required to lead our nation. It is essential that we make our voices heard in the voting booth.

KEEP THE FAITH

Let me end this chapter with some good news about activism: Although we have a long way to go, we are winning. *Time* magazine recently said that although abortion-rights activists "won an epic victory" in *Roe v. Wade*, "they've been losing ever since."[69] The years 2011, 2012, 2013 and 2014 saw record numbers of pro-life laws limiting abortion passed in states. Four states are down to one abortion clinic each: Mississippi, North Dakota, South Dakota, and Wyoming.[70] Our work matters, and we *can* make change happen.

This is not an issue that is going to solve itself. Our country is divided, and unfortunately, the issue has gotten only more divisive, with each side more deeply entrenched than ever. We need to bring rational thought, measured rhetoric, and compassion back into the conversation.

Public opinion, science, and truth are on our side. You, the Esthers of this generation, can make a difference. Don't be cowed by the handful of vocal supporters of abortion. They are either in deep denial or profiting from the industry. We are standing on the precipice of change. We have the power to engage our culture and speak for the most innocent. You can do this, and if we join hands and take on the battle, we can roll back this most scurrilous injustice. Our time is here.

Who knows, the baby you advocate for today may be tomorrow's president, the scientist who finds a cure for cancer, or the engineer who saves lives. Or she may be an average little girl. Regardless, she is beautiful and has worth because she is made in God's image. *Imago Dei!*

Day Gardner

FOUNDER AND PRESIDENT OF THE NATIONAL BLACK PRO-LIFE UNION; ASSOCIATE DIRECTOR OF NATIONAL PRO-LIFE CENTER ON CAPITOL HILL

Day Gardner has dedicated her life to fighting for the rights of unborn babies, particularly in minority communities. She became committed to the pro-life movement while running for a seat in the Maryland state legislature. While conducting research to defend her position on abortion, she became appalled by the statistics of abortion in the black community. "The very thought of the insane brutality inflicted on small children that are aborted is almost unbearable," she says. "How could I stand by and do nothing?"

Realizing that God had called her into this arena for a reason, Day responded with vigor. She served as the National Director of Black Americans for Life, and then in 2009 founded the National Black Pro-Life Union to help bring together the many pro-life groups and individuals working throughout the country. By combining resources and encouraging each other in the fight, these groups are more effective than ever before.

Day, who was the first African American woman to place as a semifinalist in the Miss America Pageant in 1977, is emblematic of the progress of conservative women in this country, and she continues to work to strengthen our voices every day. She is especially passionate about the need for African American women's voices to be heard and has devoted herself to educating conservative leaders about the importance of working with the black community.

Though she has faced struggles and pushback at many points in her career, Day continues to lead the way for conservative women and to fight for life at every turn, relying on her faith. "In every trial, God is triumphant!" she says.[71]

Marjorie Dannenfelser

PRESIDENT, SUSAN B. ANTHONY LIST

Marjorie Dannenfelser is the president of the Susan B. Anthony List (SBA List), a pro-life organization that advocates for candidates and policies that work toward ending abortion in our nation. Today the organization has more than 380,000 members and has helped elect more than 130 pro-life candidates at the state and federal levels.

Marjorie's efforts helped bring a Republican majority to the Senate in 2014, and she continues to fight for legislation to save the lives of unborn babies. Her work was critical in bringing attention to the Pain-Capable Unborn Child Protection Act, which gives legal protection to unborn babies beginning at twenty weeks. It is the most important pro-life legislation in the past decade, and Marjorie has campaigned tirelessly to enlist the support of leaders in the House and Senate.

Marjorie's passion for this lifesaving work permeates every aspect of her life. In the early days of the SBA List, she housed the group's offices within her own home in Arlington, Virginia. Although she wasn't always pro-life, Marjorie came to ardently believe in the issue in her twenties, a conviction strengthened by her conversion to Catholicism. Realizing the importance of this issue and the grave consequences of doing nothing, she threw herself into pro-life activism with determination and unrelenting focus.

Marjorie, who has five children, brings a relatability and realism to the pro-life arena. She understands the challenges of being a working mom and emphasizes the need for women to support each other. Particularly in the area of pro-life work, Marjorie is an inspiration to women who feel called to serve in significant public roles while also balancing the demands of motherhood, marriage, and community.

Though Marjorie has faced significant opposition and pushback from opponents of her pro-life message, she refused to be silenced or intimidated. In fact, she seeks out surprising audiences with the pro-life message. Marjorie was the subject of a recent article titled "The Intensity Gap: Can a Pro-life Platform Win Elections?" in *The New Yorker* magazine. The piece showcased Marjorie's political strategy and firm belief that fighting for life is not only morally right but politically smart. She has been named one of the *Washington Examiner*'s top ten "Political Women on the Move," one of Newsmax's top twenty-five most influential Republican women, and among *Newsweek*'s top ten leaders of the Christian right. The grassroots work of the SBA List continues to change minds and save lives, and thanks to Marjorie's leadership, it is more influential now than ever before.

CHAPTER 6

The Real War against Women

In the summer of 2014 I stood in Dulles airport's international terminal, waiting for my daughter, who was on her way home from a mission trip. A bit early for her arrival, I had time to observe people entering into our country, including many women from other cultures dressed in an array of interesting outfits. Many were wearing Western clothes—some in jeans and T-shirts, some in dressier pants and pretty tops. There were also Indian women in beautifully colorful saris, African women wearing gorgeous tribal fabrics, and Orthodox Jewish women wearing attractive headscarves covering their hair and graceful skirts.

Then I noticed the women in black. I love to wear black, but these women wore shapeless black robes from the top of their heads to the bottom of their feet. All I could see of their faces was their eyes. Nothing else. No smile or frown, no expression at all. I had no idea how they felt about entering our great nation. Were they missing their families left behind? Were they excited at the promise of a new adventure? I couldn't even tell for certain if they were women at all.

I had an urge to reach out and introduce myself to one of them, but held back. They were set apart from everyone else, wrangled by the men accompanying them and then corralled out the door. I watched, both fascinated and saddened. Who were these women, and what were their stories? Clearly they were arriving from Islamic nations where such clothing is often their required dress. I desperately wanted to welcome them and also let them know that it's different in the United States. "You don't have to cover your face and hide here; you're safe," I wanted to say. "Let us get to know you."

When women are forced to cover their faces, it sets them apart from everyone else. It's a barrier not just from the immodest gazes of men, as some claim, but from society at large. For if radical Islamic men can keep women separate from everyone else, keep them isolated, then they can manipulate and control them. Such oppression has been aptly named burqa apartheid, and it's a powerful tool in a full toolbox used to subjugate women into second-class citizens.

I am not talking about the oftentimes-concocted patriarchy denounced by American feminists, but the legitimate objectification and subjugation of a large group of women in the world.

As Christians, we know that, as stated in the Declaration of Independence, our rights are granted by our Creator—not by any government. Thomas Jefferson wrote, "We hold these truths to be self-evident, that all men are created equal, that they are endowed by their Creator with certain unalienable rights, that among these are life, liberty and the pursuit of happiness." No government has the authority to give or take liberty away. Therefore, we must be advocates for human rights for all people. Women living in theocratic, Muslim nations are at the mercy of men who control every aspect of their lives. In many cases, they cannot choose whom or when to marry, they cannot leave their homes without a male escort, they cannot drive, they have little legal protection from abuse or rape, many cannot vote; quite simply, they have no power.

We have to stop ignoring this reality.

A Global Problem

Human rights abuses against women occur worldwide every single day. Human trafficking of women and girls for sexual exploitation is one of the fastest-growing criminal enterprises on the globe, with women and children making up an estimated 70 percent of trafficking victims.[1] In war-torn parts of Africa like the Democratic Republic of Congo, sexual violence and rape are perpetrated against women constantly and with impunity.[2] In India, bride burnings—setting a woman on fire to punish her and her family for refusing to pay a higher dowry—occur at a rate of one every two hours, according to some estimates.[3] In China, one in four women is subject to domestic violence.[4]

Women are so devalued in much of the world that, often, female babies aren't even given the right to life. According to Nicholas Kristof and Sheryl WuDunn, "More girls have been killed in the last fifty years, precisely because they were girls, than men were killed in all the wars of the twentieth century." Such gendercide has resulted in the loss of between 60 and 100 million or more girls from the planet, with at least two million more girls lost each year from sex-selective abortions, abuse, and discrimination against girls that prevents them from receiving vaccinations, medicine, or necessary medical treatment.[5]

Much of the human rights abuses against women are condemned by the United Nations and governments around the world; collectively billions of dollars are spent in an attempt to combat violence, abuse, and sexual trafficking of women.[6] Yet there is also a huge amount of mistreatment of women that goes unnoticed and unexamined. Around the world, women suffer in silence and in the shadows.

Sadly, this is particularly true in Muslim-majority countries. In Muslim states, especially those under sharia law, the oppression of women is basically institutionalized. Women's freedom of movement, education, choices about marriage, even control over their own bodies are all restricted under sharia law. Without rights or legal recourse, women are left with few options and are subject to the mercy of the men who control nearly all aspects of their lives. They have no liberty.

The West often turns a blind eye to such realities. Not wanting to be accused of Islamophobia, many claim that the way women are treated in Muslim societies is simply cultural, and they argue that it's not our place to say anything about it. Such willful blindness of widespread, ongoing abuse of women is despicable and only allows it to continue. Any abuse of another human being is morally reprehensible, and we have a duty to speak up about it.

Honor Violence

Much has been written on the topic of honor violence recently, but it's still not a term that has penetrated the consciousness of most Christians. When we think of honor and families, we typically think of "Honor your father and your mother, so that you may live long in the land the LORD your God is giving you" (Ex. 20:12). Unfortunately, what Christians rightly understand as a requirement to respect and show kindness toward one's parents is not the meaning required by sharia law.

Under radical Islam, honor is the perception of a family's reputation. In a religion devoid of grace, any behavior (even looking at a boy) that is perceived to besmirch a family's good name is intolerable. It's so intolerable that it is expected, even demanded, that a girl who dishonors her family is punished by her father, brothers, and in some cases even her mother. Punishment can include beatings, stoning, acid attacks, mutilation, and even death.

Recently, the radical Islamic group ISIS released a video of a young Syrian woman being stoned to death by a group of men for allegedly committing adultery. Though she pleaded for her life, the group bludgeoned her with rocks, culminating in her death at the hands of her father, who had been granted the "honor" of ending her life for betraying him and her religion.[7]

ISIS is known for its widespread brutality of women—something I'll touch on further in the following chapter—but honor violence in Muslim societies is in no way limited to this single militant group. It has been a part of honor-based societies for hundreds of years, and unfortunately persists today. The United Nations has reported that an estimated 5,000 honor killings occur each year, but experts suggest that the actual number is much higher—perhaps closer to 20,000.[8] In Iraq and Jordan, honor killings are punished much less severely than other murders, and in countries like Iran, which operates under sharia law, husbands can kill wives suspected of adultery with no penalty whatsoever.[9]

Unfortunately, honor violence doesn't just happen in the Middle East. It has been reported in countries around the world, including the UK, Canada, and even right here in the United States. In 2009, a twenty-year-old girl in Phoenix, Arizona, was killed when her father ran her over with his car for becoming "too Westernized"—wearing makeup, listening to Western music, and refusing to submit to a marriage her father had orchestrated.[10] In Dallas, Texas, a father shot his seventeen- and eighteen-year old daughters eleven times for dating American boys. In upstate New York, a young woman was stabbed by her brother for being a "bad Muslim girl" when she tried to leave her family to move to New York City.[11]

Honor killings are prosecuted here, of course, but too often they aren't recognized as such. They are treated as isolated crimes, unconnected to religion or culture, and therefore very few efforts are made to combat further honor violence in Muslim communities. In the United States, low-level violence and threats against Muslim women are often ignored by authorities, either because they aren't reported or because police don't understand the phenomenon of honor violence and don't take steps to protect women before things go any farther. Authorities don't even collect data on the prevalence of honor violence in the United States.[12] As a Reuters article in June 2015 noted, "Honor violence is a crime without a name in the United States."[13]

Worse, even when they do notice something, Westerners often don't speak out against such violence because they fear being accused of racism or bigotry, or they assume that some actions, like forced marriages, are just part of Muslim culture and should not be questioned.

This is simply not true. As Ayaan Hirsi Ali, founder of the AHA Foundation, which works to end honor violence in the United States, wrote in an op-ed, "No religion, culture, or tradition can be invoked to justify violence against woman and girls." Honor violence shames us all.[14]

Women as Property

Honor violence is just one form of abuse suffered by women in many Muslim societies. It is predicated on the fact that under sharia law women are viewed as property—they belong to the male members of their families and exist to uphold family honor. This refusal to respect women precipitates some of the most insidious violations of human rights known to humanity. It removes any agency or dignity. It reduces women to slaves.

When women are treated as property, abuse and violence are too often the inevitable result. This is particularly true when it comes to radical Islamic militant groups like ISIS or Boko Haram. Women and young girls captured by these groups are raped, brutalized, sold into slavery, even given to soldiers as rewards to do with as they please. As I'll discuss in the next chapter, ISIS has institutionalized rape and slavery of women as a legitimate and even worshipful act under their religion.

The West hasn't paid much attention to the plight of these women, although some people began to realize the severity of the situation in April 2014, when Boko Haram abducted nearly three hundred schoolgirls from a boarding school in Nigeria. The kidnapping was followed by a video in which Boko Haram leader Abubakar Shekau announced he would "sell" the girls as "slaves in the market." The incident drew an outraged response from the international community and launched the Bring Back Our Girls campaign on social media. Despite the response, as of the writing of this book, the majority of those girls are still missing.

This is appalling, but it is only one kind of exploitation of women happening around the world. Let's discuss others.

Forced Marriages

Consider, for instance, forced marriages. Prevalent in Muslim states and in immigrant Muslim communities around the world, forced marriages are simply another form of slavery. I am not talking about an arranged marriage, where a bride and groom willingly consent to allow their parents to arrange a match. I know two couples whose parents emigrated from India and whose marriages were arranged. Both couples agreed to the matches, and both have happy marriages today. (Interestingly, however, both sets have declined to arrange their own children's marriages. My friend Neena says her daughter Natasha is "too American for that." Natasha's religion is Sikh, like her parents, but she has her own strong ideas on marriage, and her parents support her desire to choose for herself.)

Forced marriage is completely different. In a forced marriage the woman is promised, often from childhood, to a man she may have never met. She has no choice in the matter, no voice in the selection or the timing of the union. If she tries to resist, she may be threatened, abused, or even killed. Often, the husband she is promised to is a much older man. He may have other wives, because the Muslim religion allows and even encourages polygamy. The age of the girl when the marriage is consummated ranges; often, it is at or just after puberty.[15]

The United Nations has described forced marriage as "a form of culturally-justified violence against women as well as a violation of human rights that is endemic in many countries."[16] There is no ambiguity here; these marriages strip women and girls of rights and often push them into marriages where abuse and violence are common. They are often unable to escape because they have no support from their families or society and no other means of economic empowerment.

In some cases, families use arranged marriages to pay off debts. The US State Department's 2014 report on Human Rights Practices related an incident of a seven-year-old girl in a refugee camp in Afghanistan whose father attempted to sell her to a nineteen-year-old moneylender to cover his debt. The report also noted the phenomenon of "opium brides," where poor farming families sell their daughters in marriage to erase debts owed to opium traffickers.[17] Naturally, the girls have no say in the matter. Their lives are bargaining chips to help alleviate a family's financial situation.

Forced marriages are also disturbingly common; according to the Human Rights Watch, an estimated 70 to 80 percent of women in Afghanistan face forced marriages, and 57 percent of girls are married before the country's legal marriage age of sixteen.[18] In Iran, more than 1,500 girls under the age of ten were forced to marry in 2012 alone. Almost 30,000 girls aged ten to fourteen were forced into marriages that same year.[19] In Nigeria, it is estimated that 20 percent of girls are married by age fifteen.[20] This practice shows up in South Asia as well; Bangladesh, for instance, has the fourth-highest rate of child marriage in the world.[21] Across countries with Muslim populations, the practice persists.

The human rights violations of forced marriage are obvious, in part because of the consequences marriage and childbirth have on young girls. Girls' bodies are not made to begin having children at the onset of puberty. The risks of early pregnancies include premature labor, complications during delivery, increased chance that the baby will not survive, and a much higher risk of death for the mother.[22] In fact, girls younger than fifteen are *five times* more likely to die during pregnancy or childbirth.[23]

For girls who do survive, one of the greatest risks of early pregnancy is fistula, a complication that begins in labor when a baby's head becomes lodged in the birth canal. Because young girls' bodies haven't developed enough, the chance of such an occurrence is much greater. During labor, the continuous pressure against the birth canal damages the tissue between the vagina and the bladder or rectum, eventually creating a hole through which the girl continuously leaks urine or feces.[24] Surgery is required to repair the condition, but for many girls living in rural areas, it is not an option. Girls with fistula are often shamed by their communities and abandoned by their husbands.

Beyond the complications of pregnancy, many girls in forced marriages suffer physical and sexual abuse. As children, they are too young to give informed consent, and the power dynamics between the husband and the girl prevent her from having a say in their sexual union. According to a report presented to the United Nations, the emotional distress of forced marriages, which rob girls of their adolescence, can result in depression, lack of self-esteem, and even suicide.[25]

Like honor violence, forced marriages are a problem for Western nations as well. Across Europe, Canada, and the United States, forced marriages are imposed upon children every year. Migrant parents, mainly from the Middle East, North Africa, and Southeast Asia, carry on the traditions of their cultures and force their children to enter into marriages without choice, often sending them back to their home countries for the marriage. A report by the Tahirih Justice Center found that between 2009 and 2010, there were 3,000 known or suspected cases of forced marriage in the United States. In Europe, these figures were even higher.[26]

The *Washington Post*, reporting on the phenomenon in the United States, noted that the lack of attention to this issue makes it more difficult for women to escape such arrangements. US laws offer little legal protection, as they are "more geared to victims of kidnapping or physical violence," and neither law enforcement nor service agencies understand the depth of the problem or view pressure from families to marry as the abusive emergency it often is.[27]

Indeed, the coercion families use to force their daughters into such marriages can encompass both emotional and physical abuse. Parents pressure their children, telling them the honor of the family is at stake. As Jeanne Smoot, Senior Counsel for Policy and Strategy at Tahirih, told the *Washington Post*, "If a mother says to her daughter, 'You will be dead to your parents,' or 'This will kill your grandmother,' or 'I will kill myself if you don't marry him,' that is as coercive as a gun to the head."[28]

For girls who do object to the union, consequences can be dire. In London, an Afghani couple threatened to kill their teenage daughter when she refused an arranged marriage and told her they would "cut her head off" if she went to the authorities. The daughter sought help anyway and received a forced marriage protection order in court.[29] Many women, however, are too intimidated to seek help, and most succumb to the marriages forced upon them.

Female Genital Mutilation

It's not just women's lives that belong to their families under sharia law but their very bodies. One terrible consequence of this reality is a brutal practice euphemistically termed female circumcision. Don't be confused, however: what some call circumcision is really female genital mutilation (FGM), a practice which, according to the World Health Organization, has "no health benefits for girls or women."[30] In this horrible procedure, girls ranging in age from infancy to fifteen years have part or all of their external genitalia removed, usually with a razor. It is severely painful and can result in hemorrhaging, trouble urinating, and bacterial infection. Because the same unsterilized blade is often used for all girls being cut at one time, there is also risk of infections like HIV.[31] Over the long term, complications include infertility, urinary tract infections, increased risk of childbirth complications and infant death, and the need for further surgeries.[32]

According to UNICEF, more than 130 million girls today have been subject to FGM. This number could increase by 30 million over the next decade alone.[33]

The practice is concentrated in North Africa and the Middle East and is used as a way to ensure a girl's virginity until marriage. FGM is thought to decrease a woman's libido and help her resist sinful sexual temptation, thereby keeping her honor intact for her family and future husband. Older women are complicit in the vile practice because they are told that their daughters cannot marry without it. It is viewed as a necessary part of raising a daughter, as a way to prepare her for adulthood and keep her "clean" and "beautiful."[34]

Although the practice is incredibly harmful and serves no health benefit, it persists in many Muslim communities, where it is seen by some as a cultural tradition. Human rights groups have begun working to raise awareness about the dangerous effects, and FGM is widely recognized as a human rights violation, but the practice continues. Even in the United States, an estimated 500,000 women have either undergone FGM or are at risk of it.[35] We need more awareness about this issue, and greater dialogue with the communities who practice it. Culture is no excuse for violence against women.

Human Trafficking

An even more blatant violation of women's bodies is the widespread crime of human trafficking. Human trafficking is a modern-day form of slavery, defined by the Department of Homeland Security as "the illegal trade of people for exploitation or commercial gain."[36] Men, women, and children are smuggled within countries and often across borders, sold for profit, and typically forced to work as sex slaves or forced laborers. Estimates vary as to the number of people trafficked across international borders each year, but the United Nations suggested it may be upwards of two million.[37] As I mentioned, more than 70 percent of the victims are women and children.

Unfortunately, the industry is rapidly growing, estimated at about $32 billion a year.[38] And the situation is only getting worse. As the UN 2014 report on human trafficking worldwide stated, "Trafficking in persons remains all too common, with all too few consequences for the perpetrators." It occurs in more than 150 countries across the globe, including the United States. Recently much attention has been given to ISIS's sex trafficking of women across the Middle East, which we'll discuss in-depth in the following chapter, but ISIS is a newcomer to an already-global enterprise.

The United States should be leading the globe in preventing trafficking and prosecuting those who engage in it. Yet we are failing in this area. The State Department's Office to Monitor and Combat Trafficking in Persons office has been marginalized and suffered severe budget cuts.[39] Although the Trafficking Victims Protection Act, enacted in 2000 due in part to advocacy by CWA and its members, set up ways to pressure rogue nations who engage in trafficking, our government sometimes chooses to look the other way.

In 2014, for instance, Rep. Michael Burgess (R-TX) noted that the US government was ignoring human trafficking along the Mexican border. Burgess had visited the border and seen children under ten with signs of abuse, but federal workers had been told not to investigate or report the cases. "We're enablers right now, as far as I can see. We are co-dependents with the child traffickers, and it is not a pretty story," said Burgess during a hearing on the Hill.[40]

Despite all the money spent and all the attention on human trafficking, the worldwide numbers are not improving. As women and children are smuggled across lands to be bought and sold as property for labor and sexual abuse, we cannot simply throw money at the problem and expect methods that have not succeeded so far to start working now. It's time to find some solutions that work.

Political Correctness and Honor

The status of women in Islamic society is appalling. The abuse of women around the world is heartbreaking. But what makes me furious is that our society, and particularly Western liberals, ignore the reality of what's happening to women abroad for fear of being politically incorrect. While liberals rail against the GOP's war on women, a true and brutal battle is being waged against our sisters around the world.

Shockingly, liberal American humanitarian relief agencies are unwittingly sometimes part of the problem because they are so nervous about cultural sensitivity. I know that sounds over the top, but about two years ago I witnessed it firsthand. I was asked to come to the beautiful and historic Hay-Adams hotel to meet with two of the top people for the Bill and Melinda Gates Foundation. The Gates Foundation invests more than $3 billion annually to address global health and development issues, including a specific focus on maternal, newborn, and child health.[41]

The point of this meeting, I soon realized, was for them to crack the code of how to get American evangelicals more involved in fighting for maternal health abroad. That is certainly a worthy goal, but in the meeting the Gates' staff focused narrowly on birth control. They wanted to know how to get CWA's buy-in and evangelicals' help in the random distribution of IUDs and Depo-Provera, an injectable birth control shot.

I talked to them about the divide within the church on the use of birth control and explained that most evangelicals draw a bright line between birth control and abortifacients. I explained that most Christians do not support any practice that destroys a fertilized egg and suggested that they should not reject out of hand the idea that Christians are willing to teach married women about spacing their pregnancies and prenatal care but don't support every method of birth control. There is a range of choices, I noted, including barrier methods and others. I pointed out that, for instance, many Catholic believers support natural family planning and use simple tactics like beans in a jar to count days and monitor ovulation. This method, among others, is free or of little cost.

We also discussed that, when willing, husbands should be brought into the discussion and educational process. Women deserve the support of their husbands, and the responsibility should not be only on their shoulders. Good men care about their wives' health and the ability to feed their children. The Gates Foundation seemed to have been acting with an all-or-nothing approach to family planning, and I suggested they might be able to find new allies if they were willing to tolerate a range of views on the matter.

The conversation seemed to be going well, but then came an exchange that left me stunned.

The Gates Foundation people kept talking about the physical repercussions of young girls giving birth and their abuse at the hands of their husbands. "You give millions of dollars to these countries," I said. "Your philanthropy is sought after, and some of them depend upon it. Why are you not using your influence to pressure these nations to stop the practice of child marriage and forced marriage?"

With straight faces they replied that they could not involve themselves with the policies of another culture, because it would be "paternalistic." Paternalistic? My head almost exploded. The Gates Foundation strives to be an advocate for human rights, yet they won't go to the root of the issue and work to protect young girls from rape. Shocked, I couldn't help myself from asking, "Isn't what you're doing something like handing a rapist a condom and telling him to be careful?" That, of course, didn't go over well.

Hopefully by now they have changed their view on this issue, but regardless, the Gates Foundation is not alone in this belief. Randomly handing out birth control will perhaps decrease population, but it won't stop the suffering. Shame on anyone whose sense of political correctness stops them from being truth tellers.

Vilifying Christianity

Sadly, liberals would rather cling to political correctness and tolerance than face the status of women around the globe. They would rather spend $70 million on gender-baiting ads—as they did in the 2014 midterm elections, accusing Republicans of waging a war on women (a charge Hillary Clinton revived) for their stance on birth control and abortion—than focus on the very real and very dire circumstances of women abroad, particularly in Muslim nations.

In the view of many on the left, anyone who holds conservative, traditional views is patriarchal and misogynistic. Christians are lambasted for wanting to end abortion or for holding traditional views on marriage, yet forced marriages among Muslims in our own country are ignored because we don't want to seem culturally insensitive.

All too often, criticism of Christian conservatives is used to distract us from the real issues.

Such criticism is unfounded. People who hold the view that Christianity is antiwomen ignore the earthshaking words of the Bible, "There is neither Jew nor Gentile, neither slave nor free, nor is there male and female, for you are all one in Christ Jesus" (Gal. 3:28). Jesus demonstrated love and grace toward women who were considered outcasts and whores.

Contrast everything we have discussed about the treatment of women worldwide with Jesus' treatment of the woman caught in the act of adultery, whom we've discussed before (John 8:3–11). This woman was brought before Jesus as a test by the religious leaders who wanted to force him to condemn her to death by stoning—but he did not. Instead he knelt down and wrote in the sand. Though John doesn't tell us what he wrote, I believe that he wrote down a list of sins. Maybe he scrawled out things like lying, slander, gluttony, lust, drunkenness, slothfulness, gossip, greed, pride. After a while he calmly stood up and challenged the arrogant Pharisees, "Let any one of you who is without sin be the first to throw a stone at her" (v. 7). Then he knelt back down and continued writing his list until one by one, shamed by their own pet sins, the crowd melted away.

Then it was her turn. Jesus looked up, turning his full attention to the woman, and asked, "Woman, where are they? Has no one condemned you?" Startled and probably in shock, she told him they had all left. Jesus replied, "Then neither do I condemn you. Go now and leave your life of sin" (v. 10–11). He acknowledged her sin and called her to repentance, yet he also forgave her and showed her the deepest love she had ever received.

What?! She must have been stunned. She was dragged out of bed with her lover, and although he was dismissed, she was publicly shamed, dragged through the streets, and cast at the feet of the Messiah. Surely this holy man would have no tolerance for her grievous mistake. But no. He sees her, he loves her, and he forgives her as only God can forgive. Praise Jesus! That's the God we serve. That's the Son of God who died for my list of grievous sins. He paid both her price and mine on the cross. Jesus died for her, he died for you and me, and he died for the women deprived of their basic rights around the world. His love for them and our own blessing of freedom should compel us to look for ways to help those women whose rights are being subjugated.

Don't let anyone tell you that Christianity is somehow antiwomen. Jesus made the ultimate sacrifice for everyone regardless of race, class, or gender. There is true equality in the gospel, for it offers redemption for all. Lay down your heavy burdens right now if you have not or if you need to again. Jesus waits for you with forgiveness and hope, just as he did the woman caught in adultery or the woman at the well. I encourage you to pray, accepting his death on the cross as payment for your sins and asking him to be the Lord or Leader of your life. He waits just for you.

Jesus was the greatest believer in the value, beauty, and significance of women of anyone who has ever walked this earth. We know this to be true. But somehow many on the left missed this part of the story. It's time we turned this around and used our faith to start a movement of change for women around the world.

What Can Esther Women Do?

As Christian women, we have a particular calling to speak out about the suffering of other women. As we've seen, Jesus gave his life for the least of us, and we need to work hard to end suffering and establish liberty for women everywhere. This is too important for us to remain silent.

START THE CONVERSATION

The first thing we need to do is to stay informed and speak up. Read up on the issues facing women today, both in the United States and abroad. Particularly when it comes to the serious problem of how women are treated in Islamic societies, we must inform ourselves. So much of this oppression is kept in the shadows, never spoken about or brought into the light, which only allows it to persist. The apostle Paul tells us that the Lord "will bring to light what is hidden in darkness" (1 Cor. 4:5). We must shine a light on evil that is ongoing.

We must also reject superficial ideas about political correctness. While we must always respect others, we can't allow culture, religion, or tradition to be used to perpetuate violence and oppression of the weak. We must be brave and reject the claim that to question the practices of others is intolerant. Questioning and drawing attention to practices that seem unjust or harmful might save another woman's life.

PROMOTE OTHERS WHO ARE ALREADY WORKING IN THIS AREA

Many women are working hard to address the injustice and violence suffered by women, and part of our role can be to support them and broaden their visibility. Sign up for our alerts at www.concernedwomen.org to stay informed about the latest work here and abroad to help women living under oppression.

In 2015 Concerned Women for America hosted a screening for opinion leaders on Capitol Hill of the film *Honor Diaries*. Coproduced by Ayaan Hirsi Ali of the AHA Foundation, the film exposes the suffering of many women in Muslim-majority societies with its frank discussion of honor killings, genital mutilation, forced marriages, child brides, and the limited access women have to education and economic opportunities. It is a powerful and eye-opening film and highlights the work of women seeking to bring these issues to light. You might consider screening this film with a group of women in your church or other social circles. CWA can facilitate a screening if you contact us. Witnessing the true stories of atrocities other women endure can be a powerful tool to motivate us to respond.

On Fox News, Megyn Kelly was instrumental in raising the profile of this film and the issues it addresses, despite the fact that she was accused of spreading "anti-Muslim bigotry."[42] I applaud Megyn's brave work to continue to speak truth about these issues, and I hope that more of us can take similar stances. Despite the backlash we may receive, we have a responsibility to women who are threatened by violence to look upon them with compassion and to seek to protect them.

There are many other ways we can spread the word about efforts to end atrocities against women. In particular, social media can be a helpful tool when it comes to starting a dialogue about issues that aren't getting enough focus in the mainstream media. When the Christian writer and blogger Ann Voskamp wrote a post about the persecution of women in Iraq and Syria by ISIS, it was re-tweeted and shared thousands of times. Ann included information about an organization on the ground in Iraq providing support and resources for those fleeing ISIS. Ann's blog post inspired donations of more than $1 million in three days.[43] *That's* powerful and life changing for the women and children on the receiving end of the donations. And it all starts with a willingness to speak up.

And sometimes, we need a willingness to pay up. "For where your treasure is, there your heart will be also" (Matt. 6:21). If we value something, we should fund it. What could I do if I gave up my favorite lattes for a month? What if I skipped eating out too?

Many wonderful organizations do important work on behalf of women's rights: organizations, like Concerned Women for America, which focus on policy, and others, like Samaritan's Purse, which provide aid to the poor, sick, and suffering around the world, including women living under repressive regimes or societies. Christian nonprofit organizations work with the most vulnerable women in the world to help stop abuse, raise awareness about sex trafficking, provide for medical needs, and increase education, literacy, and economic opportunities. By supporting organizations like these, we can contribute to the restoration and well-being of women, even on the other side of the world. What do you value?

ADVOCATE TO CHANGE NATIONAL PUBLIC POLICY

A successful fight against violence and oppression of women requires comprehensive and targeted public policy changes. In the United States, we have courts that will protect women from violence. However, the laws we currently have in place are not sufficient to protect women from forced marriage. Particularly if there is no record of past abuse, women have little legal recourse. We need a broader national conversation about a bill criminalizing forced marriages.

Similarly, FGM has been illegal in the United States since 1996, but it has not always been heavily enforced. In 2012, Congress finally closed a loophole that had allowed parents to take their children abroad for the procedure—a practice known as vacation cutting—and in 2015 Congress introduced further legislation to "establish a multi-agency strategy to bring the practice to an end," but much work remains to be done.[44]

CWA is currently working with federal legislators to protect girls from another dangerous threat: sex-selective abortions. It's essential that as a world leader, the United States have laws on its books that protect the lives of baby girls. An estimated two million girls are lost each year due to sex-selective abortions and infanticide, and research shows that it is a growing trend in the United States.[45] Unless we prevent this from happening at home, we will never be able to stop the widespread practice abroad.[46] Join with CWA in advocating for the passage of this important legislation.

PUSH FOR BETTER LOCAL LAW ENFORCEMENT

These steps are important, but we can do better than what we've seen from our federal government so far. Certainly these atrocities are civil rights violations in this nation, but the most effective way to attack this issue is not at the federal level but rather closer to the victim. Concerned Women for America will be working to pass state statutes with stronger penalties for honor abuse of women. Working at the state level is important because crime is, with only a few exceptions, constitutionally handled by state rather than federal authorities. State and local law enforcement are much closer to the problem. They are the ones called when a young girl runs away from home or is bleeding uncontrollably at a hospital.

Unfortunately, as we've seen, state and local law enforcement are often uninformed about cultural abuse and the consequences of this ignorance. In many cases of honor violence or forced marriages in the United States, there were clear signs that something was amiss, but officials were uninformed or unwilling to pursue something that seemed to be a cultural issue. The movie *Honor Diaries* tells, for instance, of cases where school officials don't question truancy, bruises under a hijab, or why a fifteen-year-old is wearing a wedding ring. State criminalization gives both law enforcement and state welfare agents the tools they need to be effective.

HOLD OUR GOVERNMENT ACCOUNTABLE
FOR TRAFFICKING WORLDWIDE

In respect to international policy, we have lost many of the gains made by the Bush Administration, particularly in the area of human and sex

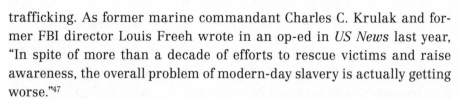

trafficking. As former marine commandant Charles C. Krulak and former FBI director Louis Freeh wrote in an op-ed in *US News* last year, "In spite of more than a decade of efforts to rescue victims and raise awareness, the overall problem of modern-day slavery is actually getting worse."[47]

In the United States, according to the *Washington Post*, we don't even know the numbers of victims trafficked within our borders.[48] This is despite the fact that in 2008 CWA worked to get the Zurita Amendment passed. Named after former CWA staff member Brenda Zurita, this amendment required the Department of Justice to identify arrests for prostitution and commercialized vice into three categories: pimps, buyers, and sellers. It was an important step, but victims continue to be trafficked.

Additionally, the US State Department releases an annual report, the Trafficking in Persons report, to rank countries on their effectiveness in fighting human trafficking. While our government has levied sanctions against some of the worst offenders in the past, including Cuba, Myanmar, and North Korea, too often we have looked the other way, allowing countries to sit on a watch list, where there is no threat of sanctions, despite ongoing abuses.[49]

We must demand that our government take a stronger, more vocal stance. The United States must require more of our allies to take significant steps in regard to protecting innocent women and children. Short of outright sanctions, smart leaders can find ways to use the bully pulpit that go beyond official policy. I am reminded of an anecdote that recently came out about Queen Elizabeth, who invited Saudi Arabia's King Abdullah (then crown prince) to tour her estate in Balmoral in 1998. Saudi women are not allowed to drive, so the crown prince was shocked when the queen invited him to get into the passenger seat and then got behind the wheel herself. According to British Ambassador Sherard Cowper-Coles, the queen sped along the Scottish roads, talking all the while, while the Saudi prince "implored" her to slow down.[50] It's a comical story, but also a powerful point about using your actions to speak for your values.

I think of this when I see female State Department officials at functions in Islamic countries with their heads covered. If officials chose to cover their heads due to their own faith, it would make sense, but as official representatives of the United States, it shouldn't happen unless at a holy site. I was heartened when Michelle Obama declined to cover her head on her trip to Saudi Arabia in 2015. This should be the normal operating procedure for our representatives unless it violates the faith of individual representatives.

As Christian conservative women, we must heighten the pressure on our government and specifically the State Department to take steps that protect women and that pressure other countries to join us in the fight. If we don't stand up for these women, who will? Let your representatives and local leaders hear from you on these issues.

SHARE THE LOVE OF CHRIST

At the end of the day, we are called to speak up for women living under oppression. When Jesus came, he overthrew the old ways of thinking about women—that they were less than men, that they were property, that they had no dignity. He spoke to them directly, healed them, offered them forgiveness, listened to their needs, and loved them deeply. The lives and well-being of women was of utmost importance to Jesus, and should be to us too.

Many admirable secular organizations work to address human rights issues, but Christians have a unique position from which to tackle this topic. We understand the intrinsic value of women based on the love of Christ for each of us as his precious daughters. And we understand that as Christians, we are called to help the widow, the poor, and the persecuted. As the Bible says, "Defend the weak and the fatherless; uphold the cause of the poor and the oppressed" (Ps. 82:3).

It's important that we emphasize the deep love and compassion of Christianity for women because by doing so we can push back against false stereotypes that Christians are intolerant or antiwomen. We must emphasize that we seek the well-being of all women from a place of love—not condemnation. We aren't anti-Muslim, by any means; we want Muslim women to receive the respect and dignity they deserve as humans created in God's image. When we show the love of Christ by fighting for the lives and liberty of women, we spread the message of the gospel.

"From everyone who has been given much . . . much more will be asked" (Luke 12:48). As women in the greatest nation on earth, we have been given so much. As Christians who know the love of our Father, we have even more. Let us use the abundance of blessings that God has given us to help the least of these around the world, calling for their freedom from oppression, violence, and fear, and then working together to achieve that goal.

Jeanne Mancini

PRESIDENT, MARCH FOR LIFE

Jeanne Mancini is the president of the largest pro-life event in the world, the March for Life. Every January, nearly half a million people join together on the National Mall and peacefully march past the Supreme Court in protest of the 1973 *Roe v. Wade* decision.

Under Jeanne's leadership, the gathering has become even more diverse and powerful. She has shepherded it into the next generation, with a focus on digital media and engaging younger women. Savvy social media changes, such as introducing the #WhyWeMarch hashtag for the 2015 march, have expanded the reach of the movement and made its message more broadly visible than ever before.

Jeanne realized God was calling her to work in the pro-life arena while studying for her master's degree at the Pope John Paul II Institute for Studies on Marriage and Family. "Everything I studied that was related to building a culture of life reverberated deeply in my soul," she says. Jeanne responded to that call, stepping up to take the reins in 2012 after the passing of the March for Life's beloved founder, Nellie Gray. And although she admits that the sheer magnitude of the march and everything that goes into it can sometimes be overwhelming, she relies on her faith and the dedicated team around her to persevere.

When it comes to encouraging other women to find their voices and speak out on issues that matter, Jeanne points to the words of the great Saint Catherine of Sienna: "Be who you are and you will set the world ablaze." She tells women to have confidence that they were created with a unique mission. Through prayer and self-reflection, she suggests, we can discern what we were made for, and we should pursue it with all our hearts.

CHAPTER 7

The Rise of Islamic Extremism
and the Need to Fight Back

In February 2015, I felt overwhelmed by the atrocities being inflicted upon innocent men, women, and children in the Middle East at the hands of the Islamic State of Iraq and al-Sham (ISIS) and others. I watched the news in horror as stories of the murder of Christians and the abuse of Yazidis (another religious minority) leaked out in the media. The president and other politicians had plenty of words about stopping the rise of jihad, but I was seeing little action. Reading about women being sold as sex slaves, young girls being physically and sexually abused, and Christians being driven from their homes and killed, I felt helpless.

And then, one morning as I brought this helpless, broken feeling before God in prayer, it hit me: Only God can protect these lambs from slaughter. On our own we are powerless, but he is all-powerful, and we needed to call on him to help. So I gathered my CWA team, and together we organized our first Day of Prayer and Fasting for the Victims of Islamic Terrorists. We chose February 15 because it was the weekend of Valentine's Day, and we thought intercessory prayer was one of the most loving things we could do. We called on our CWA members to join us and to get the word out to their friends, families, and churches.

We called, and on that day thousands of Concerned Women for America members got on our knees, abstained from food, and begged God for justice and mercy for innocents.

The handful of times that I have fasted have been spiritually meaningful and powerful, and this time was no exception. I will never know how our prayers played out in a cosmic battle between good and evil that raged that day, but I know they were timely and important. On the day of our prayer vigil, ISIS beheaded twenty-one Egyptian Coptic Christians as they knelt on a Libyan beach. These innocents were killed for their faith.

Afterward ISIS released a propaganda video of the executions, claiming that it was "[a] message signed with blood to the nation of the cross."[1]

I was appalled to learn about what had been happening at the moment we were on our knees in prayer, but I know that our prayers interceded for those Egyptians, and perhaps for others also in danger that day. I know that as those men were martyred, the prayers of faithful women half a world away surrounded them throughout the entire experience. I also know that they were met at the gates of heaven by a loving Savior who dried their tears and welcomed them into everlasting peace. Their blood stains the hands of the wicked and will be used as evidence against Jihadi John and his cowardly cohorts on judgment day. Until that time, we must continue to raise our prayers to God, our protector and deliverer.

The Rise of Islamic Extremism

The threat of global terrorism is at an all-time high today. With the rise of radical Islam, particularly in the growth of ultraviolent groups like ISIS in the Middle East and Boko Haram in Nigeria, as well as lesser-known groups, small cells, and the lone-wolf attackers they have inspired, we face an unstable international situation unlike anything we have witnessed before. As President Obama stated in his 2015 State of the Union address, the "phenomenon of violent extremism" has "metastasized and . . . penetrated communities around the world."[2]

Perhaps the best-known terrorist group operating today is ISIS, also known as the Islamic State or ISIL (Islamic State of Iraq and the Levant). Once a part of al-Qaeda in Iraq, ISIS is a Sunni extremist group driven by a radical Islamic ideology that has risen rapidly to prominence in the past few years. The stated goal of ISIS is to expand their caliphate—a sovereign Islamic state that exerts religious and political authority over the world. In short, world domination. And this is not hyperbole. Taking advantage of the chaos in Syria in 2011 when the country devolved into civil war, ISIS seized territory there and established a base of operations. Since the capture of Mosul, Iraq's second-largest city, in June 2014, ISIS has expanded its reach in much of Iraq and Syria, and now controls an area larger than Great Britain.

The group's territorial ambitions are sweeping, expanding even beyond the Levant. The Council on Foreign Relations has expressed concerns that ISIS's "ambitions to capture and administer territory have no geographic limits."[3] ISIS maintains a force of at least 30,000 fighters (although some estimates suggest it could be as large as 200,000), and it is the most well-funded terrorist organization in the world, mainly due to the Syrian oil they sell on the black market.[4] Controlling supply and communication lines and carrying out sophisticated military operations, ISIS continues to make gains as it fights against an incompetent and disorganized Iraqi army with erratic international support.

Why is this particularly important? Because ISIS's takeover of much of the Middle East is symptomatic of the dangerous rise of Islamic extremism, and it represents a threat far beyond their own borders. As a radical religious group ruled by the desire to establish a global Islamic empire and exterminate "apostate unbelievers," its ideology and actions have worldwide ramifications.[5] Global terrorism is growing, and much of it is a direct result of ISIS and groups inspired by their hard-core Islamic ideology.

Since 2000, there has been an incredible fivefold increase in the number of people killed by terrorism worldwide. This increase is concentrated in the Middle East, as you might expect, but it is not confined there. In 2013, sixty countries recorded one or more deaths from terrorist activity, including Nigeria, where the terrorist group Boko Haram has now pledged allegiance to the Islamic State; India; Thailand; and Western countries including the United States and the United Kingdom.[6] The groups that have taken root in the Middle East have spread their tentacles to inspire other attackers around the world. This danger is present everywhere, and it affects us all.

In addition to ISIS and Boko Haram, other significant terrorist groups acting right now are al-Qaeda in the Middle East and Africa; Hezbollah and Hamas in the Middle East; al-Shabaab, a group in Somalia and Kenya with links to al-Qaeda; and the Taliban, which remains a deadly force in Afghanistan and Pakistan.[7] There are others, but despite significant differences between each of these groups, they are all driven in part by radical religious ideologies based on radical Islam. Religious extremism is the single greatest driver of terrorist activity today, far surpassing nationalist, separatist, or political movements, and has become so pervasive as to threaten global security on a massive scale.[8]

With the rise of social media, we have become more aware of the kinds of atrocities perpetrated by groups subscribing to Islamic extremism. The depth of the evil we face has been brought home by videos of brutal acts, such as the beheading of Western journalists and the burning of a Jordanian pilot in Iraq. Most recently, I was brought to a new level of outrage and sorrow when the news broke that Kayla Mueller, a twenty-six-year-old American Christian aid worker who was captured by ISIS in 2013, had been raped and tortured by Abu Bakr al-Baghdadi, ISIS's leader.[9] An innocent woman, and a US citizen, Kayla was held by the group's leader as his *personal sex slave* for more than a year before she was killed in February 2015. ISIS claimed Mueller may have died in a Jordanian airstrike, but the international community has been extremely skeptical of that version of events.[10]

This was nothing less than an attack on the United States and specifically Christian Americans. I haven't the words to describe my anger for these acts of cowardice. Al-Baghdadi represents an evil so intense it's hard to conceive, and his capture and killing ought to be one of our nation's greatest priorities. His behavior is straight out of the pit of hell, and that's where he should be sent in short order.

Sadly, these broadly visible and horrific attacks are only the tip of the iceberg.

Targeting Christians and Religious Minorities

A recent report from the United Nations on abuses committed by ISIS in Iraq found that "human rights violations suffered by the people of Iraq were shockingly widespread and extremely severe," and included torture, indiscriminate slaughter of civilians, systematic slavery, rape and sexual violence, forced conversions to Islam, and forcible military training for children—some as young as twelve.[11] I can't imagine what the people of Iraq and Syria have suffered at the hands of these jihadists. It is both ghastly and infuriating.

While all civilians living in areas under threat from Islamic groups are at risk, sadly, these groups are targeting religious minorities. According to the same UN report, ISIS is "clearly intent on shattering the rich ethnic and religious diversity of Iraq, and had perpetrated appalling crimes on Christians, Kaka'es, Kurds, Sabea-Mandeans, Shi'a, Turkmen and Yazidis, for no other reason than their religious beliefs or ethnic origin."[12]

For our Christian brothers and sisters in the Middle East, the threat is severe. When ISIS took over large parts of Iraq in 2014, they implemented sharia law and began to exile and kill Christians. According to Open Doors USA, a nonprofit that works with Christians in persecuted countries, more than 140,000 Christians have been forced to flee Iraq in the year since ISIS infiltrated the country.[13] In Mosul, ISIS fighters stormed churches, burned books, and destroyed Christian homes. Christians were told they could either convert to Islam or be killed. Many of the towns on Iraq's Nineveh Plains, once home to thriving Christian communities, are now desolate.[14]

Other religious communities suffer similar fates. In particular, the Yazidis, a group that follows an ancient faith that ISIS views as devil worship, have been unrelentingly targeted. In March 2015, the United Nations reported that ISIS's attacks on the Yazidi population were beginning to approximate a genocide, with the intent to "destroy the Yazidi as a group."[15] Entire villages have been wiped of their Yazidi population, and thousands of men and boys have killed. The treatment of the women and girls, as we'll see, is beyond heinous.

In Nigeria, where Boko Haram has been fighting to overthrow the secular government since 2009, Christians face a particular threat. Because Nigeria is primarily divided between Muslims and Christians, Boko Haram is intent on removing all Christians from the country and has issued an ultimatum to Christians living in the northeast to "leave or die."[16] More than two hundred churches have been destroyed by the group, and at least 1,600 Christians have been murdered so far.[17]

One leading evangelical Christian in Nigeria, Samuel Kunhiyop, gave an interview to *Christianity Today* in the fall of 2014 in which he explained, "Pastors have been murdered in their houses. Another was murdered in the church during a prayer service. . . . They don't want Christians in the Muslim areas, so they bomb those places of worship, or refuse to give them a license to worship." And yet even in the face of unrelenting persecution and a constant threat of death, Kunhiyop noted, "The church has not declined in any way. In fact, it is growing stronger."[18] What a testament to the strength and persistence of God's people.

Women as a Weapon of War

Yes, religious minorities are suffering mightily at the hands of Islamic extremists—and the situation is particularly dire for women and girls. As we have seen, human rights violations against women occur worldwide. But in the Middle East and North Africa, where radical Islamic ideology devalues women to the point of degradation, these offenses are rampant—and they are used to advance the cause of radical Islam.

Systematic rape, enslavement, selling of women and girls, separation from families, torture, and all manner of degradation are occurring on a daily basis. And this is not random; it is, as a UN briefing on ISIS reported in May 2015, a "central aspect of their ideology and operations."[19]

Indeed, the rape, sexual abuse, and selling of girls and women as sex slaves has been "enshrined in the group's core tenets," according to a special report by the *New York Times*.[20] ISIS methodically targets women and girls, primarily of the Yazidi religion but also Christians and Jews, as a way of forcing communities into submission and securing the goals of the jihadists. By perpetrating violence against women and girls, ISIS has been able to take control of communities, destroy traditional family and social structures, and humiliate dissenters—thereby expanding their reach and power. The group also uses women to reward fighters and to generate income through selling and trafficking.[21]

ISIS fighters view women as spoils of war, which they own, to be abused and discarded.[22] Girls as young as nine are given to ISIS fighters as wives or sold as sex slaves to be passed among men as they wish.[23] The *Christian Post* reported that Christian and Yazidi girls under the age of ten are sold for $172—less than a designer pair of jeans.[24]

Women who have escaped ISIS have told horrific stories of their captivity. One UN report documented the case of fourteen young girls captured by ISIS who were forced to write their names down on slips of paper. Two ISIS fighters drew a name each from the slips and then took the girls whose names had been called into a back room and raped them, while the other girls listened to them scream.[25] In another case, a nineteen-year-old pregnant woman was captured by an ISIS "doctor" who raped her repeatedly over a period of two months, tortured her, and sat on her stomach in an attempt to kill her unborn baby, telling her, "this baby should die because it is an infidel; I can make a Muslim baby."[26]

Many of the women living through this barbarity would rather die. In an interview with the BBC World Service, one man told of a Yazidi woman who managed to make a phone call from the brothel where she was being held and begged Western forces to bomb it. "I've been raped thirty times and it's not even lunchtime," she said, according to the man. "If you know where we are please bomb us. . . . There is no life after this," she begged.[27] I don't know about you, but when I heard this, I wanted to go fight ISIS personally.

I cannot understand the depths of this evil. It emanates directly from Satan; it's utterly heart wrenching. In Nigeria, circumstances are similar; as the *New York Times* reported, Boko Haram has captured and raped hundreds of women and girls as part of "a deliberate strategy to dominate rural residents and possibly even create a new generation of Islamist militants in Nigeria."[28] That's right: Boko Haram may be raping these women and forcing them to carry their children in order to give birth to the next wave of radical jihadists. And as with ISIS, Boko Haram targets women as well as young girls; in a large refugee camp outside the Borno State capital, more than two hundred girls who had escaped were found to be pregnant, some as young as eleven years old.[29]

The brutalization of women by Islamic extremists is one of the greatest crimes against humanity of our time. And it's only getting worse; these fighters have no respect for the lives of women, and they're intent on using whatever means necessary to accomplish their goals. They justify such crimes with radical ideology, claiming that the Quran not only permits the sexual abuse of infidels or non-Muslims but in fact condones it.[30] ISIS has published policy memos establishing guidelines for sexual slavery which permit all manner of sexual abuse, including the rape of children. A *New York Times* report told of one experience of a twelve-year-old girl who was bought as a sex slave and raped repeatedly by her captor. "I kept telling him it hurts—please stop," she said. "He told me that according to Islam he is allowed to rape an unbeliever. He said that by raping me, he is drawing closer to God."[31]

How can we allow this to continue? The rise of Islamic extremism is destroying the lives of our sisters in the Middle East, and it is an offense to women everywhere. As David Jacobson, a professor at the University of South Florida, told PBS's *NewsHour*, "Women are now at the heart of the world's most dangerous quarrel."[32] It's time that the rest of us sat up and took notice.

A Growing Threat

The rise of radical Islam directly threatens the lives of millions of men, women, and children in the Middle East and North Africa. But the threat does not end there. Not only are radical Islamic groups wrecking havoc in their own lands and among their own people, they are also recruiting foreigners to come and fight for them, and they are inspiring groups in other lands, including the West.

Since declaring itself a caliphate in June 2014, ISIS has attracted more than fifteen thousand foreign fighters from eighty countries.[33]

While many of them come from neighboring and Muslim-majority countries, they have also been drawn from places like Australia, Western Europe, and the United States. Using online recruitment and propaganda spread through social media, ISIS draws disaffected young Muslims to their cause, promising recruits glory, profit, sexual and military conquest, and participation in the establishment of the true Islamic state. Last year the *New Yorker* estimated that four thousand European jihadis and more than one hundred Americans had traveled to Syria since the outbreak of the war there in 2011.[34]

More than fifteen American teenagers have been apprehended in the past year attempting to get to Syria to fight, often from ordinary, middle-class neighborhoods in places like Chicago and Minneapolis, and many more have made it to the front lines.[35] Whether we want to admit it or not, American children are susceptible, particularly those with Muslim heritage who feel that they don't belong or that their religion isn't valued in America. ISIS knows this, and it preys on young people seeking identity, community, and adventure. As one teen from Chicago who was apprehended trying to get to Syria explained in a letter to his parents, "An Islamic State has been established and it is thus obligatory upon every able-bodied male and female to migrate there. Muslims have been crushed under foot for too long. . . . This nation is openly against Islam and Muslims."[36]

The wave of recruits to ISIS from the United States and Europe is troubling, but even more threatening to the West is that some of these recruits are trickling back to their Western countries of origin to carry out terrorist acts in their homelands. Similarly, some disaffected Muslims in Western countries who haven't even traveled to the Middle East are taking inspiration from the Islamic State or other terrorist organizations and carrying out acts in their name.

In January 2015, the world was shocked by the attack on the Paris offices of *Charlie Hebdo*, a satirical newspaper, by radical Islamists who opposed the newspaper's depictions of the prophet Muhammad. The attackers, two brothers, were both French citizens, one of whom had trained with al-Qaeda in Yemen. According to witnesses, the men loudly declared their allegiance to the group as they attacked the magazine offices. They also shouted, "We have avenged the Prophet Muhammad!" and, "God is Great!" as they murdered eleven people.[37] The following week, the al-Qaeda branch in Yemen officially claimed responsibility for the massacre, calling the brothers "two heroes of Islam."[38]

Interestingly, the brothers' collaborator, Amedy Coulibaly, who killed four people in a kosher supermarket, had released a video in which he claimed allegiance to ISIS. Following his death, his wife apparently fled to Syria to join ISIS there.[39] While ISIS and al-Qaeda are rivals, the presence of both groups' extremist ideologies as motives underlying the Paris attack suggests the extent to which extremism has infiltrated the West, and how fluidly these ideologies can merge in the minds of those who hate us and our allies.

A similar story played out tragically on our own soil in April 2013, when two brothers set off a series of bombs at the finish line of the Boston Marathon that killed three and injured more than 260.[40] Although Dzhokhar and Tamerlan Tsarnaev were not officially acting with any known terrorist group, they were motivated by radical Islamic ideology and used online resources, including the al-Qaeda magazine *Inspire*, to gain knowledge about how to build bombs and carry out an attack.[41] Steeped in radical ideology and driven by anger over US wars in Muslim lands, the brothers vowed to take their revenge. "We Muslims are one body, you hurt one you hurt us all," Dzhokhar wrote in a confession while hiding from authorities before his capture.[42]

As Islamic extremism continues to grow and take hold in communities outside of the Middle East, experts fear that events like these will only become more common. In May 2015, Homeland Security Secretary Jeh Johnson warned that the United States had entered "a new phase in the global terrorist threat, where the so-called lone wolf could strike at any moment."[43]

The Just War Theory

Esther Women, are you upset by all this information? Good! We should be furious with righteous indignation. How dare these evil men be allowed to continue their quest for world domination?

This international nightmare is not going to go away on its own. Yet some people believe that what's going on in the Middle East is none of our business. They take a more isolationist approach to foreign policy, meaning that they want to concentrate on domestic policy and ignore the world around us. Certainly they make good points; we cannot be the world's police. Many of the conflicts around the globe have been happening for hundreds or even thousands of years, and when we meddle, we sometimes create unintended consequences.

The Sunnis and Shiites have fought each other on and off almost since the time of Muhammad's death. However, the conflict in the Middle East today is more complicated than just a sectarian argument. I would argue that there are some conflicts that morally demand our attention and involvement. Certainly that was true with Hitler's quest to create an Aryan society to rule the world. He was a long way from invading the United States, yet it was right for us to engage in World War II, even without the tragic bombing of Pearl Harbor in 1941.

But what should be our guiding principles about which conflicts demand our involvement? Christians have often looked to something called the Just War Theory. First developed by Saint Augustine in the fifth century and later added to by Thomas Aquinas and others, the Just War Theory holds that some wars are morally justifiable to stop evil and reestablish peace. It traditionally sets the following criteria by which to judge whether or not it is just and right for Christians to go to war:

1. **Legitimate Authority:** Wars must be initiated by a legitimate political authority and legal processes.
2. **Just Cause:** Wars must be fought for causes that are just, for instance, to resist aggression, protect civilians, or support the rights of an oppressed group.
3. **Right Intention:** Wars must be fought for the right reasons and not go beyond the pursuit of the just cause. War should advance good and avoid evil.
4. **Last Resort:** War should be the final resort after all other political and diplomatic solutions have failed.
5. **Reasonable Hope of Justice:** There must be a reasonable chance of success in order to avoid unnecessary wars.[44]

Augustine understood something critically important: not every battle is worthy, but some demand our engagement on a moral level. Christians have long understood that in some cases, force is necessary and even righteous.

Surely, a war against ISIS and perhaps others meets these criteria. What we are witnessing in the Middle East is pure evil, much like that of the Nazis against the Jews. It is unwarranted aggression against civilians and militants alike. Every day, more women and children suffer at the hands of extremists; more men are forced to take up arms or are killed.

The goal of these extremist groups is world domination, and they are openly plotting and threatening the safety of the United States. Radical Islam has been waging war against the United States for decades. This holy war came to our soil with the first attack on the World Trade Center in 1993, the *USS Cole* in 2000, and, of course, the events of 9/11. Today the threat on our soil is greater than ever, as seen in the beheading of a woman in Moore, Oklahoma, in 2014; the attack on a Jewish community center in Kansas City that same year; the 2015 attack on Pam Geller's Muhammad cartoon protest in Garland, Texas; and the murder of five servicemen at two military facilities in Tennessee in July 2015. Make no mistake. Sunni jihadists are here.

Defining the Enemy

In this extremely complicated fight, our enemy is not necessarily demarcated with any boundaries. This is not a war about land; it is about religious ideology. ISIS wants to create an Islamic caliphate at all costs; land is only relevant insofar as it helps them achieve that goal.

Groups driven by this ideology are killing and terrorizing innocent men, women, and children, giving our government legitimate cause to wage war against radical Islamic terrorists. The reality is that radical jihadists have already declared war against us. But we haven't been successful in fighting back, primarily because we haven't accurately defined our enemy or our strategy. Many, particularly our political leaders, have been reluctant to say that we are at war with Islam. Certainly, we need to distinguish between Muslims and radical Islamists. We are not at war with the millions of Muslims who practice their religion peacefully around the world. But we are at war with an ideology, one hell-bent on our destruction, and its roots are based in Islam. As journalist Graeme Wood wrote in a cover piece for the *Atlantic* last year, "The reality is that the Islamic State is Islamic. *Very* Islamic. Yes, it has attracted psychopaths and adventure seekers, drawn largely from the disaffected populations of the Middle East and Europe. But the religion preached by its most ardent followers derives from coherent and even learned interpretations of Islam."[45]

The facts are undeniable: Islamic extremists, driven by religious ideology, are persecuting Jews, Christians, and other religious minorities; exploiting and abusing women; and waging a war on the West. We need our government to get this straight. As former Defense Intelligence

Agency Director Lt. Gen. Michael Flynn has said, "You can't defeat an enemy that you don't admit exists."[46] We must admit that radical Islam is our enemy, and we must defeat them.

Americans understand the difference between our precious Muslim neighbors, who are valued members of our communities, and violent Islamic terrorists who are willing to kill others, including Muslims, in order to build their caliphate. The majority of Americans have a positive opinion of Muslims, according to a 2011 Pew Research Center poll, even while 69 percent of those same Americans expressed concern about Islamic extremism.[47] Most of us realize that these views are entirely compatible.

Unfortunately, the left doesn't understand this situation as clearly as the American people do. The radical extremists in the Middle East have made it obvious that they hate anyone who does not subscribe to their narrow worldview, and they have no interest in tolerance. We've got to stop dancing around this truth. As Governor Bobby Jindal (R-LA) has said: "If you cannot admit the problem, you cannot fix the problem. . . . Islam has a problem. There is an evil belief system that has taken root in radical Islam. It contends that many of us must be killed, women should be treated like property, some of us are eligible for slavery, and others need to be crucified."[48] This is the kind of honest rhetoric we need to be hearing from our leaders.

So here's the deal. There are American boots on the ground right now in the Middle East, and about three thousand troops in Iraq alone.[49] The problem—as is so often the case in holding back military success—is politics. Now is the time to let your leaders know that we expect them to engage and thwart this enemy. We expect that any troops committed to the Middle East be unshackled to unleash the full might of the US military on these evil men. Let me be clear. I want our military to rain hell down on these evildoers. Forget the politics. If you want that too, if you think we are morally justified in our fear and contempt for these men, then read on, sister.

Short of adding more boots on the ground, there is much we can do to help other partners in the region to fight this battle. The Kurds, the Jordanians, and the Egyptians have proven to be able partners, yet we have not aided them properly. Our air campaigns have been halfhearted, and our training and support of the Iraqi forces has been weak. As the *Washington Times* reported, in the first four months of 2015, almost 75 percent of US bombing runs in Iraq targeting ISIS never fired any weapons, "holding their fire mainly because of a lack of ground intelligence."[50] Such ineffective and disorganized action only allows ISIS to thrive. Containment for this enemy won't work.

It's time to face this threat head-on, both for the sake of those suffering in the Middle East and North Africa and for the safety of Americans here at home.

What Can Esther Women Do?

We're living in a scary, new world. Global terrorism compromises the safety of us all. We've watched this terrible reality unfold, and we know what we're facing. It's time to stand up and do something about it. We will not succumb to the evil that degrades and dehumanizes women, tears families and societies apart, and threatens our own borders.

When it comes to questions of foreign policy, it can be hard to find your voice or know what to say. But if we educate ourselves about these issues and then speak out and stand our ground, we can make a huge difference. This is too important not to. And whether we're speaking with our Christian sisters or our nonbelieving friends, we need to focus on several key things: raising awareness, relying on prayer, calling for action, and supporting those who fight for our freedom.

SOUND THE ALARM

We need to raise awareness about the peril facing our world. Sure, everyone knows that global terrorism is a threat, but the heartbreaking effects it has already caused aren't widely known or discussed. The persecution of religious minorities, violations of human rights, and perilous condition of millions of refugees in the Middle East and North Africa are ongoing travesties. We need to be speaking out about them, particularly the persecution of our fellow Christians in the Middle East. The terror that these families live under daily is real, and we cannot disregard it. The same is true of Jews and other minorities who suffer at the hands of radical Islamists: we must be their voices.

All who believe in Christ are one body (Rom. 12:5). When one part of our body is persecuted, it affects us all. As Christians, we are responsible to share in the suffering of our brothers and sisters and not to turn away. It may feel small—like you're not really doing anything in the face of such incredible suffering on the other side of the world—but by keeping ourselves informed and refusing to ignore the truth of what's happening, we can begin to create change. Don't be afraid to raise these topics with others; be emboldened. You are on the side of righteousness.

I encourage you not to limit yourself to speaking up within the church community or to fellow Christians. We need to be loud in speaking out against the atrocities ISIS and other groups are committing worldwide.

Share the principles that I have given you in this chapter. Express the belief that the United States has a moral responsibility to help. Explain the Just War Theory. Read the national news accounts and use them as an anchor to write an op-ed to your local newspaper, pass out a CWA or some other group's flier in your PTA or MOPs group. Make sure your family is aware of the atrocities being suffered. The more people we engage in this conversation, the greater chance we have of seeing God work through us to bring about change.

ACT WITH POWER: PRAY

Raising awareness is good, but it must lead to concrete action. And, as believers, we have the greatest source of power for change at our fingertips: prayer. As I discovered when CWA held its first Day of Prayer and Fasting, the most important and powerful thing we can do in the face of global terrorism is pray. For when we do, God will act. This is true throughout the Bible, and it is true today; as God told Jeremiah, "Call to me and I will answer you" (Jer. 33:3).

We should pray bold prayers for God's protection for those in the path of extremists and those who are already in their clutches. We should pray for his wisdom for our leaders. We should pray for his strength to fight against evil. Jesus himself encouraged us to pray boldly to our Father when he described a man who knocked on a friend's door at midnight asking for bread. "I say to you, though he will not rise and give to him because he is his friend, yet because of his persistence he will rise and give him as many as he needs" (Luke 11:8 NKJV). Go to God with boldness in confidence that he hears our prayers.

Even more important, don't stop at praying by yourself or with one or two others. Instead, encourage the Christians in your community to set up a day of prayer or a prayer network for those suffering at the hands of Islamic extremists.

At CWA we have designated the fourth Sunday of every month as a day in which we encourage the world to join us in prayer and fasting for the victims of Islamic terrorists. With Ephesians 6:12 in our minds, "For we do not wrestle against flesh and blood, but against principalities, against powers, against the rulers of the darkness of this age, against spiritual hosts of wickedness in the heavenly places" (NKJV), we asked others to join us in praying for the following crucial issues:

- For our enemies, that they may have a Damascus Road conversion to faith in Jesus and repent of their evil, just as Paul did.
- For justice to prevail in nations around the world.
- For victims around the world: women, children, and innocent men.
- For Israel, Jordan, Egypt, and other sovereign nations in the Middle East who are working for peace but are being threatened by Islamic terrorism.
- For the leaders of the world to stiffen their resolve to fight evil and to stand up for the weak.
- For our administration to acknowledge the seriousness of the threat of terrorism, take a strong stance against it, and once again assume a position of leadership in the world.

As we pray consistently over these topics, we may also find ourselves empowered to take greater action in our communities—particularly our church communities. Encourage your church, pastors, and leaders to take a stand on the issue of those persecuted by radical extremists. Ask them to hold a day of prayer. Print out CWA's flier on our website, www.concernedwomen.org, and ask your church to use it as a bulletin insert. Do we believe in prayer or not? If we do, then let's join together and seek God's power, petitioning him to send angel armies, carrying the fiery sword of justice on behalf of these people.

You can also ask your church to take a special offering at one of your services to raise money for refugees and victims of violence in the Middle East. The church is called to act, and part of our job as Christ's ambassadors is to ensure that the communities in which we worship are living up to their calling. As Americans blessed with safety, security, and in many cases, disposable income, we need to consider giving out of our abundance in order to help groups minister to the physical and material needs of those affected by the actions of terrorist groups.

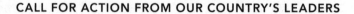
CALL FOR ACTION FROM OUR COUNTRY'S LEADERS

There is power in advocacy, and there is a lot we can do when we raise our voices together to demand change. We need to lobby our congressmen and representatives to take more action to protect both our own interests and the interests of those being persecuted abroad—and encourage others to do the same.

We also need to call for our leaders to face this threat head-on—starting by calling it by its name. No more dancing around the facts; Islamic extremists threaten our safety and that of the world at large, and we can't deny that their ideology is rooted in religion. Our leaders need to use unequivocal language to denounce radical Islam and give the American people enough credit to be able to distinguish between our radical enemies and our peaceable Muslim neighbors and friends.

Ultimately, we need to elect political leaders and a commander in chief who understands America's role in the world. Our geopolitical standing has consequences not just for us but for weaker nations too. Nations are led by people, and therefore they take on the attributes of people. Some nations are bullies and aggressors. For those of us who believe in original sin, it should be obvious that there is, as Ronald Reagan put it, "peace through strength." Weak leadership in the United States makes the entire world less safe. When the enemies of freedom no longer fear us, and our allies no longer trust that we will follow through on our promises to stand with them, then everyone loses.

SUPPORT THOSE WHO FIGHT

As we consider how to address the situation in the Middle East, we also need to look for ways to thank the troops who fight for us. Regardless of what we think of our government's strategy for fighting ISIS, we need to support the work of our troops at every level. The men and women who serve in our military are heroes. Popular culture has cheapened that word, but let's take a moment and remember the true heroes among us. I am so grateful for their willingness to sacrifice even their very lives to protect our freedom.

There are big ways to acknowledge our troops, such as institutional recognition, and small ways, such as saying "thank you for your service" to a person in uniform in the airport. You can buy them coffee in line at the coffee shop or make care packages to send abroad. When my children were small, we sent care packages to troops in Iraq and Afghanistan. My friend Barbara's son Gabe was on his second tour in Fallujah, and we wanted to thank him and his troops, so I went out and bought beef jerky, nutritional bars, candy, and Skin So Soft bath oil (to keep the sand fleas away) and boxed them up. I had my children make cards for the troops with crayons and construction paper. We wrote a little message that read, "Thank you. Freedom isn't free."

And it's not. I wanted my kids to learn early that our freedom is so very expensive. It has been paid for not just with treasure but also with the blood of our citizens and with the sacrifice of their families. Every Thanksgiving, Christmas, Easter, Passover, and Ramadan I am touched by the military families who have an empty chair at their table. They have a loved one away doing the messy work of defending our nation; even more heartbreaking, some are never coming home. As Christians, we can take it upon ourselves to reach out to those families and thank them too. People who criticize our military need to remember why they have that inalienable right of liberty. They have it because someone in a uniform was willing to sacrifice for it. As Winston Churchill is thought to have said, "We sleep soundly in our beds because rough men stand ready in the night to visit violence on those who would do us harm." I thank God for our brave, and sometimes rough, men and women.

The Power to Act

Ultimately, when it comes to the threat of Islamic extremism, we are not powerless in the face of evil. We can act, and we must. We are dealing with a kind of darkness that threatens us, our children, and the future of our nation, and which has already begun to destroy the lives and liberties of our brothers and sisters in the Middle East and North Africa.

Esther Women, we have the ability to do something about it. We have the power to speak up, to pray, to advocate for our government to intervene, to support our troops on the ground, and to cry out for justice—and we must do so. Join me in heeding the call of Isaiah: "Shout it aloud, do not hold back. Raise your voice like a trumpet," so that God's people might "loose the chains of injustice and untie the cords of the yoke [and] set the oppressed free" (Isa. 58:1, 6). God calls us to action. Let's respond.

Representative Vicky Hartzler

US REPRESENTATIVE FOR MISSOURI'S FOURTH CONGRESSIONAL DISTRICT

Conservative women are making inroads at all levels of government, and one of the most inspiring is Congresswoman Vicky Hartzler. Elected to the House in 2010, Representative Hartzler serves as the chairman of the Oversight and Investigations Subcommittee of the House Armed Services Committee, a critical position in which she ensures accountability within the Department of Defense.

Rep. Hartzler spent eleven years as a home economics teacher before being approached by members of her community about running for state representative in 1994. She prayed long and hard about it and eventually realized that God was calling her to run. She knew that this was a way for her to make a difference for the country she loved, and she stepped up to the challenge.

In office, Rep. Hartzler has been a strong advocate for families and traditional marriage. She served as the spokeswoman for the Missouri Coalition to Protect Marriage in 2004 and has continued to speak out fearlessly on the issue at the federal level, even when others won't. She also works to strengthen families by advocating for life—particularly by promoting adoption as a wonderful alternative for mothers who aren't able to raise their own children. This is a personal issue for the congresswoman, who is a mother through adoption herself.

A longtime member of CWA, Rep. Hartzler encourages women to make a difference by being informed on issues that matter, praying about them, and then acting. Most important, she says to support candidates who hold your beliefs. "As Christians, we need to back up our vision." Whether that means going door-to-door campaigning for candidates, investing money in campaigns, or even running yourself, Rep. Hartzler emphasizes the importance of being involved. "By all of us doing this, the body of Christ working together, we can change our country and impact our culture."[51]

Vicky's book *Running God's Way* is an amazing tool to help women become winning candidates.

CHAPTER 8

Beyond Our Borders
Why Israel Matters to Christians

*I*n April 2013 I made my first visit to Israel, where I walked in the steps of Jesus. I saw the Sea of Galilee and the Old City and encountered places so central to Christianity that it changed the way I read the Bible. I saw many incredible things on that trip, but the most powerful to me was Yad Vashem, the Holocaust museum. Yad Vashem has beautiful architecture, a series of structures on a hillside overlooking Jerusalem. Inside, however, it is made of concrete. The atmosphere is stark and depressing as the museum chronicles a history so outrageous it's difficult to fathom: the systematic murder of six million Jews and others.

Yad Vashem serves as a reminder to me of what happens when people of faith don't speak up against a culture moving in the wrong direction. Because with a few notable exceptions, Christians around the world averted their eyes to the evil in front of them when it came to the Holocaust. Even the United States was slow to give sanctuary to Jews, severely restricting immigration and making it difficult for refugees to obtain entry visas. Although church leaders spoke out after Kristallnacht, or the "Night of Broken Glass," on November 9, 1938, when Jewish businesses and synagogues in Austria and Germany were attacked and thirty thousand Jews were rounded up and taken away to concentration camps, few leaders demanded concrete action from the American government or from within the church community.[1] Sadly, the American church ignored its responsibility along with the rest of the country. It was not until 1944, when the United States had become aware of the extent of the Nazi policy to exterminate Jews, that President Roosevelt finally implemented a specific policy to rescue European Jews.[2] By that point, millions had already perished at the hands of the Nazis.

The one ray of light and hope at Yad Vashem is a grove of trees outside that parallels the museum's walls, where Israel recognizes Christians who tried to save the Jewish people. The trees represent "the righteous among the nations"—more than 25,000 people from many different countries who risked everything to protect Jewish people from 1933 to 1945.[3] As I walked along the avenue of trees, I couldn't help but wonder how many more lives would have been saved had the church chosen to act.

My questions increased after seeing the horrific pictures of men, women, and children victimized by the Nazis: If I had been alive during the Holocaust, who would I have been? Would I have risked being sent to a concentration camp like Auschwitz in order to do what was right? What if I had kids—would I have been willing to risk the safety of my own family in order to protect others? This question in particular nagged at me. Later on the trip I met a Jewish woman visiting from New York, and she asked me what I was learning on my trip. I told her about the question I had asked myself, "Would I have made the right choice?" She replied, "You say you are a Christian. Don't you think God would give you the grace to do the right thing?" *Of course I do*, I thought, but the question is not his character—it's mine.

Upon my return to the United States, within a day or two I was called to do a Fox News segment, and it hit me: the Jewish people need me right now, today, and I have an incredible platform from which to speak up. As I prepared for the segment, I realized that I will never know if I would have had the courage to act on behalf of the Jews during the Holocaust. Would I have been like Corrie Ten Boom, acting as a living embodiment of the love of Jesus by taking in strangers to spare them? I don't know if I would have had the courage to act as she did. But this I do know: I am responsible before God for what I know today. And what I know is that the Jewish people and the Jewish state of Israel are still in danger. Anti-Semitism is on the rise again, and I am committed to speaking out against it at every opportunity.

The United States and Israel are closely linked. Israel's welfare directly blesses us as a nation. We must send the signal to the world that American Christians will defend Israel and the Jewish people, not only because of God's everlasting, unbroken covenants with the Jewish people but because of our love for our own country.

Why Christians Must Stand with Israel

For nearly 3,400 years, the land of Israel has been the heart and soul of the Jewish people. It is the homeland from where its ancient traditions, culture, and values have emanated. As Christians, we recognize that the Old Testament serves as the Israelites' deed to their home, the Promised Land. In Genesis, God establishes a unconditional covenant with Abraham: "I will establish my covenant as an everlasting covenant between me and you and your descendants after you for the generations to come, to be your God and the God of your descendants after you" (Gen. 17:7). That covenant passed from Abraham to his son Isaac, and then to Isaac's son Jacob. In Genesis 35, God renames Jacob "Israel," and reaffirms his covenant with his people: "And God said to him, 'Your name is Jacob; your name shall not be called Jacob anymore, but Israel shall be your name.' So He called his name Israel. Also God said to him: 'I am God Almighty. Be fruitful and multiply; a nation and a company of nations shall proceed from you, and kings shall come from your body. The land which I gave Abraham and Isaac I give to you; and to your descendants after you I give this land'" (vv. 10–12 NKJV).

God gave the land of Israel to Jacob's descendants—the Jewish people of today. God's covenant is unconditional and everlasting; nothing can take away his establishment of the land of Israel or his declaration that the Jews are his precious people.

In the New Testament, the apostle Paul reaffirms this everlasting covenant: "What I mean is this: The law, introduced 430 years later, does not set aside the covenant previously established by God and thus do away with the promise" (Gal. 3:17). The Abrahamic covenant is dealt with consistently in forty-six verses, all of which confirm God's promise of the land of Canaan to the Jews.[4]

In addition to the biblically stated divine right for Israel to exist, we also have historical truth supporting the Jewish claim to their homeland. The Jewish people first established an independent nation-state, with Jerusalem as its political and spiritual capital, around 1000 BC, when Saul became the first king of Israel. In the three millennia that followed, the Jewish nation was repeatedly conquered by foreign empires, including the Persians, Greeks, and Romans. Despite intense persecution by invading foreign forces and mass expulsion from Israel, many Jews remained in their homeland, continuing the Jewish inhabitance of the land of Israel, without pause, to this day.

While many were forced into exile, the Jewish people never lost hope of one day returning to the land of their forefathers and foremothers. They dreamt of returning to their ancient capital of Jerusalem, a city mentioned more than eight hundred times in the Old Testament and nearly 150 times in the New Testament. The concluding words of Israel's national anthem, "Hatikvah" (The Hope), summarize the Jewish people's desire: "The hope of 2000 years: To live as a free people / In our own land, / The land of Zion and Jerusalem."[5]

The deep-seated yearning to return to their homeland, coupled with increasingly unlivable conditions for Jews in Europe, spawned the political movement of Zionism in the nineteenth century. Although Jews had lived in Europe for quite some time, the situation had become unimaginable; Jews were persecuted and massacred en masse, and they faced a choice. Many came to believe that they would only escape persecution and murder in a state of their own. That state was Israel.

In 1917, the British issued the Balfour Declaration, pledging to support the establishment of a national home for the Jewish people in what was then called Palestine. In 1947, the United Nations voted to partition Palestine into two states—one Arab and one Jewish. Even though more than half of the area allocated for the Jewish nation was desert, the Jewish community in Palestine immediately accepted the compromise. The Arabs, on the other hand, opposed the creation of two states and joined forces with neighboring countries to wage a war against their Jewish neighbor.

Sixty-seven years and six unwanted wars later, the state of Israel continues to fight for its existence. As Christians, we must never forget this simple fact: the Jewish people have a God-given right to live in their ancient land, and the modern state of Israel is the fulfillment of that historic right.

The Danger of Replacement Theology

Despite the clear biblical call for us to stand with Israel, differences exist within the Christian community in our outlook on the Jewish state. Some Christians adhere to the idea that the church has replaced the Jewish people. In this understanding, the Jews are no longer God's chosen people; instead, his promises to them are fulfilled in his blessings to the church. This outlook is called replacement theology.

Although some who believe this concept have never even heard this term, this idea was born centuries ago. Part of this thinking seems to come from our embrace of the New Testament at the expense of—almost the disdaining of—the Old Testament. Because of the centrality of the Gospels and Jesus' earthly ministry to our faith, some Christians elevate the New Testament and undermine the Old, even if unintentionally.

However, this replacement theology is both wrong and dangerous because it carries an undercurrent of anti-Semitism, rooted in the early years of Christianity when many held the Jewish people responsible for sending Jesus to his death. What they seemed to forget is that he was a Jewish Savior with Jewish disciples and that it was Jewish missionaries who brought the gospel to non-Jews. Despite this fact, history is plagued with enduring anti-Semitism—even though God himself chose this particular people as vessels to transmit his Scriptures, both Old and New Testament, and to provide our Savior, a Jewish rabbi, to redeem us.

Let me be clear: the belief that the Jews are to blame for Jesus' crucifixion is a distortion of Scripture. Jesus himself says, "The reason my Father loves me is that I lay down my life—only to take it up again. No one takes it from me, but I lay it down of my own accord. I have authority to lay it down and authority to take it up again. This command I received from my Father" (John 10:17–18).

Jesus' arrest, crucifixion, and resurrection were completely in God's hands. Pontius Pilate; the Jewish religious hierarchy; the high priest, Caiaphas; the Roman soldiers; and Judas Iscariot could have done nothing to prevent God's plan of salvation for his creation. Jesus had to die as a substitute for our sins. The crucifixion had to happen: "For God so loved the world that he gave his one and only Son" (John 3:16). After Jesus' resurrection and ascension his disciples and many other Jewish believers brought the gospel to the known world. Despite these facts, anti-Semitism is alive and well in the church.

I was a little girl of seven or eight the first time I was confronted with this anti-Semitic understanding of the Scriptures. I remember another child telling me that "the Jews killed Jesus." I was confused, but I knew that didn't sound right. In response, I said something about the Roman soldiers carrying out the crucifixion. But I was smart enough to go to my resident biblical authority, my dad, who was a pastor (Reverend Young recently retired after fifty-one years!). I have never forgotten his wise response. He said "Yes, Penny, the Romans nailed Jesus to the cross, but it was actually me. I killed Jesus. He willingly died as a sacrifice for my sin, and he died for yours." Wow, what an astounding reminder. *My* sin is why Jesus died. He chose to die for my redemption and yours. He chose to lay down his life of his own accord. The Jews and the Romans were carrying out his plan of salvation. He could have stopped it all with a word, but he willingly died for all of us.

It's risky business for Christians to cling to the idea that the church and Christians have replaced the Jewish people in God's covenants. If God changed his mind about the covenants with the Jewish people, might he change his promises to us as well? We mischaracterize his unchanging nature and promises when we accept the ideas of replacement theology. The truth is that Jesus completed the law without dismantling his promises, and we need to cling to the Old and New Testament promises as the word of God.

The US-Israel Relationship

It is critical that Christians stand with Israel. It is equally important that Americans support Israel because it is our closest ally in the region and reflects the democratic ideals of our home country. A beacon for humanity, light, and hope in the Middle East, Israel fervently protects all holy sites and guarantees freedom of religion for all its citizens: Jewish, Muslim, Christian, Druze, and others. Furthermore, the United States has maintained a special bond with the nation of Israel since its establishment. As Senator John McCain has stated, the most "profound tie between our two countries . . . is a moral one. We are two democracies whose alliance is forged in our common values."[6]

The US-Israel relationship is strategically important for many reasons. We have common national interests, ranging from the desire to prevent nuclear weapon proliferation to promoting stable borders among countries in the Middle East. Our close cooperation has yielded military technologies and strategies that benefit both countries, and Israel's strong military and geostrategic location are crucial to the United States' interests in the region. Our relationship with Israel is necessary in addressing the rising specters of global terrorism and radical Islam.

Unfortunately, there are constant threats to Israel's safety and preservation, as there have been for centuries. Despite its commitment to peace and freedom, however, Israel has been recognized by only two of its twenty-two Arab neighbors: Egypt and Jordan. Most of the rest refuse to accept Israel's statehood or to maintain diplomatic relations. Many are outright hostile; Iran in particular has long called for the destruction of the Jewish state.

Most recently, the negotiations between the United States and Iran over Iran's nuclear program have brought things to a boiling point. Israel was rightly concerned about this deal, negotiated up through the summer of 2015, because a nuclear-capable Iran represents the greatest possible threat to Israel's existence and its people. The White House was dismissive of Israeli concerns, and their rhetoric surrounding the deal became increasingly harsh. In the run-up to the 2015 Israeli elections, it was so bad that even the *New York Times* noted that "the unrelenting White House criticism . . . has helped sink relations between Washington and Jerusalem to a nadir not seen for more than 25 years."[7]

When Israel's prime minister, Benjamin Netanyahu, came to the United States in March 2015 to address Congress about the Iran deal, Obama refused to meet with him, claiming that the meeting would come too close to the Israeli elections. And after Netanyahu won reelection, despite US tax dollars being secretly funneled to his opponent, the president pointedly waited two days before calling to congratulate him. This dismissive, even hostile attitude toward Israel has gone too far, and is detrimental to both our great nations. If Israel is going to remain the bastion of democracy and freedom in the Middle East, America must become once again its most supportive ally.

In the midst of this tumultuous and even dangerous environment, our support as American Christians for the Holy Land and the Jewish people is more critical than ever.

Anti-Semitism on the College Campus

Last year, researchers at Tel Aviv University found that anti-Semitic incidents had risen 38 percent over the previous year. "The overall feeling among many Jewish people is one of living in an intensifying anti-Jewish environment that has become not only insulting and threatening but outright dangerous," the report concluded.[8] In the United States, this disturbing trend is particularly prevalent on college and university campuses.

The BDS (Boycott, Divestment and Sanctions) movement, begun in 2005 by Palestinian organizations in an attempt to increase pressure on Israel to acquiesce to Palestinian demands, has taken hold on campuses in recent years. Calling on the international community "to impose broad boycotts and implement divestment initiatives against Israel similar to those applied to South Africa in the apartheid era," the BDS movement has found strong support from liberal student governments and groups.[9] Student groups target companies that do business with Israel and pressure their universities to divest their interests in such organizations.

They also call on consumers not to purchase Israeli products and to boycott Israeli academic and cultural institutions.

This movement is growing. In the 2013–2014 academic year, student governments at fifteen colleges ranging from Cornell to the University of Michigan voted on nonbinding divestment resolutions against organizations conducting business in Israel.[10] In the 2014–2015 year, the number of BDS campaigns initiated on campuses had risen to twenty-nine.[11]

The trouble is not just the votes but also the anti-Semitic feeling and rhetoric behind such actions. Students for Justice in Palestine (SJP), the main group behind the BDS movement, has been spewing hatred against Israel since the group's inception. As the Anti-Defamation League (ADL) recently reported, "SJP has consistently demonized Israel, describing Israeli policies toward the Palestinians as racist and apartheid-like, and comparing Israelis to Nazis or Israel to the Jim Crow-era US."[12] Sadly, such inflammatory rhetoric plays well on college campuses, where student-led groups carry out a variety of anti-Israel events that range from disrupting speakers, holding student-led teach-ins on why Israel is an apartheid state, and even setting up mock Israeli military checkpoints around campus.

The BDS campaign has been relatively ineffective on a global scale—most boycotts are soundly defeated, and no US school has sold any stock in response to resolutions passed by student governments—but it has nonetheless created a hostile environment for Jewish students and professors.[13] As the national director of the ADL, Abraham H. Foxman wrote in the *Huffington Post*, "Regardless of the fact that the BDS campaign has not gained much traction on campus in terms of having any impact against Israel . . . it is creating a great deal of noise on campus and beyond, raising a lot of attention, and contributing to the sense of discomfort of Jewish students."[14]

At multiple universities over the past few years, including NYU and Harvard, Jewish students have been harassed by false eviction notices shoved under their dorm room doors.[15] There have also been reports of physical violence.[16] During a divestment vote at UC Davis in January 2015, students waved Palestinian flags and shouted at Jewish and pro-Israel supporters. After the vote, the Jewish fraternity on campus was painted with swastikas.[17] After a failed vote on a divestment proposal at Cornell last year, one student told the *New York Times*, "There definitely is a sharpness to the anti-Israel side that's uncomfortable."[18]

Boy, that's an understatement. Uncomfortable doesn't begin to cover it.

Anti-Semitism on a Global Scale

Make no mistake: anti-Semitism is on the rise, across America more generally and also beyond our borders. As the *Times of Israel* reported in February of last year, nearly 60 percent of all hate crimes in the United States are committed against Jews.[19] Whether verbal or physical, attacks on Jewish Americans occur at an alarming rate, and they are happening more often: the ADL reported a 21 percent increase in anti-Semitic incidents in 2014.[20] Some of these are high-profile incidents, like the 2014 shooting of four people outside a Jewish community center in Overland Park, Kansas, by a white supremacist intent on "killing all Jews." But such large acts of violence also occur alongside more everyday assaults, ranging from the painting of swastikas on thirty homes in Madison, Wisconsin, in February 2015 to the recent trend of hacking into Jewish community and synagogue websites.

The increasing anti-Semitic sentiment in the United States is worrisome; in Europe, it is downright alarming. After the January 2015 terrorist attack on the Paris offices of the satirical newspaper *Charlie Hebdo*, which we talked about in the previous chapter, the attackers proceeded to a kosher supermarket, where they killed four people and took several others hostage. The supermarket had no connection to *Charlie Hebdo*; it was merely run and patronized by Jewish people. Four weeks later, a man, possibly inspired by the *Charlie Hebdo* attacks, opened fire outside of a synagogue in Copenhagen, killing a Jewish man and wounding two police officers. That same weekend, the graves of three hundred Jews were desecrated in a cemetery in eastern France.

While highly visible, these are just three incidents in a wave of increased violence and intolerance toward Jews in Europe. As Stephen Pollard, editor of Britain's *Jewish Chronicle*, wrote, the attack on the kosher supermarket in Paris was no fluke. Home to Western Europe's largest Jewish population, France in particular has seen a huge increase in anti-Semitic sentiment and activity—the number of incidents today is seven times higher than it was in the 1990s.[21] "Every single French Jew I know has either left or is actively working out how to leave," Pollard said.[22]

Indeed, anti-Semitism has become so widespread and vicious across Europe that governments have been scrambling to respond; after Israeli Prime Minister Benjamin Netanyahu suggested that European Jews ought to come home to Israel in the wake of the Copenhagen shootings,

European leaders insisted that they would do everything in their power to protect their Jewish citizens. "An attack on the Jews of Denmark is an attack on Denmark," Prime Minister Helle Thorning-Schmidt declared. "They are a strong part of our community, and we will do everything we can to protect the Jewish community in our country."[23]

Along with a stronger vocal stance against such attacks, many countries have ramped up their security measures; in the wake of the attacks in Paris, France deployed ten thousand troops across the country to protect Jewish sites and citizens, and in Amsterdam, military police guard sites like the Anne Frank museum and the city's seventeenth-century Portuguese synagogue.[24]

Even the United States has felt compelled to speak out against the state of affairs in Europe. In February 2015, the Senate introduced a bipartisan resolution condemning the rise of anti-Semitism across Europe and calling on US authorities to work with European leaders to combat it.[25]

Incidents are continuing to pile up week after week; remaining silent is no longer an option. While visiting Germany in May 2015 to mark fifty years of relations between the two countries, Israel's president, Reuven Rivlin, delivered a dire message: "Once again, fascist and neo-Nazi movements are growing stronger and stronger on European soil. Apathy, indifference, or denial is not the answer."[26]

Jews in the Middle East and the Rise in Extremism

Where is this increased hatred toward Jewish citizens coming from? While there are a variety of factors that contribute, much of the rise of anti-Semitism in Europe has been tied to the growing population of Muslim immigrants there.[27] Although many Muslims hold no ill will toward Jews, extremists have begun to exert a greater influence. With the rise of social media and the ability of extremist groups in the Middle East to inspire and support attacks abroad, the danger has continued to grow.

As we saw in the previous chapter, the recent rise in Islamic extremism presents a severe and alarming threat to the region and to the West. Yet while this reality becomes clearer and more frightening by the day, the danger posed by these groups has long been foreshadowed in the treatment of Jews and of Israel. There is a saying in the Middle East, "First the Saturday people then the Sunday people," meaning that

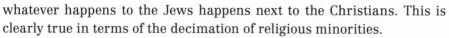
whatever happens to the Jews happens next to the Christians. This is clearly true in terms of the decimation of religious minorities.

Consider the obliteration of Jews in Iraq. In biblical times Iraq was part of ancient Mesopotamia. It was the home of the civilizations of Sumer, Babylon, and Assyria, and the site of some of our faith's earliest roots; one of its largest cities, Ur, is believed to be the birthplace of Abraham.[28] Judaism has had a significant presence in Iraq since at least the time of the Babylon captivity in 586 BC.[29]

As recently as 1950, there were 150,000 Jews living in Iraq. Today, the best estimates suggest that there are between four and ten, all living in Baghdad.[30] You read that right: less than ten Jews in the entire country. Facing extreme persecution in the 1950s, many Jews immigrated to Israel; of the several thousand who remained in Iraq, their numbers have slowly dwindled among the hostile environment and anti-Semitic atmosphere of the country.

A similar story is now playing out for Christians and other religious minorities in the region. With Israel standing as the only pillar of democracy and religious freedom in the Middle East, it is essential for those now suffering at the hands of Islamic extremists that we support our ally and work to protect Israel from threats to its homeland.

Threats to Israel

Anti-Semitism endangers Jews around the world, and radical Islam threatens religious minorities in the Middle East and abroad. But Israel's greatest threats are close to home. Terrorist groups like Hamas and Hezbollah and the antipathy of neighbors like Iran and Lebanon all pose significant dangers to our ally.

HAMAS

One of the greatest threats comes from Hamas, a Palestinian terrorist organization and political movement that has long sought the destruction of Israel. Designated a terrorist organization in 1997, it still operates as one of Palestine's major political parties, and effectively rules the Gaza Strip, an area of land Israel gave back to the Palestinians in 2005.[31] Unfortunately, that act of good will has only placed Israeli citizens in more danger due to the election of Hamas by Gaza's citizens. Hamas' founding charter from 1988 calls for the obliteration of Israel and the establishment of an Islamic state in Palestine, and Hamas has dedicated itself to this goal. It has provoked three conflicts with Israel in the past seven years and killed more than five hundred civilians in terrorist attacks.[32]

You've seen the rallies and heard the chants, particularly during Operation Protective Edge, the conflict between Israel and Gaza in the summer of 2014, when Hamas was lobbing over rockets—more than 4,500 of them—from Gaza, and Palestinians were upset that Israel fired back.[33] They yelled, "From the river to the sea Palestine will be free," meaning from the Jordan River to the Mediterranean Sea the Jews will be driven out of Israel.

Let's be clear: that is the entire width of the nation. The Palestinians want it all. They do not want a two-state solution; they want one state of Palestine.

It might surprise you to know that Hamas sending rockets into Israel isn't a new thing. There have been at least 15,200 rockets shot into Israel from Gaza in the last fourteen years.[34] I saw some of these on my last trip to Israel in April 2015. Upon my arrival, the head of security in the tiny town of Sderot drove me to the border of Gaza. It's so close, just a small swath of land a few miles away, yet a world away in terms of worldview. As I stood on a hillside looking over Gaza, I tried to imagine what it would be like to live in constant fear from my neighbors. It must be terrifying. And Hamas isn't done fighting; they are currently expanding their network of terror tunnels into Israel, assembling hundreds of rockets each week and smuggling illegal materials into Gaza for weapons building and tunnel construction.[35]

While writing this chapter, the Red Alert app on my phone went off, notifying me of rockets being shot into Sderot. Many of the elderly people living there are Holocaust survivors. I met some of them who were making cookies for Israeli Defense Forces (IDF) soldiers at the International Fellowship of Christian and Jews Senior Center I toured. They kept trying to feed me. It is such a sweet memory, and I mourn for the violence they are continually facing. The media won't cover these as acts of war because Israel refuses to fire back.

Hamas clearly states that its immediate goal is to destroy Israel. You will remember that these are the same people who condemned the United States for killing the "holy warrior" Osama Bin Laden. As long as Hamas remains armed and Gaza militarized, the six million citizens of Israel live under the shadow of further deadly conflict.

Can you imagine if even one rocket came over our borders from Mexico or Canada? What do you think our response would be? Many in the international community have condemned Israel for defending itself against this aggression, but Israel has an absolute right and responsibility to defend and protect its citizens. Furthermore, they do so with the utmost care to limit civilian casualties and provide humanitarian aid. During Operation Protective Edge, Hamas used schools and hospitals as rocket-launching sites and deliberately placed Gaza residents in the line of Israeli fire by ordering them to ignore evacuation warnings.[36] Israel, on the other hand, went out of its way to warn Gaza civilians who were in the vicinity of military targets, sent medicine and medical supplies to them, and helped restore electrical power, sewage, and water to the Gaza Strip.[37] Sadly, there are still innocent victims in Gaza who are held hostage by Hamas. Prime Minister Benjamin Netanyhu said it well: "Here's the difference between us. We're using missile defense to protect our civilians, and they're using their civilians to protect their missiles."[38]

Israel has not always done everything right, and certainly there are innocent Palestinians who deserve our compassion and prayers. But Hamas is a terrorist organization using terrorist tactics. Israel must be allowed to defend itself against this threat and deserves the support of the international community as they pursue peace. Prime Minister Netanyahu is also credited with saying, "If the Arabs lay down their arms there will be no more war, but if Israel lays down its weapons, there would be no more Israel."[39]

True that!

IRAN AND HEZBOLLAH

Hamas is not the only danger Israel must contend with on a daily basis. Iran has been hostile toward Israel since its foundation as a state. It refuses to recognize the legitimacy of Israel's statehood and has severed all diplomatic and commercial ties. More significant, Iran has set itself up in direct opposition to Israel and openly calls for the destruction of the Jewish homeland. In November 2014 Iran's supreme leader, Ayatollah Ali Khamenei, took to Twitter to demand that Israel be "annihilated," and in April 2015, an Iranian militia commander stated that "erasing Israel off the map" was "nonnegotiable." For this reason, Iran's work to obtain nuclear weapons represents perhaps the most pressing threat to Israel, and one that must be carefully considered by the United States. Iran's promises to limit their nuclear program must have immediate and verifiable results.

Iran's threat to Israel is particularly acute because of the actions of Hezbollah, the Iranian militant group based in Lebanon. US officials have described Hezbollah as the "most technically capable terrorist group in the world."[41] Established in the 1980s and pledging loyalty to Iran's supreme leader, Hezbollah opposes any Western involvement in the Middle East and, like Hamas, longs for the destruction of Israel. Their founding manifesto reads, in part: "Our primary assumption in our fight against Israel states that the Zionist entity is aggressive from its inception, and built on lands wrested from their owners, at the expense of the rights of the Muslim people. Therefore our struggle will end only when this entity is obliterated. We recognize no treaty with it, no cease-fire, and no peace agreements, whether separate or consolidated."[42]

Hezbollah's hatred for Israel is deep seated and represents a clear and constant threat to the Jewish homeland and people. Hezbollah is financed by Iran and acts as an Iranian proxy. The US State Department must remember this fact and maintain an awareness of the best interests of our ally.

These are other terrorist groups who want to destroy Israel. I don't have the space to get into all of them, but you get the point. Now is the time to stand firmly with Israel. They are facing direct threats to their homeland, and the region is awash in terrorist activity driven by radical ideology that threatens Jews, Christians, and others. We need Israel to be able to stand as a stable, democratic partner in the region and offer religious freedom in a land where almost none exists.

Increased Anti-Israel Sentiment within the US Government

Unfortunately, relations between the United States and Israel have become increasingly strained under the leadership of President Obama. The Obama administration's relationship with Israel has always been—shall we say rocky? Obama has long been accused of holding anti-Zionist views, and his links with Palestinian extremists and commentators, such as Palestine Liberation Organization spokesman Rashid Khalidi, are well known.[43] Obama has done little over the course of his presidency to acknowledge the growing threat of Hamas or Israel's other enemies in the region, and his lack of support for the nation has caused tension since the earliest days of his administration. With Obama's reelection in 2012, political commentator Daniel Pipes predicted, "the coldest treatment of Israel ever by a U.S. president will follow."[44] History has proven him correct.

We need our next commander in chief to be supportive of Israel and to maintain a strong relationship between our two nations. In most cases, what is good for Israel is good for the United States, and we need to work together to achieve our common goals.

What Can Esther Women Do?

When I reflect on the persecution of Jews and of Israel, I think that perhaps it's all evidence for God's eternal covenant with the Jews. What else can explain the vicious attacks and plots for annihilation of the Jewish people from the earliest days of history to the present than satanic vengeance against God himself? And I know how much the suffering of his chosen people must grieve God. As a parent, I suffer along with—maybe even more than—my children when they are threatened in some way. It's the same, I believe, with God and the Jewish people. Yes, God loves all of his children, but to Satan the Jews are symbolic. This is both a physical and a spiritual battle.

So what can we do? In the midst of this unstable and dangerous state of affairs, is there anything tangible that conservative women can do to make a difference?

SPEAK OUT AGAINST ANTI-SEMITISM

The most important and most direct step we can take is to address anti-Semitism on our own soil. We can't stand for the persecution of *anyone* based on their faith; as Christians, we know how crucial the freedom of religion is. We need to be aware of the anti-Semitism that is cropping up in our cities and towns and speak out against it. The BDS movement, for instance, is not a political statement; at its core, it is an anti-Semitic movement, and we ought to work to counter it. If your alma mater or your child's school has passed a divestment proposal or participates in any boycotting or censoring of Israeli academic institutions, write a letter to the president or board to alert them to the anti-Semitic underpinnings of this movement. James 2:20 reminds us that faith without works is useless. We must actively live out our faith by working against evil and those who would seek to persecute or discriminate based on religion or cultural background.

We must also speak out against anti-Semitism more globally. As Christians, we are called by God to stand against injustice, hatred, and evil. The passage by our Senate of the bill condemning anti-Semitism in Europe was an important step, and we need to continue to hear language like this from our leaders. The international community cannot remain silent, and neither can we, or history is destined to repeat itself. We should not think that because Jews are the ones being persecuted, we are not all at risk. The rising specter of radical ideology and global terrorism threatens us all, and persecution of Jews is only a harbinger of what's to come.

I'm reminded of the famous words spoken by the German pastor Martin Niemöller about the need to speak against evil, whether those who suffer share our beliefs or not:

> *First they came for the Socialists, and I did not speak out—*
> *Because I was not a Socialist.*
> *Then they came for the Trade Unionists, and I did not speak out—*
> *Because I was not a Trade Unionist.*
> *Then they came for the Jews, and I did not speak out—*
> *Because I was not a Jew.*
> *Then they came for me—and there was no one left to speak for me.*[45]

Niemöller, a Protestant pastor who opposed the Nazis, spoke these words as an indictment of the German people, particularly church leaders, who remained silent and effectively allowed the Nazis to persecute and murder millions. While it might sound dramatic to say it, we're facing a similar situation once again. None of us can afford to remain silent, or we may find ourselves left with no one to speak on our behalf when the evils of global terrorism and extremist ideology reach our doorstep.

STAND FIRM WITH ISRAEL

As Christians, we also have a particular duty to support Israel, a land and people that God loves. The Israelites are God's chosen people and always will be. We must reject the incorrect notion of replacement theology, which can slip into Christian communities without our even realizing it. And we must be active in affirming the right of Israel to exist in a region struggling under the encroaching darkness of radical extremism and religious intolerance. For as God promised Abraham, those who bless Israel and the Jewish people will be blessed, and those who curse them will be cursed (Gen. 12:3). It is in our best interest to support them, as God affirmatively promises to bless us if we do.

We also need to encourage nonbelievers to advocate for Israel. Whether one affirms the biblical basis for Israel or not, Americans recognize that it is a crucial strategic ally. Our ties with Israel are important for defense, security assistance, energy development, and cooperation in academics and business, among other things. Under the current administration, the relationship between the two countries has been strained to the breaking point. We must not stand for this any longer.

CWA took this stance in October 2014 when we hosted a Stand with Israel rally with Governor Mike Huckabee. During the war with Gaza in the summer of 2014, I watched the Palestinian student demonstrations and their threats to Jewish students. I kept waiting for Christians to rally on the side of Israel. Finally, I realized that God was calling *me* to respond. I knew that it would create a ton of work, and our CWA staff was already doing so much. So I laid a fleece before the Lord (Judg. 6:37). I said, "Lord, if you want me to do this, I need Mike Huckabee to agree to help!" Governor Huckabee was still doing his TV show, *Huckabee*, on Fox News at the time. I emailed the governor and said that I was thinking about doing a rally to give Christians an opportunity to respond and asked if he would be interested in helping.

Almost immediately, I received the governor's reply: a hearty "Let's do it!" *Okay, God*, I thought, *now I actually have to pull this off.*

Putting together an event on the National Mall is a lot of work and a lot of money I hadn't budgeted for, and getting people to show up is even harder. But Governor Huckabee was all in. He helped promote the rally on his show, and people responded. I was so proud to cohost an event in which several thousand, mostly young, Christians, along with some of our Jewish friends, linked arms and pledged to support Israel. People came from all over the nation, from as far as Iowa and North Dakota. Lee Greenwood showed up to sing, "God Bless the USA." In reporting on the rally, Jennifer Rubin of the *Washington Post* noted, "But in the sea of troubles [for Israel] there is a bright spot, namely the unflagging support for the Jewish state from American evangelicals."[46]

The proudest moment came for me at the end of the rally, when I was able to meet an elderly couple from Baltimore who are Holocaust survivors. They were accompanied by their beautiful granddaughter. Having been told they were in the audience, at the end of the event I called out to them from the stage and asked them to look around at all the Christians standing in support of Jewish people everywhere and pledged to them that they would never stand alone again. They were stunned. They had suffered so much at the hands of the Nazis, some of whom identified as Christians, and yet here we were finally getting it right. When we met face-to-face, they said to me, "We felt so loved. Thank you!" Step-by-step, I am working to answer my question from Yad Vashem.

As I saw that day on the National Mall, we can do this. We can't right the wrongs of the past, but we can work to do the right thing today, right now.

ADVOCATE FOR STRONG SUPPORT AND AID

We also need to encourage our government to get our policies right—particularly when it comes to foreign aid. This starts with increasing awareness about the countries that threaten Israel and about the dangers posed by groups like Hamas and Hezbollah. There is a lot of misinformation out there when it comes to Israel and its enemies, and being educated on this topic is important in order to bring about civil debate and encourage fellow Americans to advocate for strong support and aid to our ally.

The need to support Israel financially through foreign aid is critical. I realized this last year when I joined Yael Eckstein of the International Fellowship of Christians and Jews as we toured several military bases, including one referred to as the Lions of the North. This strategic base is staffed by Israeli Defense Forces, very young men and women whose job is to monitor the border with Lebanon for attacks against the Jewish state. These kids—well, eighteen- to twenty-five-year-olds, but I think of them as kids because many are the same age as my daughter—were so poised and resolute in their commitment to their nation. They are willing to die and know others who have died defending Israel's borders. They shoulder the tremendous responsibility of having about fifteen seconds to decide whether something they see on-screen is a missile, a commercial plane, a hijacked plane, or something else. The stakes are extremely high because they are near strategic ports and populated areas that I won't discuss further for security reasons. Remember, Israel has had ongoing conflict with Lebanon for decades, including two major wars in 1982 and 2006.

As part of my tour, I was shown the key to their safety, the American-developed-and-built Patriot missile system. A tactical air defense system, the Patriot missile system uses radar and long-range missiles to intercept and destroy enemy aircrafts and drones to protect Israeli civilians. The United States began supplying Israel with the Patriot system during the Gulf War, and we have collaborated with them since to develop a highly effective defense system.

I rounded the corner and there it was, an impressive, enormous apparatus that can take down very large threats. Seeing the missile system, I was proud of my own country's ability to innovate and create such impressive technology. However, essential defense systems like the Patriot system, or others like the Iron Dome (which protects civilians from short-range missiles and mortars) and David's Sling (which intercepts medium-to long-range threats), are very expensive. I was told by the IDF agent accompanying me that each Patriot system holds four missiles and that each missile costs Israel one million dollars.[47] Wow. Suddenly, what I already knew about foreign aid to Israel clicked in.

Despite what you may have heard, foreign aid is only 1 percent of the overall US budget, and Israel receives only 6 percent of that.[48] Of the roughly $3.1 billion they receive, at least 70 percent is invested back into the US economy by purchasing our goods, many of which are manufactured by the defense sector.[49]

Now, consider this. We are $18 trillion in debt in this nation, and $7.5 trillion of that has happened during the Obama Administration.[50] I am a fiscal hawk and strongly believe we have to get our financial house in order. However, our debt is mostly from entitlement spending (Medicaid, Medicare, and Social Security), not foreign aid. It's dishonest to suggest that we can't afford to continue to help support Israel with foreign aid. As we've seen, Israel is the only democracy in the region and an essential strategic partner in the Middle East; foreign aid there should be a no-brainer.

I joked when I left the base that if Congress tries to cut aid to Israel, I will chain myself to the Appropriations Committee door. I am only halfway kidding. We must not be penny wise and pound foolish with US resources. The money we spend helps both countries, which is not the case with many other nations.

On that note, we need to start speaking out against the millions of dollars our government sends to countries who support terrorism—countries like Pakistan, which has received almost $30 billion from the United States in direct aid in the past thirteen years.[51] Lifting sanctions on Iran will also likely free up more money to flow into the coffers of those who threaten and terrorize Israel and religious minorities in the Middle East, and our government needs to work with Israel regarding such concerns. We can't be aiding Israel with one hand while we indirectly support its gravest enemies with the other; that's ineffective and misguided.

As voting citizens of this nation, we need to demand that the administration adopt laws and policies that strengthen our relationship with Israel, not undermine it. That means advocating for things like foreign aid and strategic partnership acts. Most crucially, it means that we need to act to empower the right people. We need to vote for candidates who understand the significance of our relationship with Israel and who have a coherent view of our interests in the Middle East and the threat of Islamic terrorism. Weak leadership only allows room for our enemies to maneuver, and it threatens our nation as well as Israel. We need leaders with a clear plan and strong resolve, not haphazard policies and cloudy vision.

We aren't voiceless when it comes to this issue. There has always been strong bipartisan support for Israel in Congress, and it's important that we continue to encourage this. Congressmen across the aisle have championed to preserve our ties with our ally, something that benefits all Americans, and we can't be apathetic about using our voices to raise concerns about the direction the Obama administration has taken us. The unity I see on Capitol Hill when it comes to supporting Israel gives me great hope that our country will continue to prioritize this important relationship to make the Middle East and the world a safer and more democratic place.

Ultimately, Israel is a strategic partner and a moral ballast. And as Prime Minister Netanyahu stated in his speech before Congress last year, "The remarkable alliance between Israel and the United States has always been above politics. It must always remain above politics."[52] Our countries are bound by a commitment to peace, human rights, freedom, and democracy. As Christians, we are bound to the Jewish people by our shared heritage and faith in God. In a dark world that seems at times to be on the brink of spiraling into chaos, it is critically important that we stand with our allies in the face of evil. As Esther Women, we must raise our voices to ensure this happens.

Charmaine Yoest

PRESIDENT AND CEO, AMERICANS UNITED FOR LIFE (AUL)

Dr. Charmaine Yoest is a leading voice of the pro-life movement. She heads Americans United for Life, an organization that works through the law and legislation to stop abortion in our nation. AUL has been involved in every abortion-related case before the US Supreme Court since *Roe v. Wade* in 1973, and since Yoest took the helm in 2008, their wins have only continued to grow as they make gains in states across the country.

Dr. Yoest has always recognized the importance of political and social engagement in our nation. As a teenager, she went door-to-door for a Republican candidate for Congress, and after college she served in the White House under the Reagan administration. From there Dr. Yoest went to the Family Research Council, where she studied the breakdown of family in our country.

In 2008, Dr. Yoest took an even greater leap into the political realm, agreeing to serve as senior advisor to Mike Huckabee's presidential campaign. She and her husband took their children out of school to campaign across the country for a man who represented the conservative values and Christian morals our country desperately needed.

Following the campaign, Dr. Yoest joined AUL, where she has devoted herself to fighting for life for all human beings. Dr. Yoest has helped refine the AUL's mother-child strategy, which takes into account the well-being and interests of both the mother and the baby and seeks to protect both from the abuses of the abortion industry. A mother of five herself, Dr. Yoest knows the beauty and value of every human life, and her work in this arena is a testament to the power of conservative women when we refuse to be silenced.

CHAPTER 9

Seasons

Work, Family, Life, and the Art of Balance

As I stood before a room full of undergraduates, mostly young women, a pretty redhead sitting near the front raised her hand. The moment she began to form her question, I knew what was coming. This time I was in front of the Helms School of Government at Liberty University, but it's the same whether I'm talking to young women at other campuses, a group from the Network of Enlightened Women, or one of our Young Women for America college chapters. It happens so often that CWA staff call it "the question." The young woman looked at me and said, "So, Mrs. Nance, you're a mom and you are running the nation's largest women's public policy organization. How do you balance all of that?"

The subtext behind this question was the young woman's worry for her own future. She wants to know how on earth she is going to get her education, land her dream job, meet her dream man, get married, give birth to 2.5 children, cook healthy and delicious meals, stay in shape, earn a mom-of-the-year award, homeschool or volunteer at her kid's school, keep her husband happy, and enjoy her life, all while dressing fashionably. The answer is she's not. And Lord knows I can't either.

But here's the thing: if we can manage our own expectations, it becomes clear that women today are in a golden era. Never before have we had the opportunities and liberty to pursue the happiness that we currently enjoy. We have to get past the idea of finding a one-size-fits-all formula that works for every woman; not only are we all different, but frankly what works at one season in life won't work in another. We must instead look for fulfilling ways to serve God, our families, and our nation. At the end of the day, we are not what we do. We are so much more than that.

The Backstory

I've spoken in front of thousands of passionate and talented young women, but the truth is I am an unlikely role model. I grew up a pastor's kid. I was born in eastern Tennessee, and my family moved to Paintsville, Kentucky, population six thousand, when I was eight. My dad's church and the town were full of coal miners and kind people. Small-town life suited me just fine, but being a preacher's kid—well, that had its drawbacks.

I came to faith in Christ as a small child, and my relationship with God shaped my choices in life (that and the fact that in a small town, if you mess up, your parents know before you get home). I was a rules girl. I would have said I was saved by grace, but just in case I was going to earn God's love—and my dad's while I was at it—by being good. After a while that mindset gets exhausting. Because no matter how hard you try to be good, you can't, and you eventually get bogged down with a joyless faith that's a list of dos and don'ts.

My approach to life and faith began to change in college. I was blessed to go to Liberty University in Lynchburg, Virginia, thanks to scholarships and my parents' sacrificial generosity. What an amazing experience! I met people from all over the nation and the world. Many of my best friends today are friends I made at Liberty—intelligent, faithful women, like my lifelong friend Angel—who keep me accountable and are willing to say *anything* to me because they know all my stories and vulnerabilities.

At Liberty I was exposed to the idea that I had a world of possible career choices. Growing up, I had been offered the choice of teacher or nurse, which are both great professions, but I was not introduced to other options. But thanks to the intentional efforts of Liberty's founder, Jerry Falwell, now I was hearing from prominent female leaders like then-Secretary of Transportation Elizabeth Dole and ABC News religion correspondent Peggy Wehmeyer.

One woman in particular stood out to me: Beverly LaHaye, the president and founder of an organization I hadn't yet heard of called Concerned Women for America. Listening to her speak, I was captivated by her powerful words and message. I loved what she said about political activism based on prayer and action. I was already passionately pro-life, and I was thrilled to hear that a woman was leading an organization of other women fighting for the rights of babies. I immediately joined my campus's CWA club, a precursor to today's Young Women for America (YWA) chapters. Little did I know that Mrs. LaHaye would end up having an immeasurable impact on my life as my boss, mentor, and friend. At the time, I couldn't have planned any of that.

In fact, I wasn't planning to set the world on fire. It was only through a string of disappointments that I landed in Washington, DC, after graduation. That wasn't plan A. Plan A was a proposal from my college sweetheart, a job in public relations, and a quiet life in the suburbs.

Plan A was a bust.

My boyfriend unceremoniously dumped me, I couldn't find a PR job in Kentucky, and I was flat broke. Not Hillary Clinton broke, the kind of broke where you live on ramen noodles and pray you can make your share of the rent on your dingy apartment. The only job I could find was waitressing at Cracker Barrel. For the record, I am a horrible waitress. I was especially bad when it came to the morning breakfast shift. Other than being a mom, waitressing was the hardest work I have *ever* done. I have a deep respect for the men and women who earn their living waiting tables, but it wasn't what I had hoped to be doing.

No, things weren't looking rosy for me that first summer after graduation. It was at this point in my life, though, that I got serious with God. I was so tired of trying to earn his love. I felt like a failure. My personal life was in tatters, and my professional life wasn't panning out either. I got to the point where I just couldn't carry the burden anymore. I was exhausted, disappointed, and sad. It was then, at this lowest point of my young life, that I finally got it. All of those sermons on grace finally clicked.

I had always known that "it is by grace [we] have been saved, through faith—and this is not from [ourselves], it is the gift of God—not by works, so that no one can boast" (Eph. 2:8–9). I had known it intellectually, but somehow it hadn't seeped into my soul. I thought I could be good enough, even though I knew a holy and sinless God was the yardstick I was measuring myself against. I still wanted to work my way to heaven.

In the middle of what felt like my pitiful failure of a life, I was finally able to understand that God loved me and that Jesus died for me just as I was, just as I am. It's okay, I realized, that I am a mess—that we are all a mess. We are his mess. He died because we are broken, and he clothed us in his righteousness. What a relief!

It was after this belly-of-the-whale experience that things started to come together for me, but not through anything I did. God strung together events and people that landed me in Washington on Capitol Hill, and then as CWA's lobbyist in my twenties. If God can use me, a preacher's kid from Appalachia with no connections, no money, and little ambition to influence the nation's leaders, then he can use anyone. A life surrendered to God's plan is so much more exciting than anything we can concoct for ourselves. His plan gave me a husband who is my life's partner and children whom I adore. It gave me a career that I love. It gave me a calling.

It doesn't mean that I never have problems, nor does it mean that I won't suffer in the future. But it does mean that I have the unwavering assurance of God's mercy and love available to me—and so does anyone else who asks him for it. God has given an imperfect woman amazing opportunities, starting with the great nation to which I was born. I am so grateful.

Thank God, redemption isn't static either. It's ongoing and ever replenished. I ask for it often. But I know now that holiness isn't about rules. It's about joyful obedience. I still have to remind myself that God's plans are better than mine, even when I feel disappointment. But, oh, the joy and freedom of understanding grace!

You Are Not What You Do

It is with this backdrop that I come to the issue of career and family. As the young woman at Liberty pointed out with her question, the work-life balance for women today is incredibly difficult to manage, particularly in a world that pushes the notion that we can and should have it all. It's no longer enough to figure out what your career or calling is; we're now told we also have to do it perfectly while juggling everything else in life at the same time. I too have struggled with this false notion.

I am not even sure what having it all means. I have had many roles: single career woman, stay-at-home mom, volunteer, working part-time, working full-time. Each one has its own struggles, but it seems to me that '60s feminism created a myth of an inhuman superwoman predicated on the notion that we can and should have everything we want in our lives and careers simultaneously. That myth continues today and has piled up unmanageable pressure and unrealistic expectations for women.

Even in the Christian community, we bump up against this idea that we need to be able to do it all, inside the home and out, at church, and on the job. We beat ourselves up because we can't live up to the example of the woman in Proverbs 31, the "wife of noble character" every single day (v. 10). She is held up as an example of biblical womanhood, but can we admit that she's incredibly intimidating? She is an entrepreneur who contributes to her family financially by making and selling linen garments; she is a devoted mother and wife who "watches over the affairs of her household," and she still finds time to volunteer and "[extend] her hands to the needy" (vv. 27, 20). Seriously? How does she do it all? It's difficult for any of us to live up to the image of this ideal woman.

I think, though, that the key to the Proverbs 31 woman is found in the end of the passage: "A woman who fears the LORD is to be praised" (v. 30). She's praised or honored not only because of her work but also because she fears and loves the Lord. Everything she does points back toward him, whether she's working hard, serving her husband and kids, or helping the poor. In our culture today, we've lost sight of this idea and have elevated the appearance of being able to have it all above the reality of living humbly and devoting ourselves to whatever it is that most honors God. This only sets us up for failure. Esther Women, we need to rework this idea and reorient our mindsets.

Beverly LaHaye taught me years ago that there are seasons in life and that we should celebrate and enjoy them all to the fullest. We may not be able to live up to the world's standard of success, but so what? That doesn't mean we aren't successful. Success should not be judged by the size of one's paycheck. Life is long. Enjoy each stage, be productive, and glorify God in each one. We should strive to live a life of excellence, but we are not just what we do to earn a living.

This doesn't mean, of course, that what we do doesn't matter to God. God calls each of us to a vocation, whether that's being in the workforce, a stay-at-home mom, a missionary, or all three. Whatever the case, we should pursue that calling and seek to do it well.

Women in the Workplace

We each have a unique calling, but chances are at some point you will be working outside your home. Achievement in a career is important and admirable. However, that too must sit in proportion to everything else in our lives. Climbing the corporate ladder has taken on an outsized importance in our society, and keeping our jobs in proper proportion to the rest of our lives is often a huge challenge.

Yet women have many options today, from the kind of work we do to the level of leadership we achieve to the amount of time we spend at the office or working remotely. Women in the United States have made enormous strides in the last few generations, and if we step back and reassess, we may find that balance is more attainable today than it has ever been.

What do I mean? Well, let's start with the state of American women in the workforce. Believe it or not, I agree with Hillary Clinton on one point when it comes to this topic. At a conference in 2015, she stated that there has "never been a better time in history to be born female," and she's right—at least for females born in the United States.[1]

As "A War No More," a publication of CWA and the Beverly LaHaye Institute, perfectly sums it up, "Women from around the world come to the United States to pursue the American Dream—a concept that embodies freedom, liberty, and the pursuit of happiness along with the promise that those, including women, who are willing to sacrifice and work hard have virtually unlimited possibilities."[2] Almost 55 percent of those obtaining legal permanent residency in the United States in 2012 were women.[3] Our nation is by no means perfect, but women from all over the globe come expectantly and joyfully to our shores every year because they want something we take for granted: liberty.

Not only does our nation offer opportunity for women, it also offers a means of prosperity. Women today earn three times as much as their mothers did, and we are making more at every level of the economic spectrum.[4] We are becoming better educated as well: women today earn more undergraduate, graduate, and doctoral degrees than men.[5] Education is of course an essential building block to success for women.

Women also own more businesses than ever before. Between 1997 and 2014, the number of women-owned firms increased by 68 percent, and today there are an estimated 9.1 million women-owned businesses in the United States. During that same period, revenues of women-owned firms also increased, by a whopping 72 percent.[6]

My own family history speaks to the advancement of women we've seen in this country. My maternal grandmother had little education and supported nine children through factory work. My mother dropped out of school at sixteen and married my father. However, she eventually graduated from community college after getting her GED. Both my mother and my grandmother worked hard and made better choices than women in generations before them. As a result, in two generations I was able to rise from abject poverty to relative influence and affluence. And this is not an atypical story in our nation.

Debunking the Wage Gap: We Are Not Victims

We have so many opportunities in the workforce, yet women are often still told that we've got to run ourselves ragged and forego balance in order to break through the glass ceiling. Why?

Part of the reason work-life balance is difficult to achieve is because our society places so much weight on the financial success of one's career. For women, this has been particularly difficult because of the claim that we are underpaid compared with men and the notion that we have to work twice as hard to get to a level playing field.

The ubiquitous statistic that women earn seventy-seven cents for every dollar men earn is a compelling story that points to systemic discrimination against women. The problem is that it's untrue. In reality, in our twenties women are paid better than men—by eight cents on the dollar.[7] And overall, 72 percent of women say they have about the same opportunities to advance to top executive and professional positions in their companies as men.[8] We are now as likely as men to be company managers.[9]

Now, it is true that on average men earn more than women, and they also hold a greater number of executive positions.[10] Yet this wage gap is usually not the product of workplace discrimination but rather is the product of the choices and needs of both women and men. Here's a radical thought: women are different than men, and our priorities, demands, and career paths differ in most cases because of our own choosing. When we take into account things like education, hours worked, industry, experience, and career choice, the wage gap disappears.

Rather than pitting men and women against each other and using simplistic numbers to suggest that women are victims, we ought to acknowledge these differences and embrace the choices we make, understanding the different salaries that may result.

For instance, most women today prefer not to work full time while their children are growing up.[11] This decision naturally slows our workplace trajectory and can decrease our wages when we do return, particularly when you take into account that only 40 percent of women who take time off for children re-enter full-time work.[12] Women also work fewer hours than men on average—thirty-five minutes less per day than men among full-time workers—often due to the fact that mothers voluntarily provide more time at home caring for children.[13] I understand this desire to be home with our children; the bond of motherhood is the strongest emotion I have ever experienced. Feminism refuses to acknowledge and validate this option.

Additionally, women are more likely to be teachers and men are more likely to work in finance.[14] Women also tend to choose jobs that offer more regular hours and greater flexibility—jobs that can accommodate the demands of raising children and managing other familial demands, but which may pay less.[15]

We don't all have to be on a path to the Fortune 500. I am so encouraged by the fact that as women gain greater opportunities in the workplace, they are choosing to enter careers that interest them, even if many of these careers have lower earnings over the long run. We absolutely should encourage girls in the fields of science, technology, engineering, and mathematics (STEM). In the past there has not been enough emphasis on this opportunity, and we can do better. I also believe that it should still be their choice. Perhaps more opportunities for girls and boys at the elementary school level will orient more women toward these fields, but for now we must acknowledge that women's career choice is a factor that affects the wage gap—and that giving women choice without guilt isn't a bad thing.

As long as women recognize the financial implications of their career choices, I say, "Good for them!" No one should choose a career based on money alone. There's not enough money in the world to compensate for a job you hate. I encourage women to choose a career they love, as long as it's honest work and pays the bills. They should also look at all their options. We often limit ourselves.

Now, all of this is not to say that some fields are still difficult for women to break into or that there aren't bad bosses. Humans are still sinful, and therefore discrimination against women does still exist. However, Title VII of the Civil Rights Act of 1964 and the Pregnancy Discrimination Act have given us recourse in the courts and act as a deterrent to unfair employers. CWA recently filed an amicus brief in support of a woman who was discriminated against by UPS because of her pregnancy, and she won. We have legal recourse, and we should use it if we are wronged—including and perhaps especially when it comes to sexual harassment. I experienced sexual harassment in one job as a twentysomething, and it was disgusting and humiliating. I was highly employable and therefore sought and got another job, but sexual harassment is intolerable. Our daughters should never have to put up with that nonsense—and thankfully they don't have to. We are blessed in this country by equal protection under the law, something women in much of the world can still only dream about.

Overall, the insistence on a wage gap and on widespread discrimination against women is sometimes used by feminists to perpetuate the notion that patriarchy prevents us from attaining career success and equity with men. Victim bating is politically profitable for feminists, but it simply doesn't hold up. While choices we make about motherhood, work hours, and industry sectors may hinder our corporate-track momentum or stall our wages for a period of time, they are also opening up avenues to a work-life balance that is manageable and allows us to flourish.

And Then Come the Kids

Of course, regardless of the avenues open to us as women in the United States today, entering the workforce, blue or white collar, is hard. But you know what's even harder than simply working? Being a working mom.

According to a 2013 Pew Research Study, 56 percent of women find balancing work and family very or somewhat difficult to do.[16] I know this firsthand. Balancing my family and work has been a constant effort, and I don't always get it right. Just when I think I have it all together, *bam*, I get blindsided by life. Thank God for a 100 percent supportive husband, kind friends, and forgiving children.

One of my most scatterbrained working-mother incidents has gone down as a family legend. I had so much going on at this time in my life: I was sleep deprived and working part-time, my husband was running for state senate, my parents were coming to visit, and the kids had homework and activities I was desperately trying to support. Needless to say, I was a bit distracted. One afternoon, with a few minutes to spare before dinner, I ran by the car wash with my kids. We hopped out while the car was washed and dried and then jumped back in and zoomed up the road. About ten minutes later my cell phone rang. "Hello?" I answered, and then felt my heart jump into my throat. It was my son's voice on the other end.

"Mom, where are you?"

What? In a panic I looked into the back seat, trying to get my mind around the fact that he wasn't there. "Where are *you*?" I stumbled.

"You left me at the car wash," he said, slowly and patiently, as if explaining it to a small child. I told him I would be right there and wheeled my car around. I couldn't believe this. Not only had I left my nine-year-old son at the car wash, but I hadn't even noticed until he called me. To be fair, my daughter was in the front seat too, and she was no help in this regard. But still, how had I done this? I beat myself up all the way back. Is he going to be scarred for life? Should I call James Dobson for some family counseling as soon I get him in the car? *I am a bad, bad mother* rang in my head.

I broke the speed limit and was soon skidding into the car wash parking lot. I jumped out and raced, shamefaced, past the men who had dried my car earlier. They were polite enough to look down, but I could hear them snickering. And no wonder—what kind of a crazy woman forgets her own child? I breathlessly flung open the door to the waiting area, and there he was: my sweet son, sitting on the counter eating a lollipop, grinning from ear to ear at my discomfort.

Even now I'm a little embarrassed at my mistake, but the good news is my son was not, of course, scarred for life. In fact, he still likes to tease me about it. It's funny in hindsight, but at the time it was both terrifying and demoralizing—I felt like a failure as a mother. The reason I share this story is to say that all moms make mistakes, and we have to acknowledge that child rearing is incredibly challenging.

I can remember how, as a single woman, I used to judge moms. I'm not proud of that, but I did. I would walk by in my dry clean–only suit and matching stiletto pumps and wonder why they looked so haggard. I would think, *Fix yourself up, sister.* I specifically remember thinking how tidy the kids looked compared with the mom. Don't worry, I figured it out eventually and got a huge dose of humility to boot.

One day after having kids of my own, I was in the grocery store with my four-year-old daughter and three-month-old son. We were in line to pay, and I saw a twentysomething professional woman in the next line over, looking at me with disapproval. Suddenly, I saw myself through her eyes. I had bags under my eyes from lack of sleep, spit-up on my shoulder, my hair was a mess, I hadn't lost all my baby weight, and I was scolding my daughter for grabbing candy without asking. *Oh no*, I thought, *I've become that woman.* Of course I had! Motherhood is the absolute hardest job in the world, and I was exhausted. It got easier, and I'm so grateful for those years at home, especially now that my oldest is off to college. But let's be honest: moms deserve a medal for just keeping their sanity some days.

The reality is that we simply can't do it all when it comes to working and raising kids. There aren't enough hours in the day or energy drinks in the world to fuel us to meet the demands of work, our children's schedules, our husbands' needs, and every other family obligation without something giving way. Sometimes, as in my incident at the car wash, that something is our parenting. Sometimes it's our work products. Sometimes it's our marriages. Whatever the case, if we try to be everything to everyone while balancing work, life, and family all at once, cracks start to show up quickly.

Flexible Work Options and Career Choices

So how can we attempt to find balance? It starts with promoting flexible workplaces that take into account the realities of life for women of all stations and career paths. We need work environments that allow women choices in thoughtfully raising children, pursuing outside interests, and maintaining a balanced life. Generous flex-time plans, job sharing, telecommuting, and other innovative arrangements are important pieces of the puzzle.

These options are good for both the employee and the employer: a Boston College study has shown that greater workplace flexibility and a work-family balance results in higher employee job satisfaction, performance, and productivity, which benefit the employer as well.[17]

I was blessed to have some of these options available to me during my career. For thirteen years while my children were young, I was either at home full-time, or I worked about ten to fifteen hours per week. I am so grateful for this opportunity, which isn't available to everyone, particularly low-income women. We need to see such opportunities expanded to encompass more women; one of the things we support at CWA is legislation to amend the labor code to allow for flexible arrangements and to encourage rather than restrict work opportunities for women. Private industry should be able to enjoy the same flexibility currently allowed for federal employees.

At the same time, we need to oppose government overreach. While cottage industries and small businesses have traditionally been areas where women have had success in shaping creative and flexible work options, government regulation and burdensome oversight is decreasing these options. Regulation costs and high taxes are crushing entrepreneurs in this country. This is bad for business, and with women owning nearly 30 percent of all small businesses in the United States today, anything that hurts business hurts women.[18]

Finding What Works for You

Increased flexibility is great, but we still have to decide for ourselves what works best for us and our families. For those of us who are married with kids, when it comes to choosing the best way to balance our lives, work, and families, everyone seems to have an opinion. But only you and your husband know your situation and your family's needs. If you're a mother, God has given you the amazing responsibility of raising your children to the best of your ability. You have to answer that calling, and sometimes you've got to ignore what everyone else has to say.

I experienced this outside pressure firsthand. When I became pregnant unexpectedly with our first child, my husband and I were discussing how we would manage to pay our bills and care for our baby. A well-intentioned man from our church came up to me unsolicited to suggest that I should immediately quit work and be at home full-time from day one with our daughter. He was the father of three kids, all of whom were homeschooled by his wife. They were great kids, but even so I was a little taken aback by his presumption. He waxed eloquent about the importance of living on one income.

This man meant well, but in our case he was wrong. Will's and my annual incomes were exactly the same, and both of us worked for ministries, so neither made all that much. If I had stopped working, our household income would have been cut in half. But this man didn't know our situation (and frankly, it was none of his business). And neither do all these other people know yours. You and your husband must decide for yourselves how God is leading you to raise your family. There is no one-size-fits-all solution.

What's essential, however, is that selfish ambition isn't taking precedent over the needs of our kids. God gives us children as a gift to steward for his purposes. The Bible tells us to bring our children up "in the training and instruction of the Lord" (Eph. 6:4). This means that as your children's parents, you are responsible before God for their health and safety, education, and most important, their spiritual upbringing.

Of course, we have to be realistic when it comes to these decisions. One parent staying home isn't an option for every couple. I am always encouraged by how incredibly resourceful moms are in helping to provide for their families and putting their children's well-being first. I recently met a homeschool mom who works the graveyard, eleven-to-seven shift two nights per week in order to stay home with her children. Other women have taken to working remotely early in the morning or late at night so they can get away to pick up their kids from school. Some, like a friend of mine who's a successful doctor, may elect to have their husbands stay at home for a time. Some women rely on the help of family members or outside childcare to fill in the gaps. For all of us, the calculation is different.

When Will and I were first grappling with how to best pay our bills and care for baby Claire when she was born, I tested the waters, mostly to see what Will would say, by suggesting that I go back to work and he stay home. He at least seemed to consider it, but I was the one who shot down the idea when he suggested he could rehab and flip old houses on the side and take Claire along. I had a mental picture of him sanding or painting with Claire on his back in a baby Bjorn, overcome by fumes. I pointed out to him that when a person stays home to care for children, the kids *are* the job. I wasn't so sure he could do it right, which is to say the way *I* would do things. So after crunching the numbers, together we decided that Will would stay fully employed at Prison Fellowship Ministries and that I would go to part-time employment. Thankfully, CWA agreed to let me scale back my hours.

After Will and I made the decision, I felt great. All the baby stuff had been purchased, the nursery was arranged, and the work situation was organized. Done and done. Except it wasn't as neat and tidy as I thought. I could not have known how much motherhood would change my life. I thought that everything would stay neatly compartmentalized: at work I would be super lobbyist, and at home I would be super mom. It was a perfect plan, but, naturally, it didn't work perfectly. I dreaded going back to work when my maternity leave ended, and during those first months back, I couldn't stop worrying about how Claire was doing at home. It didn't take long to realize that I simply would never be the same person I had been before having kids. I lasted six months before resigning and beginning a consulting business that gave me an even more flexible schedule and enabled me to work from home.

Like it or not, motherhood changes everything. The way we respond to that change is different for each of us, and there is no single right answer. We have to decide for ourselves what best promotes a healthy balance for us and for our families.

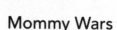

Mommy Wars

There are so many different ways women can choose to structure their lives and work in an effort to find balance, and we should encourage women to find what works for them. Yet this view is not widely embraced by our society. Many people who claim to be all about choice support only other people who choose what they want them to choose. This hypocrisy is particularly obvious when it comes to women choosing to leave the workforce to become stay-at-home moms.

Certainly, as we've discussed, this is a choice that is only available to women of certain economic means, but unlike what feminists would have you believe, they often aren't rich women. According to a 2012 Pew Research Center study, "relatively few married stay-at-home mothers [with working husbands] would qualify as highly educated and affluent." In fact, the study found that only 5 percent of stay-at-home moms had at least a master's degree and family income exceeding $75,000.[19]

In my personal experience, these are more often families who are financially intentional and are willing to sacrifice luxuries in order for Mom or Dad to spend a season at home. This was certainly true for Will and me early on. I couldn't spend a dime without really thinking about it. We were careful in how we allocated our money and in deciding how long I would work from home to be with our children.

Today, more and more women are choosing to stay at home, at least for a time. That same Pew study found that in 2012, 29 percent of all women were stay-at-home moms, a 6 percent increase from the year before. This was a reversal from the last three decades of the twentieth century, when the number of women who didn't work outside the home steadily decreased.[20]

Yet even as more women today are choosing to stay at home, feminists continue to look down on this decision as somehow indicative of not working hard enough or not being able to balance life well. In 2012, Democratic strategist Hilary Rosen said publicly that Ann Romney, whose husband was running for president at the time, had "never worked a day in her life," despite the fact that she raised five sons while encouraging Mitt's career in business and politics. Mrs. Romney responded, "My career choice was to be a mother . . . [It's] obviously an awesome responsibility to raise children. It's, to me, the most important thing we can do."[21]

And she's right. No one's going to give you a bonus or an award, but I promise you some day you will look back with a sense of satisfaction. I truly believe that Mom is the best job title there is. Stay-at-home moms don't need to apologize to *anyone* for their choices. I know you sometimes get dismissed at parties where everyone is enamored by job titles. I know that sometimes the snooty neighbor doesn't treat you with respect. But guess what? I have been there, and you don't need to give a rip. At the end of the day you get to tuck in a beautiful child who you know you did your best for. When that short window closes and they are gone, you will have no regrets. I have a few regrets about the days I left and went to Capitol Hill, but I have *none* about the days I didn't. Don't let anyone talk down to you. You have my unwavering respect and support in the public arena. There is no such thing as "just a mom."

The Single Mother

Before I go any farther, I need to make a critical point: the very idea of balance is a luxury—one that isn't available to a great number of women. When we consider work and family through the lens of single mothers, particularly single mothers in poverty, the equation changes dramatically. If we want all women to flourish and find balance, we need to recognize the challenges single women face and be willing to help them do something about it.

Most women don't choose to become a single mom. It happens for a number of reasons, including being widowed or deserted. But the fact of the matter is that single motherhood limits women's opportunities and goals. The burdens they shoulder are enormous, and unfortunately, for many this situation often leads to poor outcomes for them and their children. This isn't judgment; it's just the sad reality.

Almost half of all households run by a single mother with children under eighteen are in poverty (47.2 percent)—more than four times higher than households headed by married couples.[22] Government assistance has done nothing to alleviate the poverty associated with single women; women who grow up in homes on welfare, a 2002 study showed, are three times as likely to receive welfare as adults.[23]

For many single mothers trapped in poverty, the opportunities America offers women seem hard to access and even harder to achieve. Yet stable workplace opportunities can make all the difference. When single mothers have a full-time, year-round job, the poverty rate for such families falls to 14 percent.[24] Giving women the skills and training they need to pursue these jobs and move away from reliance on welfare benefits—through measures like vocational education programs—will dramatically increase their financial situations and benefit their children as a result.

This can best be achieved through programs run not out of Washington but rather closest to those in need. Local and state governments are better able to gauge need and success, and CWA has long advocated block-granting funds to the states. But we also need the church and other organizations to step up. We should encourage better organized church and community programs that can provide financial and parenting advice, job-skills training and career resources, and low-cost childcare. Helping single moms is essential for all communities to thrive.

What Can Esther Women Do?

For single women or married ones, those with children or without, those in big corporate careers or at home, here's the bottom line: we can't and won't be able to do it all. When it comes to career, family, motherhood, and the many other demands life places on us, we're not going to get everything right. But that doesn't mean that we can't still flourish. As I discovered when I entered the real world after college, our best-laid plans often don't succeed. But if we let go of society's insistence that our worth comes from what we do and instead surrender ourselves to the plan God has put before us, we might find that balance is possible after all.

So then, what does work-life balance look like for Esther Women today? It's different for all of us. We have to learn how to wisely and prayerfully discern what to pursue, what to sacrifice, and how best to honor God with our choices about work and family. There are a few pieces of practical advice, though, that can help guide us in this ever complicated area.

BE ROOTED IN GOD

When God is first in our lives, everything else—our jobs, our children, our volunteer work—is reduced to its proper proportion, rather than demanding an outsized place. Saint Augustine talked about "rightly ordered love," in which God holds the highest place in our hearts, and everything is secondary to our love for him. If anything takes that primary place in our lives, our loves become disordered, and we lose any sense of balance. Everything we do should be to God's glory, and if we are elevating our careers—or anything else—above the desire to please God, it's time to reassess.

As the Proverbs 31 woman was praised for her fear of the Lord, so should we be. This means carving out time to be with him—even in the midst of our busiest seasons. We cannot bear fruit if we aren't being nourished with the Word. Jesus himself showed the importance of spending time with God in order to gain strength and perspective for our work life. In Mark 1:35, we see him spending time with the Lord before he sets out to continue his ministry—the work to which God called him: "Very early in the morning, while it was still dark, Jesus got up, left the house and went off to a solitary place, where he prayed."

Even Jesus, the Son of God, set aside time for God our Father. It can look different for all of us, but whether it's in the morning, using a Bible app during your lunch break, in the car, or before you head to bed, it's critical to set aside time where we can allow God to fill us with his wisdom, reorient our hearts, and give us perspective on how we're balancing our lives so that they continually point back to him.

BE ROOTED IN CHURCH AND COMMUNITY

Work-life balance is *hard*. We all know that. So why do we try to muddle through it on our own? We can only succeed in balancing all the demands of life if we have others there to support us and help pick up the slack when we can't. We need to be connected to the community around us, particularly the Christian community, and we need to be willing both to ask for help when we need it and to offer help to others.

Galatians 6:2 tells us, "Carry each other's burdens, and in this way you will fulfill the law of Christ." As Christians, we have a built-in support network. I have seen women reach out to struggling or single moms and dads in such loving ways. One of my friends has cared for a family in which the wife suffers from clinical depression. This woman can't get out of bed some days, and my friend helps the woman's husband to make sure their daughter has everything she needs. It is a beautiful picture of the love of God expressed in community. I had similar women around me growing up. They were angels who filled the gaps in caring for me when my own mother struggled with clinical depression.

And I'm still relying on that kind of support. I so appreciate it when other moms give my kids rides, help out when media calls last minute, or give me a heads-up when there's a school function on the horizon that I somehow missed placing on my calendar. They are the room moms when I can't be or an encouragement to me when I am feeling overwhelmed. I couldn't do it without them, and any amount of success I obtain is in part theirs.

Supporting one another also means that we must be open and transparent about the difficulties we've faced searching for balance along the way. The more honesty we can bring to this conversation, the less women will feel pressure to stay in a job they hate or pretend they have it all together when really they're crumbling inside. Only when we start to speak up about the struggle to find balance will the myth of having it all finally be put to rest. And more important, we can minister to the mom who is on the brink.

COMMIT TO A SUPPORTIVE HUSBAND, AND PRIORITIZE STRONG COMMUNICATION

When we decided that I should take time off from work after Claire was born, Will and I realized the necessity of honest and prayerful dialogue with each other. It's a must when it comes to questions of work-life balance. There may be some tears and disagreement in the discussion, but these conversations have to happen. You're in this together, and you need to be able to sort through your family's specific situation with the only other person who gets it. Girlfriends, colleagues, pastors, and others can help give advice, but ultimately, these decisions come down to what you and your husband believe before the Lord will best serve your family.

If you're not yet married but hope to be someday, I encourage you to seek a husband with whom you can have this kind of dialogue. Although I may not agree with everything she writes, Sheryl Sandberg has it right in her book *Lean In* when she says, "The single most important career decision that a woman makes is whether she will have a life partner and who that partner is."[25] Wow, I couldn't agree more. I know that Paul said it's better to remain single (1 Cor. 7:8), but after all the time I have spent in an office full of young women and with our Young Women for America members, I know that the majority of young women do hope to marry. In fact, that's true across the political spectrum—84 percent of young women view marriage as important or very important to their life plans.[26] So for you single women out there, if you desire to marry, choose a man who loves God and respects how God made you.

Sandberg said, "I don't know of a single woman in a leadership position whose life partner is not fully—and I mean fully—supportive of her career."[27] I know that's true for me. Will's support is essential to my career and my work-life balance, and I hope I've provided that same support to him. As a married couple, you are one, and therefore your calling is your husband's calling and his is yours. You must be on the same team, or there will be major struggles. For this reason, it's important to look for a man who isn't intimidated by you or who would ever want to dim the light God placed in your heart.

A young, very talented woman who used to work for me had to break up with her boyfriend because he was jealous of her. He was bothered by the attention she received from her job as a spokesperson. Instead of being proud of her after her first TV appearance, he picked a fight. She told me that she realized how messed up their relationship had become when she overheard one of my phone calls in which Will was praising me (probably too generously) after a TV debate. She saw what it looked like to have a spouse who supports you and is proud of your gifts and calling. She wisely decided to wait for that kind of man. God knew who and what I needed, and he knows what you need too.

KNOW YOUR WORTH

When it comes to shaping a flexible work-life balance that works for us, we have so many options. Being aware of the various flex-time and tele-commuting options available to you, and recognizing the value you bring to your employer, can often enable you to find an arrangement that works for both sides. Liberal MSNBC morning show host Mika Brzezinski makes this point well in her book, *Knowing Your Value*: "If you don't ask for what you deserve, you won't ever find out what you're made of and what you can truly do. You undermine yourself by not developing your tools and learning what to do with them."[28] I agree. We need to recognize our value and the tools at our disposable, and put them to work for us in the marketplace.

Institutional knowledge and expertise has given women the opportunity to write their own tickets in many instances. In every job I have taken since I gave birth to my first child, I have negotiated up front the flexibility to put my kids' needs first. At CWA I work from home on Fridays. I leave work to go to soccer or lacrosse games. I can take my child to the doctor. I can even pay to bring them on a work trip with me. I certainly have it better than many, but you'll never know unless you ask. There are many options out there, and if you ask for what you need and make a good case for your value to the company, you may be able to negotiate something that works for you both.

Partly due to the years I spent at the front end of my career getting an education and then working hard to achieve success, I had developed expertise and a track record that gave me the options I have described above. I advise young women still looking for Mr. Right or without children to consider, as Sandberg puts it, to "lean in" hard at the beginning of their working lives in order to achieve advancement that will give them options later. Of course, that doesn't mean you have no social life or time for ministry. Again, we are talking about balance, not burn out.

SAVOR THE SEASON YOU'RE IN

We can't do it all at once. As Ecclesiastes 3:1 reminds us, "There is a time for everything, and a season for every activity under the heavens." God gives us opportunities both to serve and to lead, but many of those opportunities don't happen at the same time. We have to make choices, and different times will call for different responses. Some seasons we may be at home with children, some we may be working part-time or full-time, some we may be traveling or taking a sabbatical. But we must savor each season as its own, finding joy and delight in the place God has put us at that moment.

If you're in a season as a stay-at-home mom, savor every minute you have with your kids. The precious time we have with our children during those early years is irreplaceable, and there is no higher calling than to love, enjoy, and pour into our children the knowledge and love of God.

If you're in a season of working outside the home, enjoy the beauty of pursuing your vocation. Work enables us to thrive, to express ourselves and honor God through the gifts he's given us, and to bless and benefit others. As the Proverbs 31 woman shows us, it is a privilege to "work vigorously" and provide for our families, and we shouldn't lose sight of the simple pleasure of work.

If you're in a season of struggling with the question of family balance and taking time off to raise children, think in terms of what pleases God, not what pleases people. Seek God's counsel in this area. Does he want you to stay at home for a season? If so, he will provide the means. If and when you feel called to go back to work, embrace that role rather than feeling guilty or intimidated. It will take you time to come back once the little ones leave, but you can come back. I have witnessed smart women returning to the workplace, taking some time to ramp back up to successful careers.

Working full-time after having kids probably means something else gives, like time with friends or other routines—and for certain seasons, that's okay. Show yourself grace. Acknowledge that as you struggle to balance work and family you are going to make mistakes as a parent, slip up at your job, and not get everything done around the house. Children and husbands can do chores too. We are imperfect people, and we will never have it all together, no matter how hard we try. So cut yourself a little slack.

Ultimately, none of us has all the answers when it comes to the question of work-life balance. But by making God the center and realizing that there are seasons in life, we can begin to find perspective and move toward a more sustainable mode. Sure, some of us will probably still leave our kids at the car wash, but at the very least we can find the grace to admit that we've all been there and to acknowledge that finding balance is difficult. It is going to take intentional effort from all of us to erase the myth that we can be superwomen with amazing careers, perfect children, ideal marriages, and spotless homes. We can't—and you know what? That's just fine.

Representative
Cathy McMorris Rodgers

US REPRESENTATIVE FOR THE FIFTH CONGRESSIONAL DISTRICT OF WASHINGTON

Representative Cathy McMorris Rodgers is chair of the House Republican Conference, making her the fourth highest-ranking Republican in the House, and the highest-ranking woman in Congress. She has been in the House since 2004 and knows a thing or two about pursuing your potential.

Rep. McMorris Rodgers grew up in rural Washington and was the first of her family to graduate from college. "If you had told me as a little girl that one day I would . . . be sworn in as the 200th woman to serve in the House of Representatives, I never would've thought it possible," she has said.[29] But her parents taught her the value of education, working hard, and saving for her future. She took advantage of the opportunities our nation offered and refused to quit. Today, her voice helps shape the policies and direction of our country.

But she didn't just create a better future for herself; she also created one for her children. The congresswoman is a working mom with three kids, including her son Cole, who has Down syndrome. Her family comes first, but with her husband she has found ways to balance motherhood while also serving her country. These experiences have informed her work to fight for legislation offering all women more flexibility and options in the workplace.

Rep. McMorris Rodgers exemplifies the political leadership of conservative women. She serves on the Health Subcommittee, where she has worked hard to fight the skyrocketing costs and bureaucracy of Obamacare. In 2014, she delivered a brilliant Republican response to the State of the Union, one of the few women to ever do so. A role model for faithful, feminine conservatives, she is leading the movement toward a stronger and more hopeful future.

CHAPTER 10

A Vision for the Future

W hen I was in sixth grade, I memorized all the words of Helen Reddy's feminist anthem, "I Am Woman." Grinning ear to ear, I sang every line with pure enthusiasm: "I am woman, hear me roar." Little did my innocent childhood self realize that the women who embraced this anthem would one day refuse my own right to its message of female strength and victory, all because I declined to buy in to their feminist myths.

Like many other women, as I grew up, I found my voice and my views marginalized. Today, we live in an increasingly liberal and secular society, and conservative women are too often painted as two-dimensional caricatures, church ladies who don't get the real needs of women or the changing social dynamics of America.

But this representation is simply untrue. We are a dynamic, diverse group with unique experiences as business leaders, politicians, mothers, wives, doctors, teachers, and thousands of other roles. As we've seen over the course of this book, we have a lot to contribute to the national conversation on a wide range of topics, and we insist on speaking truth. Many on the left want to marginalize us into silence, but we can't allow them to do so.

The truth is that liberal politics have not made things better for women or for our country. In fact, for the first time since Gallup started asking the question, American parents say that they no longer believe their children will inherit as much opportunity as they have enjoyed in our great nation.[1] This and other cultural indicators—like the decline of marriage, staggering numbers of abortions, rate of sexual violence against women, and ever-increasing threats from abroad—suggest that our nation is in trouble.

If we have any hope of reversing the trend, brave women (and men) must be willing to step into the public square and challenge the status quo. We've got to push back against the prevailing trends in our country to make our voices heard. We've got to push back on the ways that our liberal culture has failed women and our nation, and we need to offer a new narrative—one that starts with informed, engaged, and empowered conservative women.

The Power of a Conservative Woman

Despite the scornful contempt we often receive from the media and liberal culture, conservative women are making waves, and women are rallying around those who speak truth. Conservative women candidates prevailed in local and state elections in 2010 and 2014 and are likely to do so again. There are more than one hundred women in Congress for the first time in history, and while conservative women remain outnumbered, we are steadily gaining traction. More of us are finding our voices than ever before. Within government and in the private sector, in minority communities and in local platforms, powerful female conservative leaders are emerging across all demographics.

As the profiles of FemCos—feminine conservatives—I've included throughout this book have shown, we have a diverse heritage of talented, intelligent, thoughtful, and persistent women whose leadership and vision have helped change culture and minds. From the transformative work of Beverly LaHaye and the foundation of CWA to the many incredible conservative role models in the public arena today—pro-life champions like Jeanne Mancini, Day Gardner, Marjorie Dannenfelser, Charmaine Yoest, and Lila Rose; political powerhouses like Rep. Cathy McMorris Rodgers and Rep. Vicky Hartzler; inspiring young women on college campuses like Emily Dukes and Crystal Macias—there are so many women to whom we can look for vision and leadership, and who we can be proud to work beside.

And the profiles in this book represent a small fraction of the influential female conservatives all around us. In CWA alone we have hundreds of thousands of Esther Women leading the way for the conservative movement.

Conservative women are clearly not monolithic; in fact, we are anything but. We need to stop letting the other side define us in oversimplified and false terms, and the only way to do that is to take control of the narrative ourselves.

As we've seen over the past nine chapters, the challenges facing our nation today are immense. From a culture thrown into disarray by pornography, abortion on demand, and the loss of the sanctity of marriage, to the international perils of global terrorism, radical extremism, and the violations of women's human rights, we are surrounded by issues that demand action. As educated, faithful conservative women, we can't afford to sit on the sidelines. We've got to stand up, find our voices, and speak truth about the things that matter most. We won't be marginalized because of our beliefs or values any longer; we must use them to become empowered. As my childhood anthem states, "We know too much to go back and pretend." Hear us roar!

From Inspiration to Action

There is so much we can do if we put our minds to it. God has gifted each of us with unique talents, ideas, and passions, and it's our duty to use them in service of him and our great nation. There are approximately sixty million evangelical and faithful Catholic women in this nation. If we choose to engage in an issue, we *can* effect change.

So let's engage. As Beverly LaHaye laid out clearly in the vision of CWA, engagement starts with three things: prayer, education, and action. Regardless of where we live, whether we work inside the home or out, whether we're married or single, whether we feel like we have a platform to stand on or we're just talking to the women in our book clubs, each one of us can follow these steps and together make our voices heard and inspire change.

It starts with prayer. Without being grounded in the Lord, we're not going to get anywhere. "Unless the LORD builds the house, they labor in vain" (Ps. 127:1 NKJV). Only he can truly change hearts and minds, and we must bring our concerns before him. If we do so, he will give us the wisdom about how to move forward, and he will use us to fulfill his purposes. "The prayer of a righteous person is powerful and effective" (James 5:16).

Education is the second critical piece. We've got to be informed about the important issues that threaten the values of our nation, the safety of our borders, and the future of our children. CWA publishes material intended to equip women to stay informed and to engage in the culture and challenges around us. I encourage you to subscribe to our alerts (see www.concernedwomen.org) in order to be kept informed of how you can make a difference. Follow the news, talk to people around you, and stay aware of the changes being made in Washington that affect us all.

Proverbs 24:5 tells us that "the wise prevail through great power, and those who have knowledge muster their strength." As we become more informed, we become more effective agents of change.

And finally, take action. As we've seen throughout this book, there are so many ways to get involved on a wide range of issues. Following the suggestions I've offered in each chapter, I hope you are inspired to act, whether by advocating for changes in public policy; raising awareness about issues through film screenings or passing out fliers in your church; writing a letter to the editor of your local paper; or even beginning a conversation with others who don't share your views.

Even more important, vote. If you are not registered to vote, do so today. If conservative women would vote our values, we could swing an election any way we wanted. Women have carried every presidential election since 1964.[2] How can you be too busy for that?

If you haven't already, I hope you'll begin or join a Concerned Women for America chapter too. We have four hundred adult chapters and twenty college chapters as of the writing of this book. CWA trains effective leaders, and we would love to invest in you.

Action also means supporting financially the organizations you believe in. Although the left is bankrolled by the taxpayer, the vast majority of Christian or conservative organizations don't receive any government grants. If individuals aren't led to give, such organizations wither away. Good conservative organizations need more women like Hannah More, a member of eighteenth-century abolitionist William Wilberforce's praying Clapham group and his major donor. She was a woman of means, and she changed the world through her philanthropy. Maybe you are called to give.

Made for Such a Time as This

Esther Women, God is calling you to act in some way. Whether you are engaging with your neighbor next door or your congressman in Washington, you can trust that the Lord will give you the ability to act and speak effectively. Take heart in his promise to Moses, "Now go; I will help you speak and will teach you what to say" (Ex. 4:12). You are not just doing this for yourself. You are doing this for your children and grandchildren, your nieces and nephews. And you are doing it for the glory of God.

Remember, God can work through every single one of us, and he gives us the tools to be effective. If I ever doubt this truth, I only have to recall something I saw my mother do when I was a little girl that set an example for me for the rest of my life. In the 1970s, my dad was a Free Will Baptist pastor in Tennessee. It's not a huge denomination, but every year a few thousand Free Will Baptists, mostly pastors, get together to set church policy and to network at their annual association meeting. This particular year, it was in Atlanta, Georgia. I was young and happy to be allowed to come, but quickly tired of the long meetings and sermons. I perked up, though, because of the excitement in the room for the keynote speaker that night. The governor of Georgia, Lester Maddox, was coming to address the group. I didn't really know what that meant, but everyone else seemed honored and excited he was there so I figured it must be a big deal.

I have no idea what Lester Maddox said to the group, but at the end everyone gave him an enthusiastic standing ovation. Everyone that is, except one person: my mother. She refused to stand. She sat quietly with her arms folded in silent protest of a man she clearly didn't like.

It wasn't until the tense ride home that I understood what had happened. Lester Maddox, I discovered, was a staunch segregationist who barred African Americans from eating at the restaurant he owned. As governor, he even barred Dr. Martin Luther King Jr. from lying in state in the Georgia Capitol rotunda. My mother couldn't applaud a man like that, she said.

I was amazed. Her small act of defiance was so out of character. My mother was a meek and shy pastor's wife. She never wanted attention, and she *never* wanted to embarrass my father. But she also had an immense amount of compassion for the weak. She suffered from a lack of confidence in herself, but still managed to find small ways on several occasions to make her voice heard on civil rights. She was never going to be one of those people holding signs and protesting, nor would anyone have supported her if she did. In fact, none of the women she knew even had opinions on such matters, or at least never discussed them in polite conversation. But in her heart she knew what was right, and in that ballroom in Atlanta, Georgia, she found the courage to sit in silent protest of a man whose idea of Christianity was an anathema to her.

It cost her something, believe me. My dad was very unhappy at the show of disrespect for the governor. Yet I can remember my mother saying, "There was no way I was standing for that man, and no one else should have either. He took an ax handle and wouldn't allow those students to come into his restaurant. I don't care what anyone thinks. I couldn't stand up for him." It wasn't that my father agreed with Maddox; he hated racism and would call people in his churches out for it. He successfully and intentionally broke racial barriers in worship and in our family's friendships. It was just that he was embarrassed to make a scene. But my mother fully wanted to make a scene, and in that moment found her voice.

And once I understood, I was proud. Although no one else may have been paying attention to it, I was. My mother was an Esther Woman that night. It wasn't long before my dad and eventually the entire denomination came around to my mother's view, but she led the way. Her small act of defiance was incredibly powerful, and God used her in that moment to begin to bring about change.

Esther Women, this is your chance to find your voice. In whatever sphere of influence the Lord gives you, you can choose to be a light for the things that are right and true.

It's okay if not everyone loves you for it. It's okay if people stare or say harsh things. This chapter in our nation's history is too important. Too much is at stake.

In a call to the church to stand up against the Nazis, Dietrich Bonhoeffer once said, "Silence in the face of evil is itself evil: God will not hold us guiltless. Not to speak is to speak. Not to act is to act." Today, our nation faces a tipping point. In the past decade, we've seen moral decline at an unprecedented rate, while at the same time the threats outside of our borders are rising perilously. The only way we will see change emerge is if we decide to take action, and do so with the help of our heavenly Father.

Esther Women, you are too smart, too talented, too capable of changing the world to sit back and let others define you. You are too valuable to remain on the sidelines. Your voice is needed in our culture today. Join with me to move forward in service of God's truth and his will for our nation. You were made for such a time as this.

Acknowledgments

My journey as an advocate began when I was four and used Mom's coffee table as a podium to give "sermons" to my dolls and stuffed animals. It was nourished at my family's dinner table listening to my dad opine on the news of the day and praise President Reagan. It was elevated sitting in my dad's church and living in a community of the kindest people on earth in Paintsville, Kentucky.

The late Jerry Falwell Sr. and my time at Liberty University encouraged my interest in public policy and affirmed my ability as a Christian woman to make a difference in the world. When I was a young bride, my husband's boss—and later my boss—the late Chuck Colson, encouraged my activism and refined the intellectual underpinnings of my biblical worldview.

However, the most influential person in my journey from the mountains of Appalachia to Washington is my friend and mentor Beverly LaHaye. I walked into CWA as a twentysomething with plenty of passion, but little focus. Mrs. LaHaye's example of resolute leadership and unwavering courage were formative. Her spiritual encouragement along with an atmosphere that fostered growth and creativity at CWA were transformational. Her vision and faithfulness changed the face of the conservative movement in the United States and opened doors to women like me and many other strong female voices. We stand on her shoulders. I hope to continue to honor her legacy in my work.

I am grateful to the hundreds of courageous volunteer leaders and thousands of members at Concerned Women for America. I am honored to speak on their behalf. It is an immense privilege to represent such talented and inspiring women.

The idea to write this book germinated over many years but came to fruition only through the experienced guidance and encouragement of my agent, Lisa Jackson, Alive Communications. She believed in a first-time author, helped me find the incredible team at Zondervan publishing (special thank-you to Sandy Vander Zicht and Tom Dean). Lisa also introduced me to an incredibly bright and talented young research and writing assistant, Keely Latcham Boeving. We all may be working for Keely someday. I have discovered that a book project, like most successful endeavors, is a team effort, and I have had a fabulous team.

Clearly, none of what I do professionally could be possible without the unwavering support of my husband of twenty years, Will Nance. Thank you, Will, for all the times you picked up the slack or encouraged me to live my calling. Thank you for giving me guiltless space and time to write, travel, or do that inconvenient weekend TV interview.

Finally, I am above all grateful to Jesus, my Savior, for redemption, daily grace, and mercy as I attempt to live out my faith as a broken woman in a broken world. The liberal critics will hate this book and me for writing it, but I play to an audience of one. My prayer is that this book will not sit on shelves but be marked up and dog-eared. I pray that women all over this nation will tear out pages, pop them into their purses, and study them in carpool lines at their kids' schools, at Starbucks, or between classes. My prayer is that conservative women will find their voices once again.

Notes

CHAPTER 1: FEMININE CONSERVATIVES FACE AN ESTHER MOMENT

1. "Gender Differences in Voter Turnout," Center for American Women and Politics, May 2014, http://cawp.rutgers.edu/sites/default/files/resources/genderdiff.pdf; Mark J. Perry, "Stunning College Degree Gap: Women Have Earned Almost 10 Million More College Degrees Than Men Since 1982," *Carpe Diem* (blog), American Enterprise Institute, May 13, 2013, https://www.aei.org/publication/stunning-college-degree-gap-women-have-earned-almost-10-million-more-college-degrees-than-men-since-1982/.

2. The 2014 State of Women-Owned Businesses Report, Commissioned by American Express OPEN, March 2014, http://www.womenable.com/content/userfiles/2014_State_of_Women-owned_Businesses_public.pdf.

3. Susan K. Urahn and Travis Plunkett, "Women's Work: The Economic Mobility of Women Across a Generation," *Pew Charitable Trusts*, April 2014, http://www.pewtrusts.org/~/media/legacy/uploadedfiles/pcs/content-level_pages/reports/2014/womensworkreporteconomicmobilityacrossagenerationpdf.pdf.

CHAPTER 2: THE DEVALUATION OF WOMEN

1. Michelle Lewsen, "A Letter to My Children About Fifty Shades of Grey," *Scary Mommy* (blog), accessed October 25, 2015, http://www.scarymommy.com/a-letter-to-my-children-about-fifty-shades-of-grey/.

2. "Fifty Shades of Grey" *Box Office Mojo*, accessed October 25, 2015, http://www.boxofficemojo.com/movies/?page=daily&id=fiftyshadesofgrey.htm.

3. "Estimated National Expenditures for Domestic Violence Services and Programs: Special Report," Stop Abusive and Violent Environments, January 2011, http://www.saveservices.org/downloads/Estimated-National-Expenditures-for-Domestic-Violence.

4. "Rihanna on Chris Brown: 'We Know Exactly What We Have Now,'" *Rolling Stone*, January 30, 2013, http://www.rollingstone.com/music/news/rihanna-on-chris-brown-we-know-exactly-what-we-have-now-20130130.

5. Mary Eberstadt, "Jailhouse Feminism," *National Review*, February 19, 2015, http://www.nationalreview.com/article/414022/jailhouse-feminism-mary-eberstadt.

6. Ibid.

7. Gail Dines, *Pornland: How Porn Has Hijacked Our Sexuality* (Boston: Beacon Press, 2010), 100.

8. Ibid., 102.

9. Laura Ingraham, "The Pornification of America," *Power to the People* Book Tour, Hilton DFW Lakes Executive Conference Center, Dallas, Texas, September 28, 2007. The phrase, now widely used in discussions of pornography's presence in our culture, may have first gained traction with Pamela Paul in her 2005 book, *Pornified: How Pornography Is Damaging Our Lives, Our Relationships, and Our Families* (New York: Times Books, 2005).

10. Statistic taken from Trillia Newbell, "The Secret Women's Porn Problem," *Christianity Today*, October 23, 2013, http://www.christianitytoday.com/women/2013/october/secret-womens-porn-problem.html.

11. "Fifty Shades of Grey Beats One Million Sales Record," BBC News, June 28, 2012, http://www.bbc.com/news/entertainment-arts-18618648.

12. A. Bridges et al., "Aggression and Sexual Behavior in Best-Selling Pornography Videos: A Content Analysis Update," *International Communication Association*, October 26, 2010, http://media.virbcdn.com/files/79/FileItem-273118-AgressionandSexualBehavior2010.pdf.

13. Y. Gahyun and D. Yang, "Effects of Exposure to Pornography on Male Aggressive Behavioral Tendencies," *The Open Psychology Journal*, no. 5 (2012):1–10. See also: G. M. Hald, N. M. Malamuth, and C. Yuen, "Pornography and Attitudes Supporting Violence against Women: Revisiting the Relationship in Nonexperimental Studies," *Aggressive Behavior*, no. 36 (2010): 14–20.

14. Norman Doidge, *The Brain That Changes Itself: Stories of Personal Triumph from the Frontiers of Brain Science* (New York: Viking, 2007).

15. Jennifer P. Schneider, "Effects of Cybersex Addiction on the Family: Results of a Survey," *Sexual Addiction and Compulsivity*, no. 7 (2000): 31–58, http://www.jenniferschneider.com/articles/cybersex_family.html.

16. Jean Kilbourne, *Can't Buy My Love: How Advertising Changes the Way We Think and Feel* (New York: Simon and Schuster, 1999), 133.

17. Bryan L. Wilcox et al., "Report of the APA Task Force on Advertising and Children," *American Pschological Association*, February 20, 2004, http://www.apa.org/pi/families/resources/advertising-children.pdf.

18. "Eating Disorders Statistics," *National Association of Anorexia Nervosa and Related Diseases*, accessed October 25, 2015, http://www.anad.org/get-information/about-eating-disorders/eating-disorders-statistics/.

19. Rebecca L. Collins, Steven C. Martino, and Rebecca Shaw, "Influence of New Media on Adolescent Sexual Health: Evidence and Opportunities," US Department of Health and Human Services, April 15, 2011, http://aspe.hhs.gov/hsp/11/AdolescentSexualActivity/NewMediaLitRev/.

20. Rebecca N. Dick et al., "Cyber Dating Abuse Among Teens Using School-Based Health Centers," *Pediatrics*, September 10, 2014, http://pediatrics.aappublications.org/content/early/2014/11/12/peds.2014-0537.

21. "Planned Parenthood of the Rocky Mountains," *SexEd: Dangerous Sex Advice for Kids* video, Live Action Undercover, July 15, 2014, http://plannedparenthoodexposed.com/sexed/.

22. Diane E. Levin and Jean Kilbourne, *So Sexy So Soon: The New Sexualized Childhood and What Parents Can Do to Protect Their Kids* (New York: Ballantine Books, 2009), 10.

23. "Report of the APA Task Force on the Sexualization of Girls," American Psychological Association, 2010, http://www.apa.org/pi/women/programs/girls/report-full.pdf.

24. Levin and Kilbourne, *So Sexy So Soon*, 6.

25. Ruben C. Gur et al., "Sex Differences in Temporo-Limbic and Frontal Brain Volumes of Healthy Adults," *Cerebral Cortex*, no. 12 (2002): 998–1003, http://cercor.oxfordjournals.org/content/12/9/998.full.

26. Laura A. Pratt, Debra J. Brody, and Gu Quiping, "Antidepressant Use in Persons Aged 12 and Over: United States, 2005–2008," National Center for Health Statistics Data Brief, no. 76, *Centers for Disease Control and Prevention*, October 2011, http://www.cdc.gov/nchs/data/databriefs/db76.pdf.

27. Betsey Stevenson and Justin Wolfers, "The Paradox of Declining Female Happiness," *American Economic Journal: Economic Policy* 1, no. 2: (2009): 190–225, https://www.aeaweb.org/articles.php?doi=10.1257/pol.1.2.190.

28. Erick Erickson, "You Will Be Made to Care," *Red State* (blog), March 29, 2013, http://www.redstate.com/2013/03/29/you-will-be-made-to-care/.

29. Lila Rose, email interview with author, July 13, 2015.

CHAPTER 3: SEXUAL ASSAULT AND POLITICS

1. While the widely cited "one in five women will be sexually assaulted in college" appears in the White House Task Force Report of April 2014, this statistic has been questioned by many. Work by Mark Perry of the American Enterprise Institute suggests something closer to one in thirty-two women. Regardless of the exact number, it is undeniably happening

far too often. See "Not Alone: The First Report of the White House Task Force to Protect Students from Sexual Assault," White House Task Force to Protect Students from Sexual Assault, April 2014, https://www.whitehouse.gov/sites/default/files/docs/report_0.pdf.

2. "Sexual Violence on Campus: How Too Many Institutions of Higher Education Are Failing to Protect Students," a report prepared by the US Senate Subcommittee on Financial and Contracting Oversight—Majority Staff, July 9, 2014, http://www.mccaskill.senate.gov/SurveyReportwithAppendix.pdf.

3. Richard Pérez-Peña and Ian Lovett, "California Law on Sexual Consent Pleases Many but Leaves Some Doubters," *New York Times*, September 29, 2014, http://www.nytimes.com/2014/09/30/us/california-law-on-sex-consent-pleases-many-but-leaves-some-doubters.html.

4. Ibid.

5. Jake New, "The 'Yes Means Yes' World," *Inside Higher Ed.*, October 17, 2014, https://www.insidehighered.com/news/2014/10/17/colleges-across-country-adopting-affirmative-consent-sexual-assault-policies.

6. Jed Rubenfeld, "Mishandling Rape," *New York Times*, November 15, 2014, http://www.nytimes.com/2014/11/16/opinion/sunday/mishandling-rape.html.

7. Mona Charen, "What the Left and Right Don't Get about Campus Rape," *The Federalist*, August 31, 2015, http://thefederalist.com/2015/08/31/what-the-left-and-right-dont-get-about-campus-rape/.

8. "Questions and Answers on Title IX and Sexual Violence," United States Department of Education, Office for Civil Rights, April 29, 2014, http://www2.ed.gov/about/offices/list/ocr/docs/qa-201404-title-ix.pdf.

9. Emily Yoffe, "College Women: Stop Getting Drunk," *Slate*, October 15, 2013, http://www.slate.com/articles/double_x/doublex/2013/10/sexual_assault_and_drinking_teach_women_the_connection.html; Lori Adelman, "'Dear Prudence' Columnist Publishes Rape Denialism Manifesto Advising Women to 'Stop Getting Drunk,'" *Feministing*, October 16, 2013, http://feministing.com/2013/10/16/emily-yoffe-aka-dear-prudence-publishes-rape-denialism-manifesto-tells-women-point-blank-to-stop-getting-drunk-to-avoid-rape/.

10. Emma Brown, Steve Hendrix, and Susan Svrluga, "Drinking Is Central to College Culture—and to Sexual Assault," *Washington Post*, June 14, 2015, http://www.washingtonpost.com/local/education/beer-pong-body-shots-keg-stands-alcohol-central-to-college-and-assault/2015/06/14/7430e13c-04bb-11e5-a428-c984eb077d4e_story.html.

11. Shannon Gupta, "Universities Struggle with Curbing Sexual Assaults on Campus," Fox News, April 30, 2014, http://www.foxnews.com/us/2014/04/30/universities-struggle-with-curbing-sexual-assaults-on-campus/.

12. Amanda Marcotte, "Taekwondo Is Great but Not the Solution to Campus Rape," *XX Factor: What Women Really Think* (blog), *Slate*, June 9, 2014, http://www.slate.com/blogs/xx_factor/2014/06/09/miss_usa_on_campus_sexual_assault_nia_sanchez_a_black_belt_in_tae_kwon_do.html.

13. "'Trigger Warnings' and 'Safe Spaces' When Conservative Speaks on Campus," *Fox News Insider* (blog), April 21, 2015, http://insider.foxnews.com/2015/04/21/trigger-warnings-and-safe-spaces-when-conservative-christina-hoff-sommers-speaks-campus.

14. This was a common refrain from Chuck Colson. For a comprehensive view of his position, see Charles W. Colson, "Crime and the Cure of the Soul," *First Things*, October 1993, http://www.firstthings.com/article/1993/10/001-crime-and-the-cure-of-the-soul.

15. "Rape and Sexual Assault: A Renewed Call to Action," the White House Council on Women and Girls, Report, January 2014, https://www.whitehouse.gov/sites/default/files/docs/sexual_assault_report_1-21-14.pdf.

16. Richard A. Oppel Jr., "Ohio Teenagers Guilty in Rape That Social Media Brought to Light," *New York Times*, March 17, 2013, http://www.nytimes.com/2013/03/18/us/teenagers-found-guilty-in-rape-in-steubenville-ohio.html.

17. "FY 2014 OVW Awards by Program: Stop Violence against Women," United States Department of Justice, 2014, http://www.justice.gov/ovw/awards/fy-2014-ovw-grant-awards-program#20.

18. "Accountability and Oversight of Federally Funded Domestic Violence Programs: Analysis and Recommendations," Stop Abusive and Violent Environments, Special Report, August 2010, http://saveservices.org/pdf/SAVE-Accountability-and-Oversight.pdf.

19. Janice Shaw Crouse, "A Bad Law on Life Support," *American Thinker*, March 5, 2012, http://www.americanthinker.com/articles/2012/03/a_bad_law_on_life_support.html.

20. Monica Vendituoli, "Funding Alone Can't Change How Sexual Assault Is Handled On Campus," *FiveThirtyEightLife* (blog), November 10, 2014, http://fivethirtyeight.com/features/funding-alone-cant-change-how-sexual-assault-is-handled-on-campus/.

21. John Nolte, "Investigation: Lena Dunham 'Raped by a Republican' Story in Bestseller Collapses Under Scrutiny," *Breitbart*, December 3, 2014, http://www.breitbart.com/big-hollywood/2014/12/03/investigation-lena-dunhams-republican-rapist-story-falls-apart-under-scrutiny/.

22. "Rape and Sexual Assault," White House Council on Women and Girls.

23. "Profiles in DNA: Debbie Smith," National Center for Victims of Crime, 2012, http://www.victimsofcrime.org/our-programs/dna-resource-center/profiles/debbie-smith.

24. Ibid.

25. "The SAFER Act of 2012: Section by Section Analysis," prepared by the Office of Senator John Cornyn, May 8, 2012, http://www.cornyn.senate.gov/public/?a=Files.Serve&File_id=320d1eac-9cc3-40be-8111-27c2eb151ce6.

26. "Senate Report 112-078," Departments of Commerce and Justice, and Science, and Related Agencies Appropriations Bill, September 15, 2011, http://www.gpo.gov/fdsys/pkg/CRPT-112srpt78/pdf/CRPT-112srpt78.pdf.

27. Mike DeWine and Timothy J. McGinty, "Ohio Leads the Way on Breaking Through the Rape Kit Backlog," *Washington Post*, July 6, 2014, https://www.washingtonpost.com/opinions/ohio-leads-the-way-on-breaking-through-the-rape-kit-backlog/2014/07/06/81f4f4de-03ae-11e4-8572-4b1b969b6322_story.html.

28. Justin S. Holcomb and Lindsay A. Holcomb, *Rid of My Disgrace: Hope and Healing for Victims of Sexual Assault* (Wheaton, IL: Crossway, 2011), 21.

29. "Rape and Sexual Assault," White House Council on Women and Girls.

30. "Binge Drinking on College Campuses," Center for Science in the Public Interest, December 2008, http://www.cspinet.org/booze/collfact1.htm.

31. Antonia Abbey et al., "Alcohol and Sexual Assault," National Institute on Alcohol Abuse and Alcoholism, accessed October 26, 2015, http://pubs.niaaa.nih.gov/publications/arh25-1/43-51.htm.

32. Emily Dukes, email interview with author, July 14, 2015.

CHAPTER 4: MARRIAGE AND TRUE TOLERANCE

1. Bill Maher called Sarah Palin this word during a performance in Dallas. Later, he defended it on his show and went on to call her a "dumb twat." Jeff Poor, "Report: Bill Maher Doubles Down—Calls Sarah Palin the 'C' Word," *Daily Caller*, March 29, 2011, http://dailycaller.com/2011/03/29/report-bill-maher-doubles-down-calls-sarah-palin-c-word/.

2. Penny Nance, "The Bitter Irony of the Day of Silence," *Breitbart*, April 10, 2015, http://www.breitbart.com/big-government/2015/04/10/the-bitter-irony-of-the-day-of-silence/.

3. Laura Stampler, "*Duck Dynasty* Star Compares Gay People to 'Drunks,' 'Terrorists,' and 'Prostitutes,'" *Time*, December 18, 2013, http://entertainment.time.com/2013/12/18/duck-dynasty-star-compares-gay-people-to-drunks-terrorists-and-prostitutes/.

4. Sheela Kennedy and Steven Ruggles, "Breaking Up Is Hard to Count: The Rise of Divorce in the United States, 1980–2010," *Demography*, no. 51 (April 2014): 587–98.

5. "American Householders Are Getting Older, Census Bureau Reports,"

United States Census Bureau, November 15, 2012, https://www.census.gov/newsroom/releases/archives/families_households/cb12-216.html.

6. Based on Pew Research analysis of the March 2013 Current Population Survey. See Wendy Wang and Kim Parker, "Record Share of Americans Have Never Married: As Values, Economics and Gender Patterns Change," *Pew Research Center*, September 24, 2014, http://www.pewsocialtrends.org/2014/09/24/record-share-of-americans-have-never-married/#fn-19804–3.

7. Joyce Martin et al., "Births: Final Data for 2013," *National Vital Statistics Reports* 64, no. 1 (January 15, 2015), http://www.cdc.gov/nchs/data/nvsr/nvsr64/nvsr64_01.pdf; "A War No More: The Truth Behind the 'War on Women,'" a publication of Concerned Women for America and the Beverly LaHaye Institute, 2015, http://www.cwfa.org/wp-content/uploads/2015/02/War-on-Women.pdf.

8. Molly Young, "He & He & He," *New York Magazine*, July 29, 2012, http://nymag.com/news/features/benny-morecock-throuple/.

9. *Obergefell v. Hodges*, 576 US (2015) (Roberts, J,. dissenting).

10. "The Decline of Marriage and Rise of New Families," a Social and Demographic Trends Report, *Pew Research Center*, November 18, 2010, http://www.pewsocialtrends.org/files/2010/11/pew-social-trends-2010-families.pdf.

11. Brigid Schulte, "I Do? No Thanks. The Economics behind America's Marriage Decline," *Washington Post*, September 24, 2014, http://www.washingtonpost.com/news/storyline/wp/2014/09/24/i-do-no-thanks-the-economics-behind-americas-marriage-decline/.

12. Taken from the site's homepage, "Ashley Madison: Life Is Short. Have an Affair," www.ashleymadison.com, accessed October 27, 2015.

13. Joel Hruska, "New Analysis Shows Over 99 Percent of the Women on Ashley Madison Were Fake," *Extreme Tech*, August 27, 2015, http://www.extremetech.com/internet/213019-new-analysis-shows-over-99-percent-of-the-women-on-ashley-madison-were-fake.

14. Nathan McAlone, "There Were Only 3 ZIP Codes in America without Any Ashley Madison Accounts—Here They Are," *Business Insider*, August 25, 2015, http://www.businessinsider.com/the-only-three-zip-codes-in-america-without-ashley-madison-accounts-2015-8.

15. "Expert: 400 Church Leaders Will Resign This Sunday Because Names Surfaced in Ashley Madison Hack," *Relevant*, August 27, 2015, http://www.relevantmagazine.com/slices/expert-400-church-leaders-will-resign-sunday-because-names-surfaced-ashley-madison-hack.

16. John Piper, "Marriage: A Matrix of Christian Hedonism," *Desiring God*, October 16, 1983, http://www.desiringgod.org/sermons/marriage-a-matrix-of-christian-hedonism.

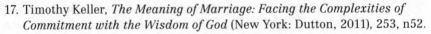

17. Timothy Keller, *The Meaning of Marriage: Facing the Complexities of Commitment with the Wisdom of God* (New York: Dutton, 2011), 253, n52.

18. Matthew Spalding, "A Defining Moment for Marriage and Self-Government," Center for Principles and Politics at The Heritage Foundation, March 8, 2013, http://www.heritage.org/research/reports/2013/03/redefining-marriage-how-changing-the-definition-of-marriage-affects-the-civil-society. See also Sherif Girgis, Ryan T. Anderson, and Robert P. George, *What Is Marriage? Man and Woman: A Defense* (New York: Encounter Books, 2012).

19. Timothy Biblarz and Greg Gottainer, "Family Structure and Children's Success: A Comparison of Widowed and Divorced Single-Mother Families," *Journal of Marriage and Family* 62, no. 2 (May 2000): 533–48; Cynthia C. Harper and Sara S. McLanahan, "Father Absence and Youth Incarceration," *Journal of Research on Adolescence* 14, no. 3 (2004): 369–97.

20. Robert Rector, "Marriage: America's Greatest Weapon against Child Poverty," Heritage Foundation, September 25, 2012, http://www.heritage.org/research/reports/2012/09/marriage-americas-greatest-weapon-against-child-poverty.

21. Barack Obama, "Father's Day Remarks (speech)," Apostolic Church of God, Chicago, IL, June 15, 2008, Transcript from *New York Times*, http://www.nytimes.com/2008/06/15/us/politics/15text-obama.html.

22. All statistics taken from Heritage Foundation's FamilyFacts.Org. "Benefits of Family for Children and Adults," accessed October 27, 2015, http://familyfacts.org/briefs/6/benefits-of-family-for-children-and-adults. Research based on "The Importance of Family Dinners II," National Center on Addiction and Substance Abuse at Columbia University, September 2005, http://casafamilyday.org/familyday/files/themes/familyday/pdf/Family-Dinners-II.pdf; and Scott J. South, Dana L. Haynie, and Sunita Bose, "Residential mobility and the onset of adolescent sexual activity," *Journal of Marriage and Family* 67, no. 2 (2005): 499–514.

23. Jamie Bryan Hall, "The Research on Same-Sex Parenting: 'No Differences' No More," Heritage Foundation, April 23, 2015, http://www.heritage.org/research/reports/2015/04/the-research-on-same-sex-parenting-no-differences-no-more. Based on research by Donald Paul Sullins, "Emotional Problems among Children with Same-Sex Parents: Difference by Definition," *British Journal of Education, Society and Behavioural Science* 7, no. 2 (January 25, 2015): 99–120.

24. Judith Wallerstein, Julia Lewis, and Sandra Blakeslee, *The Unexpected Legacy of Divorce: The Twenty-Five Year Landmark Study* (New York: Hachette, 2001), xxxv.

25. Heather Barwick, "Dear Gay Community: Your Kids Are Hurting," *The Federalist*, March 17, 2015, http://thefederalist.com/2015/03/17/dear-gay-community-your-kids-are-hurting/.

26. For further background on *DeBoer v. Snyder*, see "DeBoer v. Snyder (6th Circuit)," Constitutional Accountability Center, accessed October 27, 2015, http://theusconstitution.org/cases/deboer-v-snyder.

27. Ted Olsen, "N.M. Supreme Court: Photographers Can't Refuse Gay Weddings," *Christianity Today*, August 22, 2013, http://www.christianitytoday.com/gleanings/2013/august/nm-supreme-court-photographers-cant-refuse-gay-weddings.html.

28. Todd Starnes, "Why Does the Government Consider This Grandmother Public Enemy No. 1?" Fox News, February 19, 2015, http://www.foxnews.com/opinion/2015/02/19/why-does-government-consider-this-grandmother-public-enemy-no-1/; Sarah Larimer, "Colorado Court Rules against Baker Who Refused Same-Sex Marriage Cake Order," *Chicago Tribune*, August 15, 2015, http://www.chicagotribune.com/news/nationworld/ct-colorado-baker-same-sex-marriage-cake-20150815-story.html; Kelsey Harkness, "Here's How Religious Business Owners Could Protect Themselves against Gay Marriage Decision," *Daily Signal*, June 30, 2015, http://dailysignal.com/2015/06/30/heres-how-religious-business-owners-could-protect-themselves-against-gay-marriage-decision/.

29. David French, "The Persecution of Gordon College," *National Review*, February 2, 2015, http://www.nationalreview.com/article/397677/persecution-gordon-college-david-french.

30. Sarah Torre and Ryan T. Anderson, "Adoption, Foster Care, and Conscience Protection," Heritage Foundation, January 15, 2014, http://www.heritage.org/research/reports/2014/01/adoption-foster-care-and-conscience-protection#_ftn29.

31. Monica Davey, Campbell Robinson, and Richard Pérez-Peña, "Indiana and Arkansas Revise Rights Bills, Seeking to Remove Divisive Parts," *New York Times*, April 2, 2015, http://www.nytimes.com/2015/04/03/us/indiana-arkansas-religious-freedom-bill.html.

32. Network Indiana, "Pro-RFRA Pizza Shop Owners Shut Down, Supporters Donate," *Indiana Public Media*, April 3, 2015, http://indianapublicmedia.org/news/antigay-pizza-shop-owners-shut-raising-500k-80269/.

33. Bobby Jindal, "I'm Holding Firm against Gay Marriage," *New York Times*, April 23, 2015, http://www.nytimes.com/2015/04/23/opinion/bobby-jindal-im-holding-firm-against-gay-marriage.html.

34. Michelle Faul, "Men Attacked by Anti-Gay Mob in Nigeria," *Washington Post*, February 15, 2014, https://www.washingtonpost.com/world/africa/men-attacked-by-anti-gay-mob-in-nigeria/2014/02/15/1c313e5c-967e-11e3-9616-d367fa6ea99b_story.html.

35. Polly Mosendz, "Report: ISIS Documents Killing of Gay Man in Mosul," *Newsweek*, January 16, 2015, http://www.newsweek.com/report-isis-documents-murder-gay-man-mosul-300246.

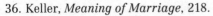

36. Keller, *Meaning of Marriage*, 218.

37. Owen Strachan spoke of the gospel's call to activism on a panel we participated in together at the National Religious Broadcasters' 2015 International Christian Media Convention. See "Protecting Marriage: How to Get the Media Message Right for This Generation," National Religious Broadcasters' 2015 International Christian Media Convention, Nashville, TN, April 1, 2015. Available at https://www.youtube.com/watch?v=MsMQVH4DOVg.

38. Hannah Wegman, "YWA President Calls El Paso Churches to Action," *Concerned Women for America* (blog), July 15, 2015, http://www.cwfa.org/ywa-president-calls-el-paso-churches-to-action/.

39. Crystal Macias, email interview with author, July 20, 2015.

CHAPTER 5: ABORTION AND THE SANCTITY OF LIFE

1. William Buckley, ed., *Issues in Adoption* (Farmington Hills, MI: Greenhaven Press, 2004), http://www.demes.teimes.gr/spoudastirio/E -NOTES/I/Issues_in_Adoption_Viewpoints.pdf.

2. Sharon Vandivere and Karin Malm, "Adoption USA: A Chartbook Based on the 2007 National Survey of Adoptive Parents," US Department of Health and Human Services, Office of the Assistant Secretary for Planning and Evaluation, November 1, 2009, http://aspe.hhs.gov/hsp/09/NSAP/chartbook/chartbook.cfm?id=1; Keith Riler, "Thirty-Six Couples Wait for Every One Baby Who Is Adopted," *Life News*, July 9, 2012, http://www.lifenews.com/2012/07/09/thirty-six-couples-wait-for-every-one-baby-who-is-adopted/.

3. "Abortion Statistics: United States Data and Trends," National Right to Life Educational Foundation, 2012, http://www.nrlc.org/uploads/factsheets/FS01AbortionintheUS.pdf.

4. "Induced Abortion in the United States: Fact Sheet," *Guttmacher Institute*, July 2014, http://www.guttmacher.org/pubs/fb_induced_abortion.html.

5. Marjorie A. England, "What Is an Embryo?" in *Life Before Birth* (London: Mosby-Wolfe, 1996).

6. "Pro-Life Action Guide: Upholding Truth, Protecting Life," *Concerned Women for America*, January 2001, http://www.cwfa.org/wp-content/uploads/2013/11/pro-life.pdf.

7. Pam Belluck, "Premature Babies May Survive at 22 Weeks If Treated, Study Finds," *New York Times*, May 7, 2015, http://www.nytimes.com/2015/05/07/health/premature-babies-22-weeks-viability-study.html?_r=1.

8. "Science Brings New Era," *USA Today*, January 22, 1998, 12A.

9. Ovide M. Lamontagne, "The Time Is Now: Defending Life 2014," Women's Protection Project, *Americans United for Life*, 2014, http://www.aul.org/wp-content/uploads/2014/03/Defending_Life_Book_FINAL_4-WPP.pdf.

10. "Pro-Life Action Guide," *Concerned Women for America*.

11. Lamontagne, "The Time Is Now."

12. Ibid.

13. Steven Ertelt, "Kermit Gosnell Found Guilty on Three First-Degree Murder Charges," *Life News*, May 13, 2013, http://www.lifenews.com/2013/05/13/ kermit-gosnell-found-guilty-of-on-three-first-degree-murder-charges/.

14. Jeanneane Maxon, "Why Big Abortion Shares Gosnell's Guilt," *Washington Times*, May 15, 2013, http://www.washingtontimes.com/news/2013/ may/15/why-big-abortion-shares-gosnells-guilt/.

15. "An Analysis of Roe and Doe," *Life Dynamics*, accessed October 27, 2015, http://www.lifedynamics.com/Pro-life_Group/Pro-choice_Women/.

16. Mailee R. Smith, "2013 State Legislative Sessions: Unabashedly Pro-Life and Pro-Woman," Women's Protection Project, *Americans United for Life*, 2014, http://www.aul.org/wp-content/uploads/2014/03/Defending_Life_ Book_FINAL_4-WPP.pdf.

17. Marisa Lengor Kwaning, "Planned Parenthood Covers Up How Its Telemed Abortions Are Four Times More Dangerous," *Life News*, March 19, 2013, http://www.lifenews.com/2015/03/19/planned-parenthood-covers-up-how -its-telemed-abortions-are-four-times-more-dangerous/.

18. Mailee R. Smith, "2013 State Legislative Sessions."

19. Eight of these studies are statistically significant. See "Pro-Life Action Guide," *Concerned Women for America*, which is based on the following studies: M. C. Pike et al., "Oral Contraceptive Use and Early Abortion as Risk Factors for Breast Cancer in Young Women," *British Journal of Cancer* 43 (1981): 72–76; Brinton et al., "Reproductive Factors in the Aetiology of Breast Cancer," *British Journal of Cancer* 47 (1983): 757–62; Rosenberg et al., "Breast Cancer in Relation to the Occurrence and the Time of the Induced and Spontaneous Abortion," *American Journal of Epidemiology* 127 (1988): 981–89; Howe et al., "Early Abortion and Breast Cancer Risk among Women under Age 40," *International Journal of Epidemiology* 18 (1989): 300–4; Laing et al., "Breast Cancer Risk Factors in African-American Women," *Journal of the National Medical Association* 85 (1993): 931–39; Laing et al., "Reproductive and Lifestyle Factors for Breast Cancer in African-American Women," *Genetic Epidemiology* 11 (1994): A300; Daling et al., "Risk of Breast Cancer among White Women," *Journal of the National Cancer Institute* 86 (1994): 1584–92; Daling et al., "Risk of Breast Cancer among White Women Following Induced Abortion," *American Journal of Epidemiology* 144 (1996): 373–80; Newcomb et al., "Pregnancy Termination in Relation to Risk of Breast Cancer," *Journal of the American Medical Association* 275 (1996): 283–87; Wu et al., "Menstrual and Reproductive Factors and Risk of Breast Cancer in Asian-Americans," *British Journal of Cancer* 73 (1996): 680–86; Palmer et al., "Induced and Spontaneous Abortion in Relation to Risk of Breast Cancer,"

Cancer Causes and Control 8 (1997): 841–49; Marcus et al., "Adolescent Reproductive Events and Subsequent Breast Cancer Risk," *American Journal of Public Health* 89 (August 1999): 1244–47; Lazovich et al., "Induced Abortion and Breast Cancer Risk," *Epidemiology* 11 (January 2000): 76–80.

20. Susan Berry, "Pediatricians Warn of Abortion-Breast Cancer Link," *Breitbart*, April 17, 2015, http://www.breitbart.com/big-government/2015/04/17/pediatricians-warn-of-abortion-breast-cancer-link/.

21. "A Risk to Avoid: Abortion's Link to Breast Cancer," *Life Notes*, Right to Life of Michigan, May 28, 2015, http://media.rtl.org/pdf/ABCLinkprint.pdf.

22. P. K. Coleman, "Abortion and Mental Health: Quantitative Synthesis and Analysis of Research Published 1995–2009," *British Journal of Psychiatry* 199 (2011): 180–86.

23. E. Joanne Angelo, "Portraits of Grief in the Aftermath of Abortion," Hope after Abortion, Diocesan Pro-Life Leadership Conference, Atlanta, GA, August 8, 2011, http://hopeafterabortion.com/?page_id=843.

24. Dr. Byron C. Calhoun and Mailee R. Smith, "Significant Potential for Harm: Growing Medical Evidence of Abortion's Negative Impact on Women," *Americans United for Life*, December 2013, http://www.aul.org/wp-content/uploads/2013/12/Abortions-Medical-Risks-2013.pdf.

25. *Doe v. Bolton*, 410 US 179 (1973), http://caselaw.lp.findlaw.com/scripts/getcase.pl?court=US&vol=410&invol=179.

26. "Doe v. Bolton," Leadership for America: Rule of Law, Heritage Foundation, 2015, http://www.heritage.org/initiatives/rule-of-law/judicial-activism/cases/doe-v-bolton.

27. "Induced Abortion in the United States," *Guttmacher Institute*.

28. Ben Johnson, "U.S., Canada among the World's Top 4% Most Permissive Nations on Abortion: Report," *LifeSite News*, February 25, 2014, https://www.lifesitenews.com/news/u.s.-canada-among-the-worlds-top-4-most-permissive-nations-on-abortion-repo.

29. Lydia Saad, "Americans Choose 'Pro-Choice' for First Time in Seven Years," *Gallup*, May 29, 2015, http://www.gallup.com/poll/183434/americans-choose-pro-choice-first-time-seven-years.aspx.

30. Steven Ertelt, "Gallup Poll: 55% of Americans Want All or Most Abortions Made Illegal," *LifeNews.com*, May 29, 2015, http://www.lifenews.com/2015/05/29/gallup-poll-54-of-americans-want-all-or-most-abortions-made-illegal/.

31. Lawrence B. Finer et al., "Reasons U.S. Women Have Abortions: Quantitative and Qualitative Perspectives," *Perspectives on Sexual and Reproductive Health* 37, no 3 (September 2005), https://www.guttmacher.org/pubs/journals/3711005.pdf.

32. "Abortion for Victims of Rape and Incest? No: They Deserve Better," pamphlet, Pro Life Action League, accessed October 27, 2015, http://prolifeaction.org/docs/RapeAbortion.pdf. The pamphlet cites the following study: Sandra Mahkorn, "Pregnancy and Sexual Assault," in *The Psychological Aspects of Abortion*, ed. D. Mall and W. F. Watts (1979), 53–72.

33. Sarah Zagorski, "58% of Millennials Believe Abortion Is Morally Wrong," *Life News*, January 26, 2015, http://www.lifenews.com/2015/01/26/58-of-millennials-believe-abortion-is-morally-wrong/.

34. Steven Ertelt, "Poll: 56% Take Pro-Life Abortion Position, 80% Want More Limits," *Life News*, January 8, 2013, http://www.lifenews.com/2013/01/08/poll-56-take-pro-life-abortion-position-80-want-more-limits/.

35. Charlie Spiering, "Poll: 60 Percent of Americans Say Abortion Is Morally Wrong," *Breitbart*, January 22, 2014, http://www.breitbart.com/big-government/2015/01/22/poll-60-percent-of-americans-say-abortion-is-morally-wrong/.

36. "Little Sisters of the Poor v. Burwell," Becket Fund for Religious Liberty, updated September 24, 2015, http://www.becketfund.org/littlesisters/.

37. Kerry Picket, "Hillary on Abortion: 'Deep-Seated Cultural Codes, Religious Beliefs and Structural Biases Have to Be Changed,'" *Daily Caller*, April 23, 2015, http://dailycaller.com/2015/04/23/hillary-on-abortion-deep-seated-cultural-codes-religious-beliefs-and-structural-biases-have-to-be-changed/.

38. "Publicly Funded Family Planning Services in the United States: Fact Sheet," *Guttmacher Institute*, July 2015, http://www.guttmacher.org/pubs/fb_contraceptive_serv.html.

39. "Planned Parenthood 2013–2014 Annual Report," Planned Parenthood Action Fund, December 2014, http://issuu.com/actionfund/docs/annual_report_final_proof_12.16.14_/0.

40. Danielle Kurtzleben, "Fact Check: How Does Planned Parenthood Spend That Government Money?" NPR, August 5, 2015, http://www.npr.org/sections/itsallpolitics/2015/08/05/429641062/fact-check-how-does-planned-parenthood-spend-that-government-money; "GAO-15–270R Funding and Health Services," Government Accountability Office, March 20, 2015, http://www.gao.gov/assets/670/669140.pdf.

41. Randall K. O'Bannon, "40 Years: Planned Parenthood Becomes Abortion Empire," *National Right to Life News*, Winter 2013, http://www.nrlc.org/archive/news/2013/201301/AbortionEmpirePage8.html#.VV5ixFnOOko; "Planned Parenthood 2013–2014 Annual Report."

42. O'Bannon, "40 Years."

43. Mark Antonio Wright, "There's More Illegality in That Planned Parenthood Video Than Just Selling Baby Body Parts," *National Review*, July 17, 2015, http://www.nationalreview.com/article/421307/planned-parenthood-altering-abortion-procedure-illegal.

44. Lori Robertson, "Planned Parenthood and Mammograms," *FactCheck.org*, October 18, 2012, http://www.factcheck.org/2012/10/planned-parenthood-and-mammograms/.

45. John Jansen, "Planned Parenthood Claims Their Own Figures Are Misleading," *Pro-Life Action League*, March 31, 2011, http://prolifeaction.org/hotline/2011/98percent/.

46. "Exposing Planned Parenthood's Cover-Up of Child Sex Trafficking," *Live Action*, 2015, http://liveaction.org/traffick/; Tristyn Bloom, "Pro-Life Group's Report: Planned Parenthood Enabling Rape, Sex Trafficking, Child Abuse," *Daily Caller*, May 28, 2014, http://dailycaller.com/2014/05/28/pro-life-groups-report-planned-parenthood-enabling-rape-sex-trafficking-child-abuse/.

47. Steven Ertelt, "79% of Planned Parenthood Abortion Clinics Target Blacks, Hispanics," *Life News*, October 16, 2012, http://www.lifenews.com/2012/10/16/79-of-planned-parenthood-abortion-clinics-target-blacks-hispanics/.

48. Kristi Burton Brown, "If You Want to Stand against Racism, Stand against Planned Parenthood," *Life News*, December 16, 2014, http://www.lifenews.com/2014/12/16/if-you-want-to-stand-against-racism-stand-against-planned-parenthood/.

49. "Pro-Life Action Guide," Concerned Women for America.

50. "Planned Parenthood 2013–2014 Annual Report."

51. O'Bannon, "40 Years."

52. Michelle Ye Hee Lee, "Does Obamacare provide federal subsidies for elective abortions?" *Washington Post*, January 26, 2015, http://www.washingtonpost.com/blogs/fact-checker/wp/2015/01/26/does-obamacare-provide-federal-subsidies-for-elective-abortions/.

53. State by State Scoreboard, Susan B. Anthony List, http://www.sba-list.org/PPScoreboard.

54. See "About Our Health Centers," National Association of Community Health Centers, accessed October 28, 2015, http://www.nachc.com/about-our-health-centers.cfm.

55. Pam Belluck, "Pregnancy Centers Gain Influence in Anti-Abortion Arena," *New York Times*, January 5, 2013, http://www.nytimes.com/2013/01/05/health/pregnancy-centers-gain-influence-in-anti-abortion-fight.html.

56. "Abundant Life: 2011 Annual Report," Alternatives Pregnancy Center, May 2012, http://youhavealternatives.org/wp-content/uploads/2012/05/APC-Financials.pdf.

57. Eight states have passed laws banning sex-selective abortion so far: Illinois, Oklahoma, Pennsylvania, Arizona, North Dakota, South Dakota, Kansas, and North Carolina, and Louisiana is currently debating

such legislation. Sex-selective abortion targets girls far more than boys, and at least 163 million girls are missing in the world because of sex-selective abortions, according to Mara Hvistendahl's book, *Unnatural Selection: Choosing Boys over Girls, and the Consequences of a World Full of Men* (New York: Public Affairs, 2011). For more information see Smith, "2013 State Legislative Sessions," and Steven Ertelt, "Louisiana Committee Passes Pro-Life Bill to Ban Sex-Selection Abortions," *Life News*, May 6, 2015, http://www.lifenews.com/2015/05/06/louisiana-committee-passes-pro-life-bill-to-ban-sex-selection-abortions/.

58. Randy O'Bannon, "Unborn Babies Feel Pain Earlier, but at 20 Weeks It's Excruciating," *Life News*, July 11, 2013, http://www.lifenews.com/2013/07/11/unborn-babies-feel-pain-earlier-but-at-20-weeks-its-excruciating/.

59. Penny Nance, "Skewing Data to Uphold Abortion," *Washington Times*, September 2, 2014, http://www.washingtontimes.com/news/2014/sep/2/nance-skewing-data-to-uphold-abortion/.

60. Smith, "2013 State Legislative Sessions."

61. "Removal of Name of Member as Co-Sponsor of H.R. 36," Congressional Record, 114th Congress, 1st Session, vol. 161, no. 9, January 20, 2015, https://www.congress.gov/crec/2015/01/20/CREC-2015-01-20.pdf.

62. J. C. Derrick, "Ignoring the Children," *World Magazine*, February 6, 2015, http://www.worldmag.com/2015/02/ignoring_the_children.

63. Frederica Mathewes-Green, *Real Choices: Listening to Women; Looking for Alternatives to Abortion* (Chesterton, IN: Conciliar Press Ministries, 1997), 11.

64. Frederica Mathewes-Green, "Abortion: Women's Rights . . . and Wrongs," *Sisterlife* newsletter, July 23, 1991, http://www.feministsforlife.org/abortion-womens-rights-and-wrongs/.

65. "Pro-Life Action Guide," Concerned Women for America.

66. P. K. Coleman, D. C. Reardon, and J. R. Cougle, "The Quality of Caregiving Environment and Child Development Outcomes Associated with Maternal History of Abortion Using the NLSY Data," *Journal of Child Psychology and Psychiatry* 43, no. 6 (2002): 743–57.

67. Lawrence B. Finer et al., "Reasons US Women Have Abortions: Quantitative and Qualitative Perspectives," *Perspectives on Sexual and Reproductive Health* 37, no. 3 (September 2005), http://www.guttmacher.org/pubs/journals/3711005.html.

68. Cindy George, "Planned Parenthood Debuts New Building," *Houston Chronicle*, May 21, 2010, http://www.chron.com/life/mom-houston/article/Planned-Parenthood-debuts-new-building-1717914.php.

69. Kate Pickert, "What Choice? Abortion Rights Activists Won an Epic Victory in Roe v. Wade. They've Been Losing Ever Since," *Time Magazine*, January 14, 2013, http://content.time.com/time/magazine/article/0,9171,2132761,00.html.

70. Esmé E. Deprez, "The Vanishing U.S. Abortion Clinic," *Bloomberg News*, updated September 14, 2015, http://www.bloombergview.com/quicktake/ abortion-and-the-decline-of-clinics.

71. Day Gardner, email interview with author, June 28, 2015.

CHAPTER 6: THE REAL WAR AGAINST WOMEN

1. "Global Report on Trafficking in Persons 2014," United Nations Office on Drugs and Crime, New York, 2014, https://www.unodc.org/documents/data -and-analysis/glotip/GLOTIP_2014_full_report.pdf; "Human Trafficking," State of California Department of Justice, Office of the Attorney General, 2015, https://oag.ca.gov/human-trafficking.

2. "Progress and Obstacles in the Fight against Impunity Sexual Violence in the Democratic Republic of the Congo," United Nations Office of the High Commissioner for Human Rights, April 2014, http://monusco .unmissions.org/LinkClick.aspx?fileticket=Gyh_dUBNGcs%3d&tabid =10770&mid=13783&language=en-US.

3. Nicholas D. Kristof and Sheryl WuDunn, *Half the Sky: Turning Oppression into Opportunity for Women Worldwide* (New York: Random House, 2008), xiv.

4. Parameswaran Ponnudurai, "Violence against Women Takes a Big Toll in Asia," *Radio Free Asia*, March 8, 2013, http://www.rfa.org/english/ commentaries/east-asia-beat/women-03082013185809.html.

5. Kristof and WuDunn, *Half the Sky*, xvii.

6. Tanis Day, Katherine McKenna, and Audra Bowlus, "The Economic Costs of Violence against Women: An Evaluation of the Literature," University of Western Ontario, 2005, http://www.un.org/womenwatch/daw/vaw/ expert%20brief%20costs.pdf.

7. John Hall, "ISIS Releases Sickening Video Clip Showing Syrian Woman Being Stoned to Death by Group of Men—Including Her Own Father," *Daily Mail*, October 21, 2014, http://www.dailymail.co.uk/news/article-2801575/ isis-releases-sickening-video-clip-showing-syrian-woman-stoned-death -group-men-including-father.html.

8. "Impunity for Domestic Violence, 'Honour Killings' Cannot Continue—UN Official," *UN News Centre*, March 2010, http://www.un.org/apps/news/ story.asp?NewsID=33971&Cr=violence+against+women&Cr1#.UKpKmrukG M4; Robert Kiener, "Honor Killings: Can Murders of Women and Girls Be Stopped?" *Global Researcher* 5, no. 8 (April 19, 2011): 185, http://faculty .maxwell.syr.edu/hpschmitz/PSC354/PSC354Readings/HonorKillings.pdf.

9. "Honor Killings By Region," *Honor Based Violence Awareness Network*, International Resource Center, accessed October 27, 2015, http://hbv

-awareness.com/regions/; "Report: Honor Killing in Iran," LandInfo Country of Origin Information Centre, May 22, 2009, http://www.landinfo .no/asset/960/1/960_1.pdf.

10. Ayaan Hirsi Ali, "Honor Killings in America," *The Atlantic*, April 30, 2015, http://www.theatlantic.com/politics/archive/2015/04/ honor-killings-in-america/391760/.

11. "Violence in the Name of Honor: North America," NPR, January 26, 2009, http://www.npr.org/templates/story/story.php?storyId=99622481.

12. Stella Dawson, "Two Girls Murdered in Texas Taxi: Were They Honor Killings?" Reuters, June 18, 2015, http://www.reuters.com/article/2015/06/ 18/us-violence-women-honourkillings-idUSKBN0OY2UK20150618.

13. Ibid.

14. Ali, "Honor Killings in America."

15. "Child, Early and Forced Marriage: A Multi-Country Study," a submission to the UN Office of the High Commissioner on Human Rights (OCHCR), Women Living under Muslim Laws, December 15, 2013, http://www.wluml .org/sites/wluml.org/files/UN%20report%20final.pdf.

16. Ibid.

17. "Country Reports on Human Rights Practices for 2014," U.S. Department of State, 2014, http://www.state.gov/j/drl/rls/hrrpt/humanrightsreport/index. htm#wrapper.

18. "Child, Early and Forced Marriage," Women Living Under Muslim Laws.

19. Ibid.

20. Ibid.

21. Nick Kirkpatrick, "Child Marriage Is As Popular As Ever in Bangladesh," *Boston Globe*, August 29, 2015, https://www.bostonglobe.com/news/ world/2015/08/29/the-saddest-bride-have-ever-seen-child-marriage -popular-ever-bangladesh/z9Nl3BbWImL9zsVuDMYzwN/story.html.

22. Ibid.

23. "Facts for Life," 4th ed., United Nations Children's Fund, New York, 2010, http://www.factsforlifeglobal.org/resources/factsforlife-en-full.pdf.

24. Faith Fookes, "Fistula, a Silent Tragedy for Child Brides," Girls Not Brides, June 12, 2013. First published in *ThisDay*, Nigeria, June 2, 2013, http:// www.girlsnotbrides.org/fistula-a-silent-tragedy-for-child-brides/.

25. "Child, Early and Forced Marriage," Women Living Under Muslim Laws.

26. Ali, "Honor Killings in America" and "Addressing Forced Marriage in the EU: Legal Provisions and Promising Practices," European Union Agency for Fundamental Rights, 2014, http://fra.europa.eu/sites/default/files/fra-2014 -forced-marriage-eu_en.pdf.pdf.

27. Pamela Constable, "Women's Groups Campaign in D.C. to Help Victims of Forced Marriages," *Washington Post*, March 21, 2015, https://www.washingtonpost.com/local/womens-groups-campaign-in-dc-to-help-victims-of-forced-marriages/2015/03/21/87e6a626-ca73-11e4-a199-6cb5e63819d2_story.html.

28. Ibid.

29. "Muslim Couple Threatened to Kill Their Daughter for Refusing Forced Marriage," *Britain First*, November 6, 2014, https://www.britainfirst.org/muslim-couple-threatened-kill-daughter-refusing-forced-marriage/.

30. "Female Genital Mutilation: Fact Sheet No. 241," World Health Organization, updated February 2014, http://www.who.int/mediacentre/factsheets/fs241/en/.

31. "Female Genital Mutilation/Cutting: What Might the Future Hold?" UNICEF, New York, 2014, http://data.unicef.org/corecode/uploads/document6/uploaded_pdfs/corecode/FGM-C-Brochure-7_15-Final-LR_167.pdf.

32. "Female Genital Mutilation," World Health Organization.

33. "Female Genital Mutilation/Cutting," UNICEF.

34. "Female Genital Mutilation," World Health Organization.

35. Ali, "Honor Killings in America."

36. "What Is Human Trafficking?" US Department of Homeland Security, updated September 14, 2015, http://www.dhs.gov/definition-human-trafficking.

37. "U.N.: 2.4 Million Human Trafficking Victims," *USA Today*, updated April 4, 2012, http://usatoday30.usatoday.com/news/world/story/2012–04–03/human-trafficking-sex-UN/53982026/1.

38. "Human Trafficking," State of California Department of Justice.

39. E. Benjamin Skinner, "How US Budget Cuts Prolong Global Slavery," *Time*, June 28, 2011, http://content.time.com/time/world/article/0,8599,2080202,00.html.

40. Sarah Ferris, "GOP Lawmaker Says Feds Ignore Human Trafficking," *The Hill*, September 11, 2014, http://thehill.com/policy/healthcare/217415-gop-lawmaker-says-feds-ignore-human-trafficking-at-border.

41. "Who We Are: 2013 Annual Report," Bill and Melinda Gates Foundation, 2014, http://www.gatesfoundation.org/Who-We-Are/Resources-and-Media/Annual-Reports/Annual-Report-2013.

42. Andrew C. McCarthy, "CAIR's Jihad against Honor Diaries," *National Review*, April 5, 2014, http://www.nationalreview.com/article/375098/cairs-jihad-against-honor-diaries-andrew-c-mccarthy.

43. "You Gave $500,000 in 3 Days!—An FAQ Interview with Jeremy Courtney,"

Preemptive Love Coalition (blog), May 21, 2015, http://www.preemptivelove
.org/you_gave_500k_in_3_days_an_faq_interview_with_jeremy_courtney.

44. "Vice Chair Crowley, Jackson Lee Introduce New Legislation Calling for
a National Strategy to Protect Girls from Female Genital Mutilation,"
Congressman Joseph Crowley Media Center, February 5, 2015, http://
crowley.house.gov/press-release/vice-chair-crowley-jackson-lee-introduce
-new-legislation-calling-national-strategy.

45. "S.138-Prenatal Nondiscrimination Act (PRENDA) of 2013," *Congress.gov*,
accessed October 28, 2015, https://www.congress.gov/bill/113th-congress/
senate-bill/138/text.

46. Valerie M. Hudson and Andrea M. den Boer, *Bare Branches: The Security
Implications of Asia's Surplus Male Population* (Cambridge, MA: MIT Press,
2005).

47. Charles C. Krulak and Louis Freeh, "Breaking a Bad Business: To
End Modern Slavery We Need to Disrupt Its Profit Cycle," *US News*,
February 19, 2015, http://www.usnews.com/opinion/articles/2015/02/19/
combat-human-trafficking-by-disrupting-its-profit-cycle.

48. Glenn Kessler, "Are There Hundreds of Thousands of Sex-Trafficked
Runaways in the United States?" *Washington Post*, July 7, 2015, http://
www.washingtonpost.com/blogs/fact-checker/wp/2015/07/02/are-there
-hundreds-of-thousands-of-sex-trafficked-runaways-in-the-united-states/.

49. "Human Trafficking," *Issues and Controversies On File*, May 15, 2009,
https://my.berkeleycollege.edu/bbcswebdav/users/gary-belkin/Course%20
Readings/Human%20Trafficking.pdf; Skinner. "How US Budget Cuts
Prolong Global Slavery."

50. Larisa Epatko, "When Queen Elizabeth Took King Abdullah for a Drive in
Her Land Rover," *PBS NewsHour*, January 23, 2015, http://www.pbs.org/
newshour/rundown/driving-king-anecdote-goes-viral.

CHAPTER 7: THE RISE OF ISLAMIC EXTREMISM
AND THE NEED TO FIGHT BACK

1. Stoyan Zaimov, "ISIS Beheads 21 Coptic Christians in 'Message to Nation
of the Cross;' Egypt Bombs Terror Group in Response," *The Christian Post*,
February 16, 2015, http://www.christianpost.com/news/isis-beheads-21
-coptic-christians-in-message-to-nation-of-the-cross-egypt-bombs-terror
-group-in-response-134142/.

2. "Remarks by the President in State of the Union Address," Office of
the Press Secretary, the White House, January 20, 2015, https://www
.whitehouse.gov/the-press-office/2015/01/20/remarks-president-state
-union-address-january-20-2015.

3. Zachary Laub and Jonathan Masters, "The Islamic State," Council on Foreign Relations, May 18, 2015, http://www.cfr.org/iraq/islamic-state/p14811.

4. Ibid.; Priyanka Boghani, "What an Estimate of 10,000 ISIS Fighters Killed Doesn't Tell Us," *PBS Frontline*, June 4, 2015, http://www.pbs.org/wgbh/pages/frontline/iraq-war-on-terror/rise-of-isis/what-an-estimate-of-10000-isis-fighters-killed-doesnt-tell-us/.

5. For discussion of ISIS's ideology, see Cole Bunzel, "From Paper State to Caliphate: The Ideology of the Islamic State," *The Brookings Project on US Relations with the Islamic World*, no. 19 (March 2015), http://www.brookings.edu/~/media/research/files/papers/2015/03/ideology-of-islamic-state-bunzel/the-ideology-of-the-islamic-state.pdf.

6. "Global Terrorism Index 2014: Measuring and Understanding the Impact of Terrorism," Institute for Economics and Peace (IEP), November 2014, http://www.visionofhumanity.org/sites/default/files/Global%20Terrorism%20Index%20Report%202014_0.pdf.

7. Ibid.

8. Ibid.

9. Adam Goldman and Greg Miller, "Leader of Islamic State Used American Hostage as Sexual Slave," *Washington Post*, August 14, 2015, https://www.washingtonpost.com/world/national-security/leader-of-islamic-state-raped-american-hostage/2015/08/14/266b6bf4-42c1-11e5-846d-02792f854297_story.html.

10. Adam Goldman, "Kayla Mueller, American Hostage of the Islamic State, Is Confirmed Dead," *Washington Post*, February 10, 2015, https://www.washingtonpost.com/world/national-security/us-believes-kayla-mueller-hostage-of-islamic-state-is-dead/2015/02/10/76eef7f0-b12e-11e4-886b-c22184f27c35_story.html.

11. "Human Rights Council Discusses Report on Abuses in Iraq Committed by the So-Called Islamic State in Iraq and the Levant," United Nations Office of the High Commissioner for Human Rights, March 25, 2015, http://www.ohchr.org/EN/NewsEvents/Pages/DisplayNews.aspx?NewsID=15755&LangID=E.

12. Ibid.

13. "World Watch List: Iraq," *Open Doors USA*, 2015, https://www.opendoorsusa.org/christian-persecution/world-watch-list/iraq/.

14. Lara Logan, "Iraq's Christians Persecuted by ISIS," transcript, *60 Minutes*, CBS, March 22, 2015, http://www.cbsnews.com/news/iraq-christians-persecuted-by-isis-60-minutes/.

15. "IS Yazidi Attacks May Be Genocide, says UN," *BBC News*, March 19, 2015, http://www.bbc.com/news/world-middle-east-31962755.

16. "Global Terrorism Index 2014," Institute for Economics and Peace.

17. Robert Windrem and Alexander Smith, "200,000 Christians at Risk of Massacre in Nigeria," NBC News, February 14, 2015, http://www.nbcnews.com/storyline/missing-nigeria-schoolgirls/boko-haram-200-000-christians-risk-massacre-nigeria-n306211; Timothy C. Morgan, "How Boko Haram's Murders and Kidnappings Are Changing Nigeria's Churches," *Christianity Today*, October 16, 2014, http://www.christianitytoday.com/ct/2014/october-web-only/boko-haram-chibok-hostages-persecution.html.

18. Morgan, "How Boko Haram's Murders and Kidnappings Are Changing Nigeria's Churches."

19. "Senior UN Official Warns of 'Widespread and Systematic' Sexual Violence in Syria, Iraq," *UN News Centre*, May 7, 2015, http://www.un.org/apps/news/story.asp?NewsID=50794#.VgVLctOrRsM.

20. Rukmini Callimachi, "ISIS Enshrines a Theology of Rape," *New York Times*, August 13, 2015, http://www.nytimes.com/2015/08/14/world/middleeast/isis-enshrines-a-theology-of-rape.html?_r=0.

21. "UN Official on Life under ISIS: 'Girls Are Being Stripped Naked, Examined in Slave Bazaars,'" *Jerusalem Post*, May 10, 2015, http://www.jpost.com/Middle-East/UN-official-on-life-under-ISIS-Girls-are-being-stripped-naked-examined-in-slave-bazaars-402611.

22. "Report of the Office of the United Nations High Commissioner for Human Rights on the Human Rights Situation in Iraq in the Light of Abuses Committed by the So-Called Islamic State in Iraq and the Levant and Associated Groups," United Nations Human Rights Council, Twenty-Eighth Session, March 13, 2015, http://www.ohchr.org/EN/HRBodies/HRC/RegularSessions/Session28/Pages/ListReports.aspx.

23. Samuel Smith, "ISIS Sex Slave Price: 1- to 9-Y-O Christian, Yazidi Girls Sold for $172," *Christian Post*, November 7, 2014, http://www.christianpost.com/news/isis-sex-slave-price-1-to-9-y-o-christian-yazidi-girls-sold-for-172-129266/.

24. Ibid.

25. "Report of the Office of the United Nations High Commissioner," United Nations.

26. Ibid.

27. John Hall, "'I've Been Raped 30 Times and It's Not Even Lunchtime': Desperate Plight of Yazidi Woman Who Begged West to Bomb Her Brothel after ISIS Militants Sold Her into Sex Slavery," *Daily Mail*, October 21, 2014, http://www.dailymail.co.uk/news/article-2801353/i-ve-raped-30-times-s-not-lunchtime-desperate-plight-yazidi-woman-begged-west-bomb-brothel-isis-militants-sold-sex-slavery.html#ixzz3bjQGX6Uq.

28. Adam Nossiter, "Boko Haram Militants Raped Hundreds of Female Captives in Nigeria," *New York Times*, May 19, 2015, http://www.nytimes.com/2015/05/19/world/africa/boko-haram-militants-raped-hundreds-of-female-captives-in-nigeria.html#NYT.

29. Ibid.

30. Callimachi, "ISIS Enshrines a Theology of Rape."

31. Ibid.

32. "How Islamic State Uses Systematic Sexual Violence against Women," transcript, *PBS NewsHour*, October 7, 2014, http://www.pbs.org/newshour/bb/islamic-state-uses-systematic-sexual-violence-women/.

33. Audrey Kurth Cronin, "ISIS Is Not a Terrorist Group," *Foreign Affairs*, March/April 2015, https://www.foreignaffairs.com/articles/middle-east/2015-02-16/isis-not-terrorist-group.

34. Ben Taub, "Journey to Jihad: Why Are Teen-agers Joining ISIS?" *New Yorker*, June 1, 2015, http://www.newyorker.com/magazine/2015/06/01/journey-to-jihad.

35. Kevin Sullivan, "Three American Teens, Recruited Online, Are Caught Trying to Join the Islamic State," *Washington Post*, December 8, 2014, https://www.washingtonpost.com/world/national-security/three-american-teens-recruited-online-are-caught-trying-to-join-the-islamic-state/2014/12/08/8022e6c4-7afb-11e4-84d4-7c896b90abdc_story.html.

36. Ibid.

37. Eric Schmitt, Michael S. Schmidt, and Andrew Higgins, "Al Qaeda Trained Suspect in Paris Terror Attack, Official Says," *New York Times*, January 9, 2015, http://www.nytimes.com/2015/01/09/world/europe/paris-terror-attack-suspects.html; "Charlie Hebdo: Gun Attack on French Magazine Kills 12," *BBC News*, January 7, 2015, http://www.bbc.com/news/world-europe-30710883.

38. Eric Schmitt, Mark Mazzetti, and Rukmini Callimachi, "Disputed Claims over Qaeda Role in Paris Attacks," *New York Times*, January 15, 2015, http://www.nytimes.com/2015/01/15/world/europe/al-qaeda-in-the-arabian-peninsula-charlie-hebdo.html.

39. "Charlie Hebdo: Paris Attacker's Widow Living in Syria Under Islamic State," *Express Tribune*, February 13, 2015, http://tribune.com.pk/story/837665/charlie-hebdo-paris-attackers-widow-living-in-syria-under-islamic-state/.

40. Michael Pearson, "Official: Suspect Says Iraq, Afghanistan Drove Boston Bombings," CNN, April 23, 2013, http://www.cnn.com/2013/04/23/us/boston-attack/.

41. Michael Cooper, Michael S. Schmidt, and Eric Schmitt, "Boston Suspects Are Seen as Self-Taught and Fueled by Web," *New York Times*, April 24,

2013, http://www.nytimes.com/2013/04/24/us/boston-marathon-bombing
-developments.html.

42. "A Closer Look at Tsarnaev's Message on Watertown Boat," *Boston Globe*,
March 10, 2013, http://www.bostonglobe.com/metro/2015/03/10/images
-show-tsarnaev-message-watertown-boat/HFmuYj0uK3SJUfTvNyiPPL/
story.html.

43. Karen Tumulty, "DHS Secretary: 'New Phase' in the Global Terrorist
Threat," *Washington Post*, May 10, 2015, http://www.washingtonpost
.com/blogs/post-politics/wp/2015/05/10/dhs-secretary-new-phase-in-the
-global-terrorist-threat/.

44. Criteria summarized from Roger Dawson SJ, "Just War Theory," *Thinking
Faith*, October 11, 2013, http://www.thinkingfaith.org/articles/20131011_2
.htm#_ednref4. For further information on the just war theory, see James
F. Childress, "Just War Theories: The Bases, Interrelations, Priorities, and
Functions of Their Criteria," *Theological Studies*, no. 39 (1976): 427–45;
Mark Evans, ed., *Just War Theory: A Reappraisal* (Edinburgh: Edinburgh
University Press, 2005).

45. Graeme Wood, "What ISIS Really Wants," *The Atlantic*, March 2015,
http://www.theatlantic.com/features/archive/2015/02/what-isis-really
-wants/384980/.

46. Justin Koski, "Lt. Gen. Michael Flynn: 'You Can't Defeat an Enemy You
Don't Admit Exists,'" *Western Journalism*, February 9, 2015, http://www
.westernjournalism.com/lt-gen-michael-flynn-cant-defeat-enemy-dont
-admit-exists/.

47. "Muslim-Western Tensions Persist: Common Concerns about Islamic
Extremism," *Pew Research Center*, July 21, 2011, http://www.pewglobal
.org/2011/07/21/muslim-western-tensions-persist/.

48. Bobby Jindal, "Louisiana Governor: ISIS Threat Reveals Obama's Failure as
Commander in Chief," Fox News, February 23, 2015, http://www.foxnews
.com/opinion/2015/02/23/louisiana-governor-isis-threat-reveals-obama
-failure-as-commander-in-chief.html.

49. Eric Bradner, Barbara Starr, and Jim Acosta, "White House Authorizes
Up to 450 Additional Troops in Iraq," CNN, June 10, 2015, http://www.cnn
.com/2015/06/09/politics/u-s-considering-1000-additional-troops-in-iraq/.

50. Jacqueline Klimas, "US Bombers Hold Fire on Islamic State Targets
amid Ground Intel Blackout," *Washington Times*, May 31, 2015, http://
www.washingtontimes.com/news/2015/may/31/us-bombers-hold-fire-on
-islamic-state-targets-amid/.

51. Vicky Hartzler, phone interview with author, June 25, 2015.

CHAPTER 8: BEYOND OUR BORDERS

1. Rafael Medoff, "Op-Ed: Christians Mostly Failed to Act in Response to Kristallnacht," *Jewish Telegraphic Agency*, October 31, 2011, http://www.jta.org/2011/10/31/news-opinion/opinion/op-ed-christians-mostly-failed-to-act-in-response-to-kristallnacht.

2. "United States Policy toward Jewish Refugees, 1941–1952," *Holocaust Encyclopedia*, United States Holocaust Memorial Museum, Washington, DC, June 20, 2014, http://www.ushmm.org/wlc/en/article.php?ModuleId=10007094.

3. According to the Yad Vashem website, "The numbers of Righteous are not necessarily an indication of the actual number of rescuers in each country, but reflect the cases that were made available to Yad Vashem." More information can be found at "Righteous among the Nations," *Yad Vashem*, accessed October 28, 2015, http://www.yadvashem.org/yv/en/righteous/index.asp.

4. "The Abrahamic Covenant," *IsraelAnswers.com*, International Christian Embassy Jerusalem, accessed October 28, 2015, http://israelanswers.com/christian_zionism/the_abrahamic_covenant#What is the significance of the Abrahamic Covenant?.

5. "Hatikvah ('The Hope')," Naphtali Herz Imber, 1886, accessed October 28, 2015, http://www.stateofisrael.com/anthem/.

6. John McCain, "The Future of US-Israel Relations" (speech), Herzliya Conference, January 23 2007, http://www.mccain.senate.gov/public/index.cfm/speeches?ID=f1f4afa6-911f-f7da-5896-c0306e335620.

7. Jodi Rudoren, "Rebukes from White House Risk Buoying Netanyahu," *New York Times*, March 25, 2015, http://www.nytimes.com/2015/03/25/world/middleeast/white-houses-rebukes-risk-buoying-netanyahu.html.

8. Dina Porat, ed., "Antisemitism Worldwide, 2014: General Analysis," Kantor Center for the Study of Contemporary European Jewry, Tel Aviv University, 2014, http://www.eurojewcong.org/docs/Doch2014_(130415).docx.pdf.

9. "Why You Should Join USACB: Mission Statement," US Campaign for the Academic and Cultural Boycott of Israel, accessed October 28, 2015, http://www.usacbi.org/mission-statement/.

10. "BDS on American College Campuses: 2013–14 Year-in-Review," Anti-Defamation League, June 3, 2014, http://www.adl.org/israel-international/anti-israel-activity/bds-on-american-college.html#.VW3drlnOOko.

11. "ADL Voices Concern about Increase in Anti-Semitic and Anti-Israel Activity on Campus (press release)," Anti-Defamation League, May 29, 2015, http://www.adl.org/press-center/press-releases/anti-semitism-usa/adl-voices-concern-about-increase-in-anti-semitic-anti-israel-activity-on-campus.html#.VW3dJ1nOOko.

12. "Students for Justice in Palestine," Anti-Defamation League, March 10, 2015, http://www.adl.org/assets/pdf/israel-international/sjp-2015 -backgrounder.pdf.

13. Rachel Zoll, "Anti-Israel Divestment Push Gains Traction at US Colleges," *Washington Times*, February 28, 2015, http://www.washingtontimes .com/news/2015/feb/28/anti-israel-divestment-push-gains-traction -at-us-c/?page=all.

14. Abraham H. Foxman, "Anti-Semitism on Campus: Old Wine in New Bottles," *Huffington Post*, April 29, 2015, http://www.huffingtonpost.com/ abraham-h-foxman/anti-semitism-on-campus-o_b_7172986.html.

15. Alina D. Sharon, "Campus Eviction Notices Are Fake, but Their Anti-Semitism Is Real, Experts Say," *JNS.org*, June 22, 2014, http://www.jns.org/ latest-articles/2014/6/22/campus-eviction-notices-are-fake-but-their-anti -semitism-is-real-experts-say#.VXEjNlyrT6Y=.

16. Tzvi Ben-Gedalyahu, "Video Exposes Massive and Violent Anti-Semitism on Campuses," *Jewish Press*, October 10, 2014, http://www.jewishpress. com/news/breaking-news/video-exposes-massive-and-violent-anti-semitism-on-us-campuses-video/2014/10/06/.

17. Adam Kredo, "Hamas on Campus," *Washington Free Beacon*, February 2, 2015, http://freebeacon.com/issues/hamas-on-campus/.

18. Zoll, "Anti-Israel Divestment Push Gains Traction at US Colleges."

19. Cathryn J. Prince, "Anti-Semitism Now 'Fashionable' in the US, Warn Experts," *The Times of Israel*, February 18, 2015, http://www.timesofisrael. com/anti-semitism-now-fashionable-in-the-us-warn-experts/.

20. "2014 Audit of Anti-Semitic Incidents," Anti-Defamation League, accessed October 29, 2015, http://www.adl.org/anti-semitism/united-states/c/2014 -audit-of-anti-semitic-incidents.html.

21. "French Anti-Semitism and French Aliyah Skyrocket on Parallel Tracks," *JNS.org*, April 7, 2014, http://www.jns.org/latest-articles/2014/4/7/ french-anti-semitism-and-french-aliyah-skyrocket-on-parallel-tracks#. Vi9PDY9Vikp=.

22. Martin Robinson and James White, "'Every Single French Jew I Know Has Left Paris': Editor of Britain's Jewish Chronicle Claims People Are Fleeing Terror-Hit French Capital," *Daily Mail*, updated January 12, 2015, http:// www.dailymail.co.uk/news/article-2903600/Every-single-French-Jew -know-left-Paris-Editor-Britain-s-Jewish-Chronicle-claims-people-fleeing -terror-hit-French-capital.html#ixzz3ZwGl2Gvc.

23. Naftali Bendavid, "European Jews Rebuff Netanyahu's Call to Migrate to Israel," *Wall Street Journal*, February 18, 2015, http://www.wsj.com/ articles/european-jews-rebuff-netanyahus-call-to-migrate-to-israel -1424297472.

24. Griff Witte and Anthony Faiola, "France Sends 10,000 Troops across Country, Protecting Hundreds of Jewish Sites," *Washington Post*, January 12, 2015, https://www.washingtonpost.com/world/hollande-calls-crisis-meeting-10000-extra-forces-sent-to-protect-people-of-france/2015/01/12/63610982-9a34-11e4-a7ee-526210d665b4_story.html; "Fear of a New Darkness," *The Economist*, February 21, 2015, http://www.economist.com/news/europe/21644242-copenhagen-shootings-paris-terror-attacks-are-raising-new-worries-about-jew-hatred.

25. "US Senators Introduce Resolution Condemning Anti-Semitism in Europe," *Ynetnews.com*, February 27, 2015, http://www.ynetnews.com/articles/0,7340,L-4631022,00.html.

26. Eldad Beck, "Rivlin in Berlin Warns of Re-emergence of 'Rampant Anti-Semitism," *Ynetnews.com*, May 11, 2015, http://www.ynetnews.com/articles/0,7340,L-4656175,00.html.

27. "Anti-Semitism in France: Dark Days," *The Economist*, July 22, 2014, http://www.economist.com/blogs/charlemagne/2014/07/anti-semitism-france.

28. Sinan Salaheddin, "Home of Abraham, Ur, Unearthed by Archaeologists in Iraq," *Christian Science Monitor*, April 4, 2013, http://www.csmonitor.com/Science/2013/0404/Home-of-Abraham-Ur-unearthed-by-archaeologists-in-Iraq.

29. "Iraq, Babylon, and Baghdad in Jewish History and Thought," AJC, November 12, 2012, http://www.ajc.org/site/apps/nlnet/content3.aspx?c=7oJILSPwFfJSG&b=8482195&ct=12481123&notoc=.

30. Stephen Farrell, "Baghdad Jews Have Become a Fearful Few," *New York Times*, June 1, 2008, http://www.nytimes.com/2008/06/01/world/middleeast/01babylon.html.

31. "Foreign Terrorist Organizations: Hamas," Country Reports on Terrorism 2011, Office of the Coordinator for Counterterrorism, US Department of State, July 31, 2012, http://www.state.gov/j/ct/rls/crt/2011/195553.htm#hamas; Zachary Laub, "Hamas," *Council on Foreign Relations*, August 1, 2014, http://www.cfr.org/israel/hamas/p8968.

32. "Hamas," American Israel Public Affairs Committee, accessed October 28, 2015, http://www.aipac.org/learn/issues/issue-display?issueid=%7B4399EDFB-3F50-4744-819A-CD491B3FA7DC%7D.

33. "The Conflict in Gaza," American Israel Public Affairs Committee, August 2014, http://www.aipac.org/~/media/Publications/Policy%20and%20Politics/AIPAC%20Analyses/One%20Pagers/HR%20abuses_one%20pager%20(4).pdf.

34. "Israel under Fire: Rocket Attacks on Israel from Gaza," *Israel Defense Forces* (blog), accessed October 29, 2015, https://www.idfblog.com/facts-figures/rocket-attacks-toward-israel/.

35. "Hamas: Rearming and Rebuilding for Future Conflict," American Israel Public Affairs Committee, May 6, 2015, http://www.aipac.org/~/media/ Publications/Policy%20and%20Politics/AIPAC%20Analyses/Issue%20 Memos/2015/AIPAC%20Memo%20%20Hamas.pdf.

36. "The Conflict in Gaza," American Israel Public Affairs Committee.

37. Ibid.

38. Michael Hausam, "Netanyahu on Hamas: Terrorists 'Using Their Civilians to Protect Their Missiles,'" *Independent Journal Review*, July 15, 2014, http://www.ijreview.com/2014/07/156651-netanyahu-hamas-theyre-using -civilians-protect-missiles/.

39. Mohammad S. Dajani Daoudi, "A Plea for Empathy and Moderation in the Middle East," *The Atlantic*, August 13, 2014, http://www.theatlantic .com/international/archive/2014/08/a-plea-for-empathy-in-the-middle -east/375990/.

40. Marissa Newman, "Iranian Supreme Leader Calls for Israel's 'Annihilation,'" *The Times of Israel,* November 9, 2014, http://www .timesofisrael.com/iranian-supreme-leader-calls-for-israels-annihilation/; Lazar Berman, "Iran Militia Chief: Destroying Israel Is 'Nonnegotiable,'" *The Times of Israel*, March 31, 2015, http://www.timesofisrael.com/ iran-militia-chief-destroying-israel-nonnegotiable/#ixzz3VySUViWe.

41. Jonathan Masters and Zachary Laub, "Hezbollah (a.k.a. Hizbollah, Hizbu'llah)," *Council on Foreign Relations*, January 3, 2014, http://www.cfr .org/lebanon/hezbollah-k-hizbollah-hizbullah/p9155.

42. "An Open Letter: The Hizballah Program," *Council on Foreign Relations*, January 1, 1988, http://www.cfr.org/terrorist-organizations-and-networks/ open-letter-hizballah-program/p30967.

43. Daniel Pipes, "Obama's Anti-Zionism," *National Review*, January 22, 2013, http://www.nationalreview.com/article/338278/obamas-anti-zionism -daniel-pipes.

44. Ibid.

45. "Martin Niemöller: First They Came for the Socialists," *Holocaust Encyclopedia*, United States Holocaust Memorial Museum, Washington, DC, August 18, 2015, http://www.ushmm.org/wlc/en/article. php?ModuleId=10007392.

46. Jennifer Rubin, "Mike Huckabee and Other Evangelicals Rally for Israel," *Washington Post*, September 2, 2014, http://www.washingtonpost.com/ blogs/right-turn/wp/2014/09/02/mike-huckabee-and-other-evangelicals -rally-for-israel/.

47. Other estimates put the cost of a MIM-104F Patriot PAC-3 missile at $3.43 million. See Joakim Kasper Oestergaard Balle, "About Patriot and PAC-3," Aerospace and Defense Intelligence Report, updated December 22, 2014, https://www.bga-aeroweb.com/Defense/Patriot-PAC-3.html.

48. Poncie Rutsch, "Guess How Much of Uncle Sam's Money Goes to Foreign Aid. Guess Again!" NPR, February 10, 2015, http://www.npr.org/sections/goatsandsoda/2015/02/10/383875581/guess-how-much-of-uncle-sams-money-goes-to-foreign-aid-guess-again. The Israeli aid expenditures and 6-percent figure come from Jeremy M. Sharp, "US Foreign Aid to Israel," Congressional Research Service Report, June 10, 2015, https://www.fas.org/sgp/crs/mideast/RL33222.pdf. Sharp cited $3.1 billion in aid, out of a total foreign aid budget of $50 billion.

49. Steve Rothman, "Israel Aid Pays US Dividends That Exceed Cost," *Bloomberg News*, April 6, 2010, http://www.bloomberg.com/apps/news?pid=newsarchive&sid=a7jrhCxvqlfg.

50. Daniel Halper, "$7.5 Trillion in Debt Added under Obama," *Weekly Standard* (blog), January 20, 2015, http://www.weeklystandard.com/blogs/75-trillion-debt-added-under-obama_824147.html.

51. Susan B. Epstein and K. Alan Kronstadt, "Pakistan: US Foreign Assistance," Congressional Research Service Report, July 1, 2013, https://www.fas.org/sgp/crs/row/R41856.pdf.

52. Benjamin Netanyahu, speech before joint meeting of Congress, Washington, DC, March 3, 2015, transcript accessed via *The Washington Post*, http://www.washingtonpost.com/blogs/post-politics/wp/2015/03/03/full-text-netanyahus-address-to-congress/.

CHAPTER 9: SEASONS

1. Ross Barkan, "Hillary Clinton Talks Women's Rights in Manhattan as Controversy Swirls," *The Observer*, March 9, 2015, http://observer.com/2015/03/hillary-clinton-talks-womens-rights-in-manhattan-as-controversy-swirls/.

2. "A War No More: The Truth behind the 'War on Women,'" a publication of Concerned Women for America and the Beverly LaHaye Institute, 2015, http://www.cwfa.org/wp-content/uploads/2015/02/War-on-Women.pdf; "US Naturalizations: 2012," Annual Flow Report, March 2013, Table 4, https://www.dhs.gov/sites/default/files/publications/ois_natz_fr_2012.pdf.

3. Ibid.

4. Ibid. Report referenced is Susan K. Urahn and Travis Plunkett, "Women's Work: The Economic Mobility of Women Across a Generation," *Pew Charitable Trusts*, April 2014, http://www.pewtrusts.org/~/media/legacy/uploadedfiles/pcs/content-level_pages/reports/2014/womensworkreporteconomicmobilityacrossagenerationpdf.pdf.

5. Mark J. Perry, "Stunning College Degree Gap: Women Have Earned Almost 10 Million More College Degrees Than Men Since 1982," *Carpe Diem* (blog), American Enterprise Institute, May 13, 2013, https://www.aei.org/

publication/stunning-college-degree-gap-women-have-earned-almost
-10-million-more-college-degrees-than-men-since-1982/.

6. "The 2014 State of Women-Owned Businesses Report," Commissioned
by American Express OPEN, March 2014, http://www.womenable.com/
content/userfiles/2014_State_of_Women-owned_Businesses_public.pdf.

7. Carrie Lukas, "There Is No Male-Female Wage Gap," *Wall Street Journal*,
April 12, 2011, http://www.wsj.com/articles/SB1000142405274870441510457
6250672504707048.

8. "A War No More," Concerned Women for America.

9. Francine D. Blau and Lawrence M. Kahn, "Female Labor Supply: Why
Is the US Falling Behind?" *American Economic Review* 103, no. 3 (2013):
251–56, http://www.nber.org/papers/w18702.pdf; Kay Hymowitz, "Think
Again: Working Women," *Foreign Policy*, June 24, 2013, http://foreignpolicy
.com/2013/06/24/think-again-working-women/.

10. "The Simple Truth about the Gender Pay Gap: 2015 Edition," American
Association of University Women, Spring 2015, http://www.aauw.org/
files/2015/02/The-Simple-Truth_Spring-2015.pdf; Hymowitz, "Think Again."

11. "A War No More," Concerned Women for America.

12. Paulette Light, "Why 43% of Women with Children Leave Their Jobs,
and How to Get Them Back," *The Atlantic*, April 19, 2013, http://www
.theatlantic.com/sexes/archive/2013/04/why-43-of-women-with-children
-leave-their-jobs-and-how-to-get-them-back/275134/.

13. Sarah Jane Glynn, "Explaining the Gender Wage Gap," *Center for American
Progress*, May 19, 2014, https://www.americanprogress.org/issues/
economy/report/2014/05/19/90039/explaining-the-gender-wage-gap/.

14. "A War No More," Concerned Women for America.

15. Lukas, "There Is No Male-Female Wage Gap."

16. "Modern Parenthood: Roles of Moms and Dads Converge As They Balance
Work and Family," *Pew Research Center*, March 14, 2013, http://www
.pewsocialtrends.org/2013/03/14/modern-parenthood-roles-of-moms-and
-dads-converge-as-they-balance-work-and-family/.

17. "A War No More," a publication of Concerned Women for America.

18. "Fact Sheet on Women-Owned Businesses," *National Women's Business
Council*, accessed October 29, 2015, https://www.nwbc.gov/facts/
women-owned-businesses.

19. D'Vera Cohn, Gretchen Livingston, and Wendy Wang, "After Decades of
Decline, a Rise in Stay-at-Home Mothers," *Pew Research Center*, April 8,
2014, http://www.pewsocialtrends.org/2014/04/08/after-decades-of-decline
-a-rise-in-stay-at-home-mothers/.

20. Ibid.

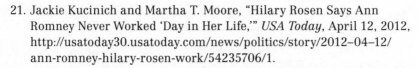

21. Jackie Kucinich and Martha T. Moore, "Hilary Rosen Says Ann Romney Never Worked 'Day in Her Life,'" *USA Today*, April 12, 2012, http://usatoday30.usatoday.com/news/politics/story/2012–04–12/ann-romney-hilary-rosen-work/54235706/1.

22. "A War No More," Concerned Women for America.

23. Robert Rector and Jennifer A. Marshall, "The Unfinished Work of Welfare Reform," Heritage Foundation, January 22, 2013, http://www.heritage.org/research/reports/2013/01/the-unfinished-work-of-welfare-reform.

24. Katie Wright, "5 Things to Know about Single Mothers in Poverty," *Center for American Progress*, May 11, 2012, https://www.americanprogress.org/issues/poverty/news/2012/05/11/11634/5-things-to-know-about-single-mothers-in-poverty/.

25. Sheryl Sandberg, *Lean In: Women, Work, and the Will to Lead* (New York: Knopf, 2013), 110.

26. K. Hymowitz, J. S. Carroll, W. B. Wilcox, and K. Kaye, "Knot Yet: The Benefits and Costs of Delayed Marriage in America," the National Campaign to Prevent Teen and Unplanned Pregnancy, 2013, http://twentysomethingmarriage.org/in-brief/.

27. Sandberg, *Lean In*, 110.

28. Mika Brzezinski, *Knowing Your Value: Women, Money, and Getting What You're Worth* (New York: Weinstein Books, 2012), 9.

29. "State of the Union GOP Response: Cathy McMorris Rodgers," *Politico*, January 28, 2014, http://www.politico.com/story/2014/01/state-of-the-union-2014-cathy-mcmorris-gop-response-102772.html.

CHAPTER 10: A VISION FOR THE FUTURE

1. Andrew Kohut, "What Will Become of America's Kids?" *Pew Research Center*, May 12, 2014, http://www.pewresearch.org/fact-tank/2014/05/12/what-will-become-of-americas-kids/.

2. Maureen H. Beasley, *First Ladies and the Press: The Unfinished Partnership of the Media Age* (Evanston, IL: Northwestern University Press, 2005).